D1376077

Working to Rule

This publication is based on research that forms part of
the Paragon Initiative.

This five-year project will provide a fundamental reassessment
of what government should – and should not – do. It will put
every area of government activity under the microscope and
analyse the failure of current policies.

The project will put forward clear and considered solutions to
the UK's problems. It will also identify the areas of government
activity that can be put back into the hands of individuals,
families, civil society, local government, charities and markets.

The Paragon Initiative will create a blueprint for a better,
freer Britain – and provide a clear vision of a new relationship
between the state and society.

WORKING TO RULE

The Damaging Economics of UK Employment Regulation

J. R. SHACKLETON

Institute of
Economic Affairs

First published in Great Britain in 2017 by
The Institute of Economic Affairs
2 Lord North Street
Westminster
London SW1P 3LB
in association with London Publishing Partnership Ltd
www.londonpublishingpartnership.co.uk

The mission of the Institute of Economic Affairs is to improve understanding
of the fundamental institutions of a free society by analysing and expounding
the role of markets in solving economic and social problems.

Copyright © The Institute of Economic Affairs 2017

The moral rights of the authors have been asserted.

All rights reserved. Without limiting the rights under copyright reserved above,
no part of this publication may be reproduced, stored or introduced into a retrieval
system, or transmitted, in any form or by any means (electronic, mechanical,
photocopying, recording or otherwise), without the prior written permission of
both the copyright owner and the publisher of this book.

A CIP catalogue record for this book is available from the British Library.

ISBN 978-0-255-36743-1

Many IEA publications are translated into languages other
than English or are reprinted. Permission to translate or to reprint
should be sought from the Director General at the address above.

Typeset in Kepler by T&T Productions Ltd
www.tandtproductions.com

Printed and bound in Great Britain by Hobbs the Printers Ltd

CONTENTS

THE AUTHOR

J. R. Shackleton is Professor of Economics at the University of Buckingham and Research and Editorial Fellow at the Institute of Economic Affairs. He edits the journal *Economic Affairs*.

FOREWORD

The costs of employment regulation are difficult to measure. Indeed, regulation itself is difficult to measure. It cannot simply be measured by its volume – many long and complicated regulations might be trivial in impact, while those that severely constrain behaviour might be very brief. It is, though, undeniable that the scope of labour market regulation has increased in recent years.

How is the scope of regulation in this area best assessed, if not measured? The best way to think about regulation in the economic sphere is to consider the way in which freely agreed bargains are prevented by the government or about how the nature of the bargains has to be changed. By these measures, in the modern era almost every aspect of labour market behaviour is very heavily regulated. The government is soon to control the pay of over 20 per cent of the workforce; it controls hiring and firing procedures, entry into pension schemes, the number of holidays, sick pay, maternity pay, the number of hours that can be worked and so on. The list is more or less endless.

As Professor Shackleton shows, the costs of labour market regulation tend to fall on employees and consumers. However, these costs are largely hidden. The benefits of regulation, on the other hand, tend to be obvious. For example, guaranteed paid holidays and protections against firing may lead to lower wages (which it is not possible to observe directly, because there is no counterfactual), but the compensating advantages are obvious to the employee. Furthermore, many of the costs of labour market regulation are borne by those who are unable to get jobs, such as the low skilled and the young. Again, they have no means of knowing about those costs – there are simply fewer opportunities for them. Meanwhile, human resources departments and regulators obtain direct benefits from regulatory complexity and some businesses may see regulation as a useful barrier to entry to potential new competitors. And so labour market regulation, once conceived, is very difficult to roll back.

Indeed, since 2010 the Coalition and Conservative governments have been responsible for a huge increase in labour market regulation, including some of the most expensive pieces of regulation conceived in the post-war era. And the list of potential challenges to freedom of contract continues to grow. Despite the fact that the gender pay gap largely arises from the free choices of employees who choose jobs that suit their own circumstances, more action in this field seems inevitable. Only very recently, it has been ruled that Uber drivers should be treated as employees and be subject to all the regulation that implies, despite the fact that Uber and other similar services have provided many people with a supplementary income, with the opportunity to become integrated into the labour market while retaining flexibility.

This is a depressing picture, not least given what we know about those groups who suffer from the downside of employment regulation. Things could be worse, however. If the UK labour market were to become as unwelcoming for younger people, older workers and immigrants as the labour markets of many continental European countries, much economic and social devastation would follow.

But Professor Shackleton, at the end of his excellent analysis of the problem, suggests some solutions. Sunset clauses, more regulatory competition and a complete review, and then repeal, of much of the labour market regulation that we already have could help to create many more economic opportunities while increasing economic welfare, growth and real wages. The best protection for employees is a competitive labour market. The exceptions to this general rule are few and we should have correspondingly few interventions in the labour market.

Professor Shackleton has spent many decades studying labour markets and this book provides an excellent analysis of the problems created by governments as well as solutions to those problems.

The views expressed in this monograph are, as in all IEA publications, those of the author and not those of the Institute (which has no corporate view), its managing trustees, Academic Advisory Council members or senior staff. With some exceptions, such as with the publication of lectures, all IEA monographs are blind peer-reviewed by at least two academics or researchers who are experts in the field.

PHILIP BOOTH

Professor of Finance, Public Policy and Ethics and Director of Research and Public Engagement at St Mary's University, Twickenham, and Senior Academic Fellow at the Institute of Economic Affairs

March 2017

SUMMARY

- Legal restrictions on the terms and conditions under which employment takes place have a long history in the UK. Since the mid 1960s, however, regulation has substantially increased and now permeates all aspects of work. The costs of this are huge. Just one element relates to the direct burden on firms. For example, the direct cost of running human resources departments is now likely to be over £15 billion per year: much of this relates to compliance with employment law. Most of the costs of regulation are, however, much more subtle and not easy to calculate.

- The European Union has regulated many aspects of labour markets including: restrictions on working hours; holiday leave; parental leave; pro-rata payments for part-time workers; information and consultation requirements (including European Works Councils for large multinationals); consultation over collective redundancies; equal conditions for permanent and agency workers; maintaining conditions for workers transferred between undertakings; and the outlawing of discrimination not just between men and women, but also on grounds of ethnic origin, religion, sexual orientation, disability and age. Some estimates have suggested that the repatriation of powers, especially in relation to the Temporary Agency Workers Directive and the Working Time Directive, could lead to the creation of at least 60,000 jobs. However, in practice, Brexit is unlikely to make a great difference to the regulatory impulse of UK politicians and interest groups: recent UK governments have been responsible for large extensions of employment laws going far beyond those ordained by the EU.

- Increasing the minimum wage through the implementation of the National Living Wage will have considerable effects on labour markets. By the government's own estimates it will costs tens of thousands of jobs and 4 million working hours in the next few years. It is likely to lead to over 20 per cent of all private sector workers having their pay set directly or indirectly by the government – in addition to those on public sector pay scales. The academic literature suggests that minimum wage laws have a small but significant negative effect on overall employment levels, with the effect being greater for young adults, greater in recessions and greater in the long term. Given that 60 per cent of those who are believed to earn less than a 'living wage' work part time and 44 per cent are in the top half of the household income distribution, any benefits from the National Living Wage as an anti-poverty measure are questionable.
- There is much concern over high pay as well as low pay, and new restrictions are being contemplated. Although the earnings distribution has not become more unequal in general over the last thirty years, those at the very top have seen large increases in their earnings. However, the evidence suggests that (despite assertions to the contrary) high pay *is* linked to performance. Artificial restrictions on top pay may lead to knock-on effects which end up penalising poorer workers.
- A stronger case needs to be made to emphasise the benefits of free labour markets in generating employment, growth, productivity and higher living standards. Furthermore, it is important that it becomes more widely understood that the effects of employment regulation and mandated benefits ultimately fall on employees, consumers, the unemployed and taxpayers, *not* on employers. The new

Apprenticeship Levy is an example of regulation which will almost certainly reduce pay levels in the long run without any obvious corresponding benefit. And some elements of regulation raise significant issues about personal freedoms and opportunity in addition to narrowly economic concerns.

- Well-meaning employment regulation often has significant and perverse downsides: anti-discrimination laws, for example, may lead to falling job opportunities for some protected groups. Employment protection laws lead to less hiring, more temporary contracts and worsened employment prospects for young workers and other disadvantaged groups. Middle-aged male workers benefit most from such laws.

- There have been moves to extend employment protection laws still further by restricting or even banning outright 'zero-hours' contracts. This would be a great mistake. Many people on such contracts are both well-off and have good job security. Many others find it suits their lifestyle and other obligations. Indeed, evidence suggests that those on zero-hours arrangements are happier with their employment conditions than those who are not. It is easy to be sanguine about the effects of yet more employment regulation because of the low level of unemployment in the UK. However, youth unemployment remains worryingly high and it is often the most vulnerable groups who lose out from restrictive legislation.

- There are strong vested interests against reform. Employers see labour market regulation as a sunk cost and a useful barrier to potential competitors with different business models. Employees suffer from the 'endowment effect', well-known from behavioural economics, which leads them to value the benefits regulation brings more highly than the potentially bigger benefits of reform. Regulators and human resource managers benefit from regulatory complexity, which increases the demand for their services.

- A case can be made for greater regulatory competition: apart from repatriation of regulation to the UK from the EU, there is an argument for devolution within the UK – for instance, allowing Scotland to set its own minimum wage. More fundamental reforms should involve adding a 'sunset' clause to a large body of existing employment legislation, followed by a major review of regulation with the default of scrapping laws which can no longer be justified. This could lead to a dramatic reduction in the categories of employment regulation from around 100 currently to perhaps just 5.

- Some have argued for less reliance on legislation but more emphasis on 'voluntary' measures such as the promotion of the Living Wage, or setting targets for women members on boards. These measures, however, are not an improvement on compulsion if the policy itself is damaging. Such pressures blur the boundaries of legitimate state power: businesses and individuals should not be cajoled into changing their priorities in line with often transient government objectives.

TABLES, FIGURES AND BOXES

PART 1

IDEAS

1 INTRODUCTION

Back when trade unions were a power in the land, a phrase activists often bandied around was 'working to rule'. In a dispute, unions might avoid a strike (and thus lost pay) but still put pressure on management by insisting on a literal reading of contractual rules. UK employers found their room for manoeuvre and innovation was substantially reduced, and productivity was held back.

Those days are gone, but in a different sense we are all 'working to rule' today: the state places myriad restrictions on the freedom of employers and workers to form contractual arrangements and to change them as economic circumstances alter.

Governments seem unable to stop intervening in labour markets. Some such regulation may be beneficial to individuals or groups, and even where there are obvious downsides it may be a reasonable judgement that the benefits of particular interventions outweigh their costs. However, regulation can be carried much further than is economically sensible. Despite occasional acknowledgment that excessive regulation can choke off enterprise and reduce job opportunities – as the current high rates of unemployment in many continental European countries demonstrate – our political classes show no sign of letting this inhibit proposals for further intervention.

The recent recession and its labour market consequences have encouraged politicians of all parties, in their never-ending search for scapegoats and easy solutions, to propose further restrictions on employers and employees. The EU referendum result seems to have added further fuel to the fire. In the last few years we have seen legislation or proposals to raise minimum wage rates, put ceilings on company executive and public sector pay, eliminate zero-hours contracts, extend flexible working arrangements, add worker representatives to boards, give longer and better-paid parental leave, impose stronger equality obligations, require firms to pay an apprenticeship levy, provide automatic access to pension schemes and prioritise British workers over those from other countries.

This book outlines the historical development of labour market regulation, offers a primer on the UK's current employment legislation and examines economic theory and international evidence on the effects of different types of intervention.

I argue that policymakers often misunderstand the situations which they attempt to regulate. Their interventions do not always benefit those they are intended to help. They have unforeseen and often undesirable consequences, and are usually more costly to implement than anticipated. Compliance is difficult, expensive and in some cases impossible fully to achieve. Loosely drafted legislation increases uncertainty and encourages litigation. The effect may be to reduce overall wages and employment, raise prices, discourage innovation and inhibit economic growth, while particularly penalising young people and others on the fringes of the labour market.

But it should also be emphasised that, apart from a narrowly economic calculus, many forms of regulation raise important issues about individual freedom to pursue legitimate personal and societal goals, to enter occupations or to start businesses, and to make use of individual and collective assets in preferred ways.

Although there is a classical liberal case – which I will discuss – for complete freedom of contract, few now argue that there should be no employment regulation at all. So we need to go beyond a black-and-white interpretation of government involvement. I therefore attempt to identify what is necessary and what is unnecessary. Recognising that much current legislation – though less than many imagine – ultimately derives from the European Commission, I consider the implications of Brexit for future policy.

The problem

In order for people to be able to get jobs, somebody must create opportunities for work. In order for the number of jobs to grow as the population expands, most of this expansion has to come from the private sector,[1] primarily from firms and individuals who see employing others[2] as a means of generating output which can be sold at a profit sufficient to justify their investment and supervisory commitment. Historically, this has required access to capital, a flair for spotting opportunities to sell goods and services, and the drive and ability to recruit, organise and motivate employees to assist in this endeavour. For their part, potential employees must be able and motivated to supply their skills and effort for an employer whose interests, while different from their own, make mutually beneficial 'trade' possible in the labour market.

These factors still matter very much. Under modern conditions, however, they are often insufficient. Labour markets have always been regulated, as I shall show, to some degree. But in the last fifty years the range and extent of regulation in the UK has continually expanded. For motives which at first glance seem

---

1   Public sector employment is very important in any conceivable modern economy, although its appropriate scale – and employment conditions – are hotly disputed. Some authors (Mazzucato 2013) argue that strategic state investment is important for stimulating private sector growth. But public spending of all types ultimately depends on extracting a surplus from the voluntary productive activities of the private sector, and there is increasing reluctance to pay more in taxes to do this.

2   Self-employment is an important feature of modern economies, and I discuss it in Chapter 11. But although growing in importance, it remains a minority activity largely confined to areas where economies of scale and scope are limited.

unimpeachable, governments have laid down conditions under which employment can or cannot take place, and have placed a huge variety of obligations and prohibitions on employers and a significant amount on employees. They have also imposed taxes and other financial imposts on both parties.

Potential employers, therefore, nowadays have a complex maze of regulations to navigate when offering employment. Moreover, the effects of government interventions are often poorly understood by the general public. Their alleged benefits are extolled by headline-grabbing politicians, while even the more predictable costs are downplayed. The unintended consequences of intervention only emerge some time afterwards, and often fall on apparently unconnected individuals and areas of the economy. In many cases, however, costs fall heavily on precisely those people whom the legislation was ostensibly intended to benefit.

In a world where government intervenes everywhere, the business of creating jobs – and, indeed, of finding employment by individuals – becomes much more difficult. Potential employers are faced with all sorts of constraints on the conditions under which they can employ people: how they recruit them, how much they can pay them, how much they must pay the government, how many hours employees can work, what leave arrangements they must be offered, what kind of safety regime they must operate under, how and under what circumstances unsatisfactory employment contracts can be terminated. Employers must keep extensive records and are required to return a great deal of data to government departments.

Compliance with these requirements involves using significant resources in administration and monitoring. The costs of compliance are inflated as firms try to diminish the uncertainty involved in badly drafted and frequently amended[3] legislation, which often

---

3 A particular problem arises when a law is passed which lacks clarity and detail. It is then amended by regulations which are not fully discussed in Parliament and poorly publicised.

requires subjective assessments of what constitutes reasonable or appropriate behaviour by employers and employees. In the UK alleged breaches of employment law can lead to employees taking out an employment tribunal case. Although the number of such claims has fallen dramatically since the introduction of charges in 2013, they are still an ever-present danger to employers. They are time-consuming, costly and stressful, and impose a significant burden on employees as well as employers. Their judgements may also lead to unanticipated and expensive extensions of the law beyond what Parliament may have originally intended.

This is worth emphasising, for while much business rhetoric focuses on the problems faced by employers, regulation also places restrictions on employees. At a minimum they must be prepared to pay taxes and national insurance; less obviously they must often possess qualifications and submit to checks which the government (rather than the employer) imposes. Such rules can prevent them from competing with others. They may be forbidden from undertaking tasks which they would be capable of and happy to contract to perform. They may not be allowed to negotiate arrangements which do not conform to those mandated by government or imposed on employers by trade union pressures facilitated by government. Employees may be prevented from working the hours they wish to work, and obliged to take leave which they have not chosen. With few exceptions, they cannot waive their employment rights (the cost of which they often largely bear themselves in any case) in order to secure what they would regard as a preferable deal.[4] And of course some workers may suffer because of privileges granted to others; for example, employment protection rules which benefit 'insiders' – those existing employees with secure jobs – may reduce opportunities for 'outsiders' seeking a toehold in the labour market.

---

4   Employment rights are therefore unlike property rights, which can be bought or sold to increase efficiency and economic welfare.

Employment regulation is often justified in terms of some category of 'market failure' – an increasingly popular term which is interpreted to mean that free contracting by individuals and firms leads to economically or socially undesirable outcomes. Such problems are frequently exaggerated. Situations are sometimes honestly misunderstood: with markets already being distorted by pre-existing regulation, deregulation may be more appropriate than further interventions. Proposed regulation can be badly designed, and will not produce the expected outcome. Worse, it may involve knock-on consequences which create new problems. Even quite sensible interventions can be mishandled and incompetently administered.

Moreover, such interventions, given our imperfect political process, in reality often serve particular interests, including privileged sections of the workforce, politicians who play on anti-employer prejudice and bureaucrats who benefit from larger regulatory budgets.

So we should never take as axiomatic that a 'market failure' will be overcome or alleviated by government action. 'Government failure', as we shall see, is also possible, even likely, in a world where incentives to honest and competent governance are often inadequate, and where even honest and competent governments do not have the detailed information necessary to perform efficiently.

Outline of this book

In what follows, I examine the nature and consequences of employment regulation, defined as *legal restrictions on the terms and conditions under which employment takes place*. There are a number of related policy areas which impact on the labour market, such as education, taxation and benefits regimes, regional policies, international trade and schemes to subsidise employment or 'create' jobs. These are all important areas of study with implications for overall employment (as, to take an even wider view, are macroeconomic fiscal and monetary policies), but they are not the focus of attention here.

The next chapter begins, however, by outlining how labour markets might be expected to work in the absence of any government regulation. While this highly simplified and idealised view of the workings of labour markets, and their contractual basis, is a useful first step to understanding the benefits which they produce, the chapter also points to complications which arise in the real world.

Chapter 3 gives a perspective to current concerns by briefly sketching the UK's historical experience. While the form and content of employment regulation has dramatically changed over the centuries, there have always been rules to constrain the buying and selling of labour power.

Chapter 4 sets out the main areas of employment regulation in the UK today, and explains how regulation is enforced. Some general ideas about the costs of regulation are introduced. The role which our membership of the European Union has played in determining employment law is outlined and assessed in Chapter 5, while subsequent chapters examine particular types of regulation in more detail. This section draws on the theoretical analysis which economists have used in assessing the consequences of regulation, and reviews the insights from a large and ever-growing body of empirical evidence.

Finally, all this is all pulled together in a conclusion which summarises the findings and suggests a way forward.

2 HOW LABOUR MARKETS WORK, AND WHY PEOPLE WANT TO REGULATE THEM

To set the scene for discussing regulation of labour markets, we need to think about how such markets might behave in the absence of regulation. The economic analysis of labour markets can be made very complicated, but most mainstream economists would argue that they are best understood through the general framework of demand and supply. Elementary 'textbook' analysis is oversimplified – as I will explain later – but simplified models can nevertheless serve as powerful guides to thinking.

Demand, supply and labour market equilibrium

The demand for labour services in a market economy is primarily the result of profit-seeking firms employing people as a means to an end, that of creating goods and services to be sold at a profit.

Economists define a useful piece of jargon, the *marginal revenue product* of labour input. This is the addition to a firm's total revenue resulting from employing one extra unit of labour – dependent on the *additional output created* and the *price at which it can be sold*. The marginal productivity of labour tends to decline as employment increases:[1] adding extra workers, or extra hours of

---

1 In the 'perfectly competitive' economy envisaged by textbooks, the marginal revenue is constant as the firm is a 'price taker'. Its output is too small to have an impact on the market price of goods and services, so each extra unit sold brings in the same revenue as the previous unit. In these circumstances, the term *value*

work, to a task is likely to add to output but at a decreasing rate. This generates a downward-sloping demand curve for labour. Profit-maximising enterprises will employ labour up to the point where the marginal revenue product is equal to the cost of an extra hour of labour services – the wage rate. Of course, firms don't always prioritise profits, but in a competitive environment managements which are insufficiently concerned with the bottom line will be under shareholder pressure as share prices dip. So profit maximisation is a not-altogether-unreasonable simplifying assumption.

In the UK currently just under two thirds of the employed population is employed by for-profit businesses. What of the rest? Slightly under 20 per cent are employed in the public sector, with the remainder being self-employed, working for charities or other not-for-profits, or in domestic employment. Even in these areas, although people are not employed to make profits, reasoning suggests that the demand curve for labour will slope downwards: a government department or a charity will have a limited budget and, other things being equal, will tend to offer less employment at a higher wage rate. Similarly, the employment offered by families to cleaners, nannies or gardeners will be inversely related to the wage paid per hour.

Look at the market now from the viewpoint of potential employees. The number of hours of paid work which individuals want to supply, and the number of individuals who wish to supply them, will be affected by the wage rate, although the reasoning is subtle. Economic theory makes a distinction between the 'substitution' and 'income' effects of a change in the wage rate. As the wage rate increases, paid work becomes more attractive and we tend to *substitute* market work for other uses of waking time, such as caring for children or other dependants, domestic

---

marginal product is sometimes used instead. But if the firm dominates the relevant product market, there is a second reason for the labour demand curve to decline, as increased output is associated with a lower price per unit sold (falling *marginal revenue*).

unpaid work, study and leisure activities. On the other hand, rising wages mean that our *income* increases, so we may also wish to take advantage of this to spend more time with our families or otherwise enjoy the fruits of our efforts. So the substitution and income effects move in opposite directions, and for different groups in the population the balance of these effects may be positive or negative. There are variations by age group, but for males overall the income effect appears to dominate – that is, higher wage rates lead to reduced hours (Borjas 2013: Chapter 2). For females the substitution effect is on average the greater (Keane 2011): women work more hours in the labour market as wage rates rise.

However, even if a wage rate increase in a particular industry or region were to mean that existing workers supply fewer hours, there would probably be an influx of potential employees from other industries or regions where wage rates had remained static or fallen. So the assumption of an upward-sloping supply curve remains a reasonable hypothesis for any particular subset of the labour market.

The combination of a downward-sloping demand curve and an upward-sloping supply curve is pictured in Figure 1. In the absence of restrictions on the working of the labour market, the wage will tend to move towards 0W, with employment 0Q. Conventional economic analysis teaches that this wage and employment 'equilibrium' combination is optimal, in the sense that the value of the extra output to the employer is just equal to the subjective benefit obtained by the provider of the marginal hour of labour. This is a bit of a mouthful: what it means is that there will be (1) an employer for whom the benefit from an extra hour's input is just equal to its cost and (2) somebody who is just as well off working an extra hour in this job as he or she would be working in some other job or subsisting on some other income source, such as welfare benefits. All the other ('intramarginal') hours supplied make their providers subjectively better off.

Figure 1   Demand, supply and 'equilibrium' in the labour market

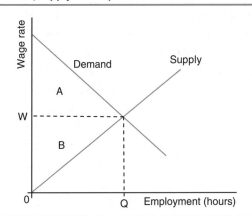

The employer gain from employment (the 'employer surplus') is the area of the triangle A, while the employees' total gain from employment is area B. Society as a whole gains the area A + B from allowing this employment to take place. This is a static picture. But, as an early IEA writer explained, 'it is an essential assumption behind a labour market that it will work to adjust the deployment of the labour force to the changing demands upon it' (Robertson 1961: 25). Demand – and supply – conditions are constantly changing, and in a free market this will lead to changes in the wage rate and the hours employed. Suppose for instance that initially wage rates in pubs and in coffee shops are equal, and supply and demand for each type of employee is in balance, with all who wish to work at going pay rates being able to find a job.[2] Now the demand for beer drinking falls while the

---

2   In much of what follows I am assuming that there is no 'Keynesian' unemployment resulting from a deficiency of *aggregate demand*. This may be argued to be a strong assumption, though I would defend it. In any case, if there *were* any such problem of a shortfall in aggregate demand, it would not be alleviated by the sort of regulation discussed in this book.

demand for coffee drinking increases. Other things being equal, wages and hours offered by pub employers will tend to fall, leading some staff to leave and move into cafes, where the increased demand has temporarily raised wages. Over time wages will adjust back to parity, but with a changed workforce composition: there will be more coffee shop staff and fewer pub staff than before. Again, supply and demand in each field will be in balance and all who wish to work at prevailing wages will be employed.

Admittedly this is a hugely simplified picture of the labour market, and needs a whole clutch of implausible assumptions to make it strictly correct – but it gives a general picture of how mainstream economists visualise the way in which things work. To the extent that it suggests that competitive pressures tend to generate efficient outcomes, it is not seriously misleading.

One limitation of this approach, however, is that it concentrates on equilibrium short-run positions to which the market tends. This can be attacked on several grounds, some spurious, but one worth thinking about is that it describes an essentially 'spot' market, that is, one where employment decisions are made for one (short) period, say a day or a week.

In reality, people typically stick with jobs for quite long periods. In the UK the average worker will have been in his or her current job for around five years (Faggio et al. 2011; Gregg and Gardner 2015). Worker search for a job is time-consuming and often costly, as is employer search for employees. There are also costs of negotiating pay, of moving house, of changing children's schools and so on. These 'transaction costs' mean that it is normal[3] for workers and employers to have *contracts* which commit them to a continuing relationship.

---

3 Though not universal. In the past many casual labour markets, for example, those on the docks, had some characteristics of spot markets. Arguably the development of the internet and social media, reducing transaction costs, together with the development of the 'gig economy' (see Chapter 11) is making the spot market model relevant once more.

Contracts

What can we say about these contracts? A completely voluntary market in labour services would involve what Americans call the 'contract at will'. This, according to the distinguished US legal academic, Richard Epstein (1984), is a common law doctrine which characterised American labour markets until eroded by twentieth-century legislative developments which protected collective bargaining and, later, civil rights.

A contract at will allows employers to hire and fire without legal restrictions,[4] and similarly allows employees to change employers whenever they want. Epstein (1992: 149) believes that the law should stay out of the determination of such contracts:

> [T]he terms of an employment contract are the business of only the parties to it. Freedom of contract on this matter is no different from freedom of speech or freedom of action. Unless and until the contract in question poses the threat of harm to third parties ... or is procured by fraud or sharp practice, then each person is his or her own best judge both of the private costs incurred by contracting and of the private benefits obtained from that contract.

Within this type of framework, a wide variety of contracts could exist depending on the preferences of employers and employees and their relative bargaining power. Contracts could include

---

4 Although in principle US employers can still fire workers 'for good cause, bad cause or no cause at all', in practice their autonomy is nowadays reduced by statutory exemptions at the state and/or federal level. In many states, a long-term contract can be inferred from the behaviour of employers, and this gives some protection against dismissal without formal procedures. A refusal by an employee to commit illegal or immoral acts is a defence against dismissal in most states, and discriminatory dismissal (on racial, gender or disability grounds) is illegal everywhere. Workers covered by recognised collective bargaining also have some protection against arbitrary dismissal.

lengthy periods of notice, compensation to employees for dismissal or compensation to employers for early leaving (for instance, where expensive training has been provided), and various mixtures of pay and conditions, including fringe benefits and risk-sharing. But no *standard* or *minimum* set of contractual conditions would be set by law.[5] This would allow freedom for firms to choose the cheapest way to produce output in competitive markets, and avoid shackling them with legal commitments to preserve jobs and conditions for a given set of workers. It would allow freedom for individuals to choose between different types of employment and different conditions, without restrictions on hours worked or holidays or pension arrangements.

Epstein thus makes a powerful liberal case for freedom of contract for its own sake. This complements the pragmatic arguments which mainstream economists tend to rely on.

It would be ridiculous to claim that the contracts emerging from such a voluntarist environment will always be ideal from the point of view of the employee – but they will not necessarily be too great for the employer either. Those pushing for regulation make much of the inequality of market power: employers are said to dictate conditions which workers are forced to accept. There are certainly cases like this, though they are less frequent than is sometimes claimed. In a tight labour market, *employees* can be in a strong position. This is glaringly obvious in the case of leading entertainers, sports stars, writers, some professionals and top executives,[6] but it is also the case more

---

5   Whatever voluntary contractual arrangements are in place must be legally enforceable, but the law should recognise that breach of contract is sometimes inevitable as economic conditions change (Campbell 2008). Thus damages for contractual breach should reflect measurable losses to the party concerned and should also be conditional on attempts made by complainants to mitigate these damages (for example, by dismissed workers actively seeking another job where this is feasible).

6   See Rosen (1981) for an analysis of the factors which give such individuals market power. Since Rosen wrote, the trends he discerned have become much more prevalent.

often than is credited even with less glamorous jobs. If there is a shortage of skilled workers in a particular field, wages tend to rise and other aspects of the job may be enhanced. Employers can and do offer better pensions, holidays, parental leave, health insurance and fringe benefits where they need to attract and retain workers.[7] As for job security, it is in many firms' interests to retain staff rather than fire them at the slightest downturn in sales. Even in the absence of employment protection laws, it is costly[8] to lose productive and experienced workers, in whom there may have been a good deal of investment in training, only to have to search for, recruit and train new workers in an upturn.

Employees may also be protected to some degree by the reputational risk to employers associated with arbitrary or opportunistic behaviour. As Epstein (1984: 967–68) argues, such behaviour damages an employer's reputation with both existing and potential future employees. The best of those currently with the firm, seeing how colleagues have been mistreated, are likely to seek – and find – new jobs. Potential employees may be put off applying, especially since knowledge of employer practices is now widely disseminated through the internet and social media – an important development since Epstein was first writing on this subject. Sites such as glassdoor.com, for example, post reviews of employers by current and past employees.

---

7   Our earlier analysis concentrated simply on the hourly wage rate as the determinant of hours supplied. Clearly, the world is a bit more complicated than this. Apart from these other non-pay benefits from a job, we also have to consider the inherent attractiveness of jobs in terms of pleasant or unpleasant working conditions, the cost of acquiring necessary skills and so on. It is the *net advantage* of jobs which determines labour supply, not just pay.

8   One recent report puts the cost of replacing staff in Britain at over £30,000 on average, made up of the logistical cost of recruiting and absorbing a new employee and the cost of lost output while the replacement gets up to speed. http://www.hr review.co.uk/hr-news/recruitment/it-costs-over-30k-to-replace-a-staff-member/ 50677 (accessed 29 March 2016).

In the US, where employment protection laws were historically non-existent, temporary layoffs (where it is expected that workers are rehired as demand picks up) were much commoner than was the case in Europe, where legal requirements about dismissal and compensation meant that either workers were kept on the payroll ('hoarded' labour) despite producing little saleable output, or else dismissed permanently. In the recent recession, however, US employers seem to have made rather less use of temporary layoffs (Groshen 2011), perhaps reflecting increasing regulation.

Whatever the relative balance of power within a contract at will, however, it is axiomatic that 'each party to the agreement regards himself or herself as better off with the agreement than without it' (Epstein 1992: 149). This is a powerful argument which is familiar to all economists, as it forms the justification for free trade between countries and for free markets more generally. The labour market, in Epstein's argument, is fundamentally no different – whatever politicians and activists may claim.

A word of warning, though: Epstein's view of the pre-twentieth-century US labour market is oversimplified. For instance, laws enforcing racial discrimination in the American South meant that contracts for black workers were distorted by state and federal actions. And certainly in the UK, as we shall see in the next chapter, 'close analysis shows that there was no period of laissez-faire, during which the labour market was governed by the general precepts of private law' (Deakin 2003: 8). Nowadays, there are considerable restrictions on the form a 'contract of service' can take in the UK, with a wide range of legally enforceable rights and obligations.[9]

So Epstein's analysis may be better considered as an abstract model of a contractual regime rather than a literal description of

---

9 Self-employed freelancers can work under a 'contract *for* services' which, while still subject to various legal restrictions, is much less prescriptive.

a prelapsarian era, and so is on a par with the simple economic model sketched in the previous section. It still provides a most useful benchmark which should be much more prominent in public debate.

'Market failure'

The view that unconstrained labour markets can work well is rejected by those who believe that such markets are inevitably riddled with problems of 'market failure' (Wachter 2012). For politicians and others, this expression is often a catch-all for everything which people don't like about markets on egalitarian, religious or even aesthetic grounds. For economists, however, it has a more precise meaning, albeit a problematic one.

It is based on an analysis of the ways in which a market – in this case the market for labour services – fails to meet the assumptions of *perfect competition*, the model derived from the neoclassical revolution of the latter part of the nineteenth and first half of the twentieth century, and embedded in standard textbooks ever since.

The first formal definition of market failure was supplied by Francis Bator (1958: 351), who saw it as

> the failure of a more or less idealized system of price-market institutions to sustain 'desirable' activities or to estop 'undesirable' activities.

This 'idealized system'[10] has pedagogical significance, but as a literal description of a feasible economy it is a non-starter. Critics

---

10 It involves assumptions such as the market being characterised by large numbers of firms and consumers, each insignificant in relation to the market as a whole; perfect information; technology displaying diminishing returns to a variable factor of production and constant returns to scale; consistent and transitive consumer preferences – and so on.

include economists of the Austrian School, who see markets as a discovery process where participants are never in possession of the full information assumed by the model, and where change is a recurrent feature preventing economies from settling at an idealised equilibrium of the sort which Bator uses as a reference point.[11]

Be that as it may, those economists who continue to use the concept of market failure have pointed to several areas where labour markets seem to perform badly.

They include *externalities,* where private decisions by employers and employees focus on private concerns and do not consider the wider costs or benefits of employment.[12] One might be the provision of workplace training which, though potentially benefiting the employer and the employee, might also spill benefits over into the wider economy, for instance if trained workers subsequently move quickly to new employers who do not pay for the training. This 'free rider' argument suggests that training will be underprovided where employers think only of their own or shareholders' interests.

Such reasoning is often used to support proposals for government funding for training, or requirements placed on employers to provide training or offer time for off-site training or education, or the UK's new Apprenticeship Levy (see Chapter 10). It is a rather weak argument: as Becker (1993: Chapter III) has suggested, if the training has a value elsewhere – it is 'general' rather than specific to the firm providing it – the cost will tend to fall on the employee through reduced wages during the training period, as under traditional apprenticeship systems. The employee bears the costs, but reaps the reward of higher pay in the future.

---

11 For a short popular critique of the concept of market failure, see Booth (2014).

12 The concept of externalities was formalised by A. C. Pigou (1920) almost a century ago. In some ways it is an economist's extension of John Stuart Mill's classical liberal principle that we should be free to do what we want unless our behaviour causes harm to others.

However, if the government intervenes, by for instance putting a floor on apprentice pay through a minimum wage, this may be difficult to achieve. This is an example of the way in which government intervention to resolve one perceived labour market problem (low or even negative[13] pay) adds to another (shortage of training opportunities).

A second frequently mentioned category of potential market failure is *information asymmetry* – which exists where the parties to a contract have access to different amounts of information. For instance, suppose an employer knows that a production process is hazardous to health, while potential employees are unaware of this. Such a possibility is held to justify government intervention on health and safety grounds. Note, though, that if employees are aware of the risk and are prepared to run this risk for a higher rate of pay, then (as we shall see later) it may be socially optimal to allow the production process to continue without strict regulation. Many jobs are widely known to carry a higher-than-average risk of injury or death (the fire service, working on oil rigs, scaffolding work, for example). As I shall argue later, such jobs typically carry what economists call a 'compensating differential': other things being equal, pay or other conditions of employment are enhanced so that the employee finds the job attractive notwithstanding the risk. At the same time, the extra cost of hiring workers in dangerous conditions provides an incentive for employers to improve safety without government being involved.

In this view, any information asymmetry may only require government intervention to make full information available to potential employees, rather than banning the activity or insisting on costly modifications of the production process. Even this

---

13 Historically, parents or other benefactors would often pay employers to provide an apprenticeship but such a system is no longer feasible given minimum wage laws. In modern conditions internship schemes similarly tend to involve a net cost to workers or their families, and thus many such schemes are now being held to breach minimum wage law.

may be unnecessary in an environment where information is widely available through the internet, and where trade unions, other pressure groups and active news media disseminate new findings quickly. There are grounds to protect vulnerable individuals, particularly children, from taking risks which they do not fully understand, but the case needs to be clearly made. As I shall suggest, a 'health and safety culture', if carried to excess, can generate hefty financial and other costs for minimal gains in safety.

Another possible market failure arising from asymmetric information may occur in relation to private work-related insurance schemes. Individuals taking out private insurance against sickness or unemployment[14] are aware of their own motivation and commitment in a way which the insurer is not. A problem of *moral hazard* is thus created: some insured workers, aware of the cushion which insurance provides, may increase their probability of being sacked by working less diligently. If unemployed, they may search for work less vigorously than if they had no fall-back income. If sick, they may take longer off work than necessary. Over time, insurance premiums then have to rise, which discourages the more hard-working and highly committed workers, whose probability of unemployment or time off work is lower than average, from taking out insurance in the first place. Insurers will be left with the bad risks, those workers who are particularly likely to make claims. This is the problem of *adverse selection*, which can undermine the viability of private insurance schemes.

In practice, though, such private schemes have worked in many cases in the past: nineteenth-century friendly societies and early trade unions provided some such protection.[15] Moral

---

14 A further problem with private unemployment insurance may be the lack of an actuarial basis for calculating the risk of unemployment.

15 As Ronald Coase argued in the famous case of the lighthouse, theoretical cases of market failure (or 'blackboard economics' as he put it) often turn out to be less of a problem in the real world. See Veljanovski (2015: Chapter 2).

hazard issues were reduced by members usually being known to each other or to officials of what were small-scale operations. Even today some limited unemployment insurance is available to protect mortgage payers (albeit under very restrictive conditions). But state provision of unemployment benefits has largely crowded out private provision.[16]

Another variant of market failure arises from *market power*. While the idealised competitive market outlined above assumes many buyers and sellers of labour services competing furiously with each other, in practice one or both sides of the market may be in a rather stronger position. Think about employers: if there is only one (*monopsony*) or just a few (*oligopsony*, perhaps in the guise of an employers' association) in a particular geographical or occupational area, wages may be forced down below the level that would prevail in a more competitive market.

An interesting historical example[17] is English professional football, which for many years enforced a maximum wage, never reaching more than £20 a week even as late as the early 1960s. It also maintained the archaic 'retain and transfer' system, which (until a High Court ruling in the case of George Eastham) gave clubs the power to retain the contracts of players indefinitely.

On the other hand, a particular group of workers who can control the supply of labour (perhaps through a trade union or a professional body) may themselves exercise some *monopoly*[18]

---

16 Self-employed people, though, typically cannot access state benefits as easily as employees. In the Netherlands, freelance workers have therefore formed small groups to run mutual sickness fund schemes (*broodfunds*) to remedy this deficiency, suggesting that there is greater scope for private employment insurance than is often assumed. See http://www.theguardian.com/money/2015/jan/14/freelance -payment-sickness-leave (accessed 25 February 2016).

17 Something similar seems to persist in the US college sports set-up: http://www .washingtontimes.com/news/2012/mar/30/the-free-market-case-against-the-ncaa -chokehold-on/?page=all (accessed 20 May 2015).

18 A few such groups may form an *oligopoly*. If market power exists on both sides, we have *bilateral monopoly*. An extensive literature on bilateral monopoly has, however, produced few public policy implications.

power to force wages up. Of course, this market power may be in part the result of government occupational regulation (see Chapter 6) which, deliberately or otherwise, entrenches such a monopoly position: it might be better to remove that support rather than engage in further regulation. On the other hand, Austrian economists point out that positions of market power tend to be undermined over time through innovation and unanticipated ways of doing things. For example, containerisation largely put an end to the power of dockworkers' unions. Paradoxically, excessive regulation intended to offset market power may inhibit the emergence of new forms of competition.

There are other theoretical angles from which to criticise the orthodox economic model.[19] Probably the most fundamental argument for intervention in employment, however, does not lie in technical issues about the assumptions of 'perfect' competition. Rather it lies in the claim that labour market outcomes are intrinsically *unfair*, that they offend against some conception of social justice. Not strictly a market failure in economists' terms, this is rather a moral or political reaction against labour market outcomes such as extreme inequalities in pay.

F. A. Hayek famously called social justice 'a mirage', on which no two people could ever agree.[20] It is, however, a powerful mirage, and has led to very many attempts to interfere with the workings of labour markets – for example, income policies for thirty years after World War II, and more recently minimum wage and equal

---

19 Arguments drawn from behavioural economics are claimed to undermine models based on rational economic actors. For instance, as we shall see in Chapter 9, Jolls (2012) puts a case for anti-discrimination legislation to offset unconscious biases such as those which recruiters and other labour market actors display in experimental situations.

20 'No agreement exists about what social justice requires ... there is no known test by which to decide who is right if people differ, and ... no preconceived scheme of distribution could be effectively devised in a society whose individuals are free ... though a great many people are dissatisfied with the existing pattern of distribution, none of them has really any clear idea of what pattern he would regard as just' (Hayek 1976: 58).

pay legislation. After a period when such attempts to manipulate labour market outcomes had been de-emphasised in favour of income redistribution through taxes and benefits (including in-work benefits such as tax credits and housing benefits), we are now in a period when 'predistribution' is high on the agenda – a recognition of the limited scope for 'tax and spend' policies at a time of high public indebtedness.

'Government failure'

What all these rationalisations for government action downplay or ignore, however, is the possibility – even probability – of 'government failure'. This term, introduced by Roland McKean (1965), reflects the weaknesses of government regulation in practice.

For government intervention, often so seductive in theory, may be ineffective in reaching its ostensible objectives. First, governments cannot, any more than the private sector, know everything relevant to economic decisions. Indeed, private firms may be better placed to gather useful information as it is in their direct financial interest to do so. For example, even a well-intentioned and hard-working government employment agency may be worse at finding you a job than a private agency.

Second, there are often knock-on, second- or third-order effects from a decision to intervene: it changes the market and creates incentives for new forms of behaviour which may turn out worse than those that the intervention sought to improve. Imposing a minimum wage may lead employers to worsen other aspects of a worker's job: compromising safety to save money, or reducing fringe benefits, or intensifying shift work. Or it may force workers onto benefits or out into the black or shadow economy where wages are lower than legitimate businesses are allowed to pay. I examine the knock-on effects of various types of regulation in later chapters.

Third, rules and regulations may be unduly influenced by interested parties to secure advantages for themselves at the expense of other firms, workers and consumers. Economists call this 'rent-seeking'. A suggestion that nursery staff need more training, for example, may be hijacked by training providers, trade unions and other commercial interests with an agenda of their own which does not coincide with the perceived problem. As they are concentrated sources of influence, they tend to do better at getting their way than widely dispersed interests such as those of parents and their children.

Fourth, government employees themselves may try to influence political decisions which favour the expansion of their remit, and thus lead over time to larger budgets and more power. A related problem in the UK is the creation of non-governmental bodies (QUANGOs) to administer the spending of public money or the regulation of activities: such bodies are typically headed by people with political agendas. There has also been the growth of what Snowdon (2012) calls 'sock puppets': charitable bodies largely funded by government to press for increasing intervention.[21]

And finally, democratic politicians responding to 'the vote motive' (Tullock 2006) will always be drawn to policies that appeal to the median voter, even though they may be quite conscious at one level that such policies are likely to be ineffective or even counter-productive – for example, pressuring firms to alter their remuneration systems for executives.

Such behaviour is perhaps not as reprehensible as it is often painted. In a party system it is always necessary for politicians to compromise, accepting some policies which they dislike in return for support over other issues which they consider more important – as the experience of the Conservative–Liberal

---

21 As a result of the publicity surrounding Snowdon's work, the government has introduced new rules on how charities spend its grants in order to reduce the use of public money to proselytise.

Democrat coalition demonstrated. Nevertheless, it is another reason to adopt a sceptical attitude towards proposals for government intervention in labour markets.

Conclusion

In this chapter I have set out the case for a free labour market and freedom of contract, while recognising that the analysis depends on assumptions which may be challenged. Those who do not accept that free markets are usually optimal can point to a range of potential 'market failures'; some arguments, moreover, raise more fundamental issues about the elusive concept of 'social justice'. But advocates of government intervention to offset problems allegedly associated with freedom of contract need to recognise that government intervention cannot be assumed to be benign or effective, and it often brings new problems in its wake.

Having sketched in general terms the way in which economists analyse the workings of labour markets and the rationale for regulation, I need to examine the economics of particular regulatory interventions in more detail. First, however, a detour to look at the growth of regulation historically.

PART 2

**EMPLOYMENT REGULATION:
THE BIG PICTURE**

3 A HISTORICAL PERSPECTIVE ON UK LABOUR MARKET REGULATION

While much of our labour market regulation is of fairly recent origin, governments have never allowed a complete free-for-all in employment. While much early legislation appears to have regulated markets to favour employers, in more modern times intervention has been intended primarily to benefit workers or to serve the needs of the state.

Governments are known to have interfered with the determination of the terms and conditions of employment for thousands of years. Back in the Babylonian empire in 1770 BCE, the Code of Hammurabi[1] laid down precise rates of pay for various classes of artisans and labourers (Schuettinger and Butler 1979). Throughout the ancient world, rulers placed restrictions on pay and on labour mobility. Chattel slavery was widely practised, even in otherwise quite sophisticated marketised and monetised economies such as ancient Athens, with high-falutin' ideas about freedom and democracy.

So in one sense there is, as Ecclesiastes tells us, nothing new under the sun. In this chapter a rapid flit through more than six hundred years of British history is intended to highlight the roots of contemporary attitudes towards employment regulation. This regulation has clearly intensified in recent decades, but its distant origins suggest that the urge to intervene is not a purely modern fad.

---

1 Preserved on a monolith (now held in the Louvre) which has lasted rather longer than ex-Labour Party leader Ed Miliband's notorious 'Edstone'.

The Early Modern period

In medieval Europe the guilds, the first privileged non-governmental actors in the labour market, were given powers to control entry into trades, apprenticeships and rates of pay. These powers at times acted as a significant constraint on commercial activity. Even in Adam Smith's day the famous inventor, James Watt, was forbidden by the instrument makers' guild to work in the city of Glasgow, because he had been apprenticed in Greenock, some 25 miles away. Fortunately, Glasgow University was outside the city limits and Watt could be employed as the university's instrument maker.[2] In England some legal restrictions on carrying out trades in cities survived the effective demise of the guilds and were reinforced by magistrates, but over time there were increasing gaps in the fabric of regulation. This allowed new enterprises to develop, particularly in unincorporated towns and in the countryside (Weingast 1995).

There were, however, more general controls on labour mobility and some other aspects of employment. For instance, take the Ordinance of Labourers of 1349, a response to the extraordinary circumstances of the Great Plague, in which between 1347 and 1349 it is estimated that a third to a half of the English population died. The Ordinance (which became the Statute of Labourers two years later) placed new constraints on movement between localities and jobs, and on pay increases. This pro-employer legislation was designed to shift the balance of power back in favour of employers after pay had risen following the labour shortage resulting from the Black Death.

The Ordinance is notable for the way in which idle men and women aged less than 60 could be forced into employment for anybody who was prepared to pay them the customary wage.

---

2   http://www.egr.msu.edu/~lira/supp/steam/wattbio.html (accessed 29 February 2016).

The labour 'contracts' resulting from these obligations were long-term and unbreakable, making the situation of some supposedly free labourers little different from that of serfs.

Such obligations, repeatedly fine-tuned over succeeding decades, endured for hundreds of years. They were incorporated into the Statute of Artificers of 1563, the Elizabethan attempt to tackle the alleged evils of beggary and vagrancy.[3] They were not finally removed from the statute book until 1814 – and then only after fierce debate (Bennett 2010). Alongside this legislation there were the Elizabethan Poor Laws, which had obvious impacts on incentives to work and on the mobility of labour. The Settlement Acts, which confined entitlement to Poor Law relief to those 'settled' in a parish by birth, apprenticeship or having completed a successful year's hiring,[4] were attacked on these grounds by Adam Smith. Modern commentators, for example Deakin (2003), have pointed to the way in which geographical employment patterns were strongly influenced by the Settlement principle.[5]

The nineteenth century

By the time Smith was writing, the English law on conspiracy could be used against combinations of workers, the forerunners of trade unions. More specific Combination Acts were passed in 1799–1800 in response to heightened political tensions during

---

3 The Statute of Artificers also allowed magistrates to set maximum wages and confirmed the regulation of apprenticeship in specified trades. Apprenticeships were for seven years and masters could only employ a maximum of three apprentices for each journeyman.

4 This requirement led to employment contracts being typically set for a year at a time, a practice which was only slowly eroded in the nineteenth century.

5 Something similar still exists (though it is being reformed) in modern China. The *hukou* system, where welfare benefits depend on place of registration, has been described by *The Economist* as comparable to apartheid in discriminating against rural workers who wish to move to cities. http://www.economist.com/news/special -report/21600798-chinas-reforms-work-its-citizens-have-be-made-more-equal-end ing-apartheid (accessed 29 February 2016).

the Napoleonic Wars. These Acts, always controversial, were eventually repealed in 1824, after prolonged debate in which economists both in and out of Parliament played an important role (Grampp 1979; Fetter 1980).

In the eighteenth and nineteenth centuries, relations between employers and employees were also regulated by Master and Servant laws. These laws required obedience from contracted employees[6] to their employers – with tough penalties for breaches. The 1823 Master and Servant Act, for example, specified prison sentences of up to three months for absconding from work. And this legislation was not just symbolic: there were some 10,000 prosecutions a year as late as the 1860s. During that decade, judges were interpreting this law to cover nascent trade union organisation, with some union officials being jailed for leading strikes.

The later nineteenth century, however, saw various attempts to define a legitimate role for unions, beginning with the Trade Union Act of 1871, which (following the recommendations of a Royal Commission report) effectively legalised them, with further legislation in 1875 clarifying that strikes might give rise to civil damages but not to criminal prosecution. Early in the twentieth century the Trades Disputes Act of 1906 went further by establishing that the funds of unions engaged in lawful strikes were exempt from damage liabilities for tort resulting from breach of contract. This was a response by the Liberal government of the day to the famous Taff Vale judgement, where a railway company had won damages against the Amalgamated Society of Railway Servants (a name very much redolent of its era).

It's worth emphasising that the principle under which unions were protected was one of immunity from being sued for damages, rather than any notion of a 'right to strike'. As Douglas Brodie (2003: 116) has commented:

---

6   Strictly, this did not cover all employees in the modern sense. Managers, agents and even clerks were treated as 'office holders' and had a different relationship to their Principals.

It may be that a significant factor was the absence of a written constitution in the UK and, as a consequence, a lack of tradition of bestowing positive rights. Given such a culture, the enactment of a positive right to strike would not have been viewed as an option.

There is a contrast here with continental European systems which lay emphasis on positive rights, a difference which, as we shall see, lies behind some of the tensions between the UK and the EU over employment legislation.

The nineteenth century also saw the development of law covering what we now think of as health and safety at work, although at the time other issues of morality and decency were frequently adduced in debate. The process began with the 1802 Factories Act, the first of ten major pieces of factory legislation in the nineteenth century.[7] The Act was intended to protect children, a recurring theme in early legislation. In 1833 the Factory Inspectorate was set up with a brief to inspect factories, the aim being to prevent injury to child textile workers. Protection was gradually extended to women: adult males, however, were not directly covered until the twentieth century (although they benefited to some degree as a by-product of changing work organisation consequent on earlier legislation). Similarly, the Mines and Collieries Act of 1842,[8] which banned women and young children

---

7   There had been earlier attempts at regulating working conditions, for instance, legislation on child chimneysweeps. The 1802 Act required some minimum educational provision by employers of young children. Interestingly, as far back as 1788 the view had been expressed that regulation of working conditions would damage international trading competitiveness (Engerman 2003: 30).

8   This Act followed a Royal Commission and extended the principle of inspection to mines. As with earlier legislation, issues of morality were frequently emphasised. For instance, in the House of Lords debate on the bill, reference was made to females working semi-naked underground and child workers being deprived of both secular and religious education. See http://hansard.millbanksystems.com/lords/1842/jul/14/mines-and-collieries#s3v0065p0_18420714_hol_51 (accessed 27 January 2015).

from working underground, did nothing directly to improve the conditions of adult male miners.

The incursions of factory legislation into the principle of Victorian laissez-faire were attacked at one time or another by many of the leading economists of the day. Robert Torrens saw the consequent rise of costs associated with legislation as undermining competitiveness: attacking the Ten Hours Bill of 1847, he argued that (quoted in Blaug 1958)

> one of two events must inevitably ensue: the manufactures of England will be transferred to foreign lands, or else the operatives must submit to a reduction of wages of 25 per cent.

A similarly over-the-top position was taken by Nassau Senior, who thought profits would diminish directly in line with cuts in working hours – an argument parodied by Karl Marx as the 'last hour' fallacy (Johnson 1969). Senior, Henry Fawcett and J. S. Mill were also concerned with the implications for women's employment of limiting their hours of work while leaving those of men unchanged. In a striking anticipation of modern criticisms of employment regulation, they thought that this would lead to women losing jobs, as employers would prefer to hire men who could work longer hours. Senior even went so far as to suggest that women displaced from mining by regulation should be given financial compensation.

A further concern which emerged towards the end of the nineteenth century concerned the low level of wages and long hours in what were called 'sweated' trades – for example, clothing piecework carried out in the home or in squalid workshops. In 1891 the House of Commons passed the Fair Wages Resolution,[9] which required contractors working for the government to observe terms

---

9 Amended in 1909 and 1946, the Resolution was scrapped by the Conservatives in the 1980s.

and conditions which were no less favourable than those which emerged from collective bargaining in higher-paying sectors (quoted in Brodie 2003: 50):

> [I]n the opinion of this House it is the duty of the Government in all Government contracts to make provision against the evils which have recently been disclosed before the House of Lords Sweating Committee, and to insert such conditions as may prevent the abuses ... and make every effort to serve the payment of the rate of wages generally accepted as current for a competent workman in his trade.

The early twentieth century

This concern also led, in the early years of the twentieth century, to the setting up of Trade Boards to regulate conditions in the sweated trades. Winston Churchill, as President of the Board of Trade, introduced the Trade Boards Act 1909, which covered four areas – ready-made tailoring, paper box making, machine lace-making and chain-making – employing 200,000 workers, 70 per cent of whom were women (Addison 1993: 78). These Boards, renamed Wages Councils from 1945, covered more and more trades over time. At their peak, well over three million workers in 66 separate trades had their pay set by representatives of employers and unions, together with independents.[10]

The Trade Boards Act was just one manifestation of the 'New Liberalism', involving innovative forms of state intervention in the workings of the labour market. Inspired in part by William Beveridge's favourable impressions of post-Bismarckian Germany

---

10 The Councils were abolished under John Major's government in 1993, with the exception of the Agricultural Wage Board which, remarkably, survived until 2013 – indeed rump versions remain in Scotland and Northern Ireland. Labour MP Owen Smith, in his bid for the party leadership, recently called for the revival of Wages Councils.

(Harris 1998), David Lloyd George and Winston Churchill led such developments as labour exchanges, old-age pensions and unemployment insurance. These Liberal Party measures were supported by the Labour Party and were usually unopposed by the Conservatives.

It was, however, during World War I that state intervention really took off. During the course of the struggle Parliament granted the government unprecedented powers – including powers to mobilise and direct labour. Conscription was not introduced until 1916, but from early in the conflict the government aimed to control the expansion of the volunteer army so that essential production should not be stripped of workers. A National Register was compiled, with groups of key workers being held back from military service. As the war progressed, the government began to allocate labour across the economy. Controls were placed on movement between civilian jobs, powers were taken to limit wage increases, and agreements were negotiated with unions to relax restrictive practices and permit the 'dilution' of skilled jobs by the employment of unskilled men and, increasingly, women. A new Ministry of Labour was created to oversee employment issues and to coordinate some of the pre-war functions dispersed between the Home Office, the Board of Trade and the Local Government Board (Parker 1957).

Although many of these powers were relinquished at the end of the war, a precedent had been set which would be built on for much of the twentieth century. Shortly after the war ended, for example, an Industrial Courts Act gave the government permanent powers to arbitrate in industrial disputes, subject to both parties agreeing (Brodie 2003: 166–69). These powers were to be used repeatedly in the years to come.

The end of the war also saw the beginnings of international regulation of labour with the formation of the International Labour Organization (ILO) as part of the League of Nations, set up by the 1919 Treaty of Versailles. UK officials and trade unionists played a large part in the formation of the ILO: the commission devising its constitution[11] worked from a British draft. Conventions and recommendations developed by the ILO (nowadays a UN agency) are adopted by a two-thirds majority vote at the annual International Labour Conference, which meets in Geneva. National delegations consist of one employer representative, one union representative and two government officials.

States are not obliged to ratify ILO conventions, and the UK, despite initial enthusiasm for the principle, was ambivalent from the start about such supranational regulation in practice. The first ILO convention covered the 48-hour working week. The UK never ratified this convention, which predates by 75 years the EU directive which led the UK (very reluctantly) to regulate in this area. At the time – and this was a recurring theme in the UK until Mrs Thatcher's day – the argument was that the government preferred agreements to be reached by collective bargaining rather than being imposed by law. World War I had established the respectability of unions as part of the fabric of national life, a development which would be strengthened during World War II.

However, the early part of the inter-war period saw considerable industrial unrest (most notably in the General Strike of 1926) and high unemployment. In the aftermath of the General Strike new restrictions on sympathetic strikes and picketing were introduced by the 1927 Trade Disputes Act. On the other hand, the scope of unemployment insurance was widened and other benefits, such as widows' pensions, were introduced to assist the needy. Safety legislation was consolidated and extended by the Factories Act 1937: with more than 150 clauses this Act

---

11 This included the assertions that 'labour is not a commodity' and that 'lasting peace can be established only if it is based upon social justice'. It sets out an agenda for a wide range of employment regulation. See http://ilo.org/dyn/normlex/en/f?p=1000:62:0::NO:62:P62_LIST_ENTRIE_ID:2453907:NO (accessed 30 December 2016).

was already concerned with the sort of detailed technical and administrative requirements which accompany much of today's health and safety legislation.

World War II and its aftermath

The 1939–45 conflict saw government intervention in labour markets reaching new heights, with 'manpower planning' now covering much of the adult female, as well as male, population, and with the state taking powers to amalgamate and close businesses in the interests of directing labour to the war effort. Trade unions were given a privileged position as a result of their cooperation with such wartime measures as wage restraint. One of their most able leaders, Ernest Bevin, became Minister of Labour and National Service in Churchill's coalition government.

There was some enthusiasm for continuing with these measures after the war was over. The Control of Engagement orders (which gave the government power to direct labour) were renewed until 1950,[12] though little used. Wage restraint (buttressed by food subsidies) had seemingly been relatively successful in keeping wartime inflation under control, and under the Attlee government attempts were made to continue with this. A White Paper in 1948 set the scene by arguing that wages had to be kept down to help the export drive. A period of restraint lasted until the inflation of the Korean War made it impossible to sustain, but this episode was the forerunner of a succession of more or less formal prices and incomes policies which lasted with little break from 1957 to the collapse of the 'Social Contract' in 1978–79. Nearly 40 years later, it is difficult to recall just how much detailed government control over the

---

12 One of Margaret Thatcher's earliest campaigns, as a young parliamentary candidate, was to draw attention to what she saw as the iniquities of these powers. See http://www.margaretthatcher.org/document/100834 (accessed 17 January 2015).

decisions of private businesses was entailed by prices and incomes policies.[13]

Perhaps the most important legacy of the war years was the indulgence shown by governments of both major parties towards the trade unions. The consensus of the time was that unions were a legitimate and key part of civil society, entitled to representation on everything from the Board of Governors of the BBC to Royal Commissions. Not just Commissions concerned with employment matters, either. For example, by the 1970s David Basnett of the National Union of General and Municipal Workers was serving on the Royal Commission on the Constitution, while Jack Jones of the Transport and General Workers Union – voted the most powerful man in Britain in a 1977 Gallup Poll – was a member of the Royal Commission on Criminal Procedure.

Under the Macmillan government in the early 1960s the Trades Union Congress was invited to be part of the National Economic Development Council (NEDC) alongside representatives of the nationalised industries and the Confederation of British Industries (CBI). Loosely modelled on a similar, seemingly successful, institution in France, the NEDC was an economic policy forum which discussed strategies for reversing the economic decline troubling all politicians and opinion formers at the time. It expanded to play a role in Harold Wilson's short-lived National Plan, and was an enduring feature of the UK's somewhat half-hearted attempts at corporatism until cold-shouldered by Margaret Thatcher and finally abolished by John Major's government in 1992.

So the unions grew in power and influence over the 1950s and 60s (Owen 1999: Chapter 16), and this development was attacked by many commentators as being detrimental to the prospects of the UK economy. Unions were seen as establishing

---

13 For a salutary reminder of the powers of the National Board for Prices and Incomes under Harold Wilson's administration in the 1960s, see Pickering (1971) and Liddle and McCarthy (1972).

or condoning such restrictive practices as overstaffing ('featherbedding') and unnecessary demarcation between different skills and trades. Another perceived problem was the strength of shop-floor organisation. In the UK's two-tier system of industrial relations, factory-based shop stewards, rather than full-time officials from union headquarters, frequently called the shots. A strike or other 'unofficial' industrial action (at the time still protected by the general immunity of unions from actions for breach of contract) could be called by a show of hands. Rather than face disruption, employers might settle with one group of workers, only to find that a rival union organising another group then took action over a claim to emulate or even leapfrog over the first group.

Concern over these issues led the Wilson government to set up the Donovan Commission on Trade Unions and Employers Associations. Reporting in 1968, this body was strongly influenced by the Oxford School of industrial relations, an academic orthodoxy which approved of 'joint regulation' of the labour market by unions and employers, with the state playing only a limited back-up role. Accordingly, the Donovan Commission, while making a number of recommendations for change, did not significantly challenge the power of unions. It rejected the view that collective agreements should be legally binding but looked instead to regularise the two-tier system by explicit recognition of shop stewards as legitimate employee representatives.

In response to this milk-and-water report, Harold Wilson and his combative Secretary of State, Barbara Castle, put forward a White Paper called *In Place of Strife*, which would have required strike ballots and imposed financial penalties on unions for infractions. These proposals were, however, defeated by a coalition of unionists and rebel members of the parliamentary Labour Party. Similar ideas lay behind the Heath government's 1971 Industrial Relations Act. This Act, which imposed a legal framework under a National Industrial Relations Court, strike ballots, cooling-off periods and registration of trade unions, was bitterly opposed by the unions. It was repealed by the incoming Labour government in 1974, setting the scene for the rising tide of militancy which peaked in the 1978–79 'winter of discontent'. At this peak of its influence in post-war Britain, trade union membership reached 13.3 million in 1979, well over half those in employment: 5 million of these unionists were in closed shops,[14] where membership was compulsory.

In reaction, the Thatcher and Major years saw a dramatic rolling back of trade union power, with eight important industrial relations acts[15] which enforced ballots, abolished the closed shop, severely limited picketing, proscribed sympathy strikes and ended victimisation of non-striking employees by their unions. Although Tony Blair's New Labour legislated to provide a procedure for balloting workers on union recognition, they left the Conservatives' industrial relations legislation largely unchanged. Today union power and influence, while still far from negligible, are much less significant in the economy than they were 35–40 years ago: membership has fallen to less than 6.5 million, just 25 per cent of employees. Strike activity (despite recurrent short strikes in parts of the public sector) remains far below that of the 1970s.[16]

14　An arrangement which was often acquiesced in by many employers, who argued that it brought greater predictability and stability to industrial relations. Maybe so, but this is dangerously close to the view that the Kray brothers kept East End streets safe for old ladies. Eventually, arguments in defence of closed shops were undermined by European Court of Human Rights judgements.

15　The Employment Acts 1980, 1982. 1988, 1989 and 1990; the Trade Union Act 1984, the Wages Act 1986 and the Trade Union Reform and Employment Rights Act 1993. See Shackleton (1998) for an overview of the legislation of this period.

16　The 1975–79 annual average was 2,345 strikes and 11.6 million working days lost. In 2015, the last full year for which we have data at the time of writing, there were only 106 stoppages and 170,000 days lost – although this was a particularly quiet year. In 2016 the days lost seem to have risen sharply, but were still only a tiny fraction of the numbers experienced in the 1970s.

Newer forms of regulation

Yet the 1980s reductions in the power of unions, and other measures to increase labour market flexibility, such as scrapping the Fair Wages resolution and Wages Councils, have been offset by a very considerable increase in other forms of government intervention. As should now be apparent, it is difficult to argue that there was ever in the UK a period of labour market laissez-faire of the sort which Richard Epstein has extolled. But undoubtedly the quantity of regulation has greatly increased in recent decades as the scope of government involvement in employment matters has widened.

Why has this happened? As suggested earlier, the intellectual orthodoxy of the 1950s, 1960s and 1970s (on both the left and, to a now surprising degree, the right) was that 'free collective bargaining' by powerful unions could secure any necessary protection of employees, with the state merely playing a residual role in areas where unions were weak. UK unions used to be very wary of labour market regulation by the state. A national minimum wage would interfere with bargaining between employers and unions: this was opposed. Wages Councils were only tolerated in sectors where, for various reasons, unions were weak. The development of other employment rights was treated with suspicion, as they might be a means by which governments undermined unions. This wasn't too wide of the mark: it was part of the reason why the Conservatives introduced Unfair Dismissal legislation (originally proposed by the Donovan Commission and rejected by the union movement) in the early 1970s.

Today, however, a dramatically weaker trade union movement sees government intervention as a positive development and devotes much campaigning energy to push for tighter employment regulation. It is tempting to suggest that the decline in union membership has simply led the left to switch tactics from supporting industrial militancy to the promotion of state action. But there are other factors in play, such as the changing structure of the economy (which has broken up huge concentrations of workers in heavy industry with common interests), the rise of women's employment (which has emphasised different issues about equal pay, discrimination and caring responsibilities) and the greatly increased ethnic diversity of the workforce.

As early as 1963, Harold MacMillan's government had brought in the Contracts of Employment Act, one of the first of these new cross-economy interventions. It required employers to give a minimum period of notice when terminating employees' contracts, and written particulars of any verbal contract when a written contract was not already provided. Then the first Wilson government set up industrial tribunals (renamed employment tribunals from 1998), and brought in the Redundancy Payments Act 1965, which required firms to consult unions prior to redundancies, while giving employees a statutory right to notice and financial compensation. Labour also brought in the Race Relations Act of 1968 and the Equal Pay Act of 1970. The Conservatives under Edward Heath introduced the concept of Unfair Dismissal in 1971, and later in the 1970s we had the Health and Safety at Work Act 1974 (which codified and extended existing factory and other safety legislation), and the Sex Discrimination Act 1975.

The advent of the Thatcher and Major governments did not stop the gradual expansion of the role of government in the labour market, augmented by the occasional demands of the European Commission. The European influence was accentuated when Labour returned to power in 1997 and opted in to the Social Chapter, leading to an expansion of anti-discrimination legislation, the imposition of the Working Time Directive and greater rights for part-time workers, and the incorporation of the European Convention on Human Rights into UK law for the first time. But the Blair and Brown governments also took independent steps to increase regulation with the introduction of a National Minimum Wage in 1998 and the introduction and later expansion of parental and other carer leave. Despite occasional attempts at deregulation, the Conservative–Liberal Democrat Coalition also added substantially to employment regulation through extension of family leave and flexible working, auto-enrolment in pension schemes, rules on setting executive pay, raising the effective school-leaving age and widening yet again the scope of anti-discrimination legislation. Following their general election victory in 2015, the Conservatives added the National Living Wage and an Apprenticeship Levy.

Government intervention has also continued to grow in the ever-contentious area of immigration. After the end of World War II, the British Nationality Act was passed in 1948 to allow British subjects worldwide to live and work in the UK without a visa. Some were specifically encouraged to come to the UK to fill perceived gaps in the labour market. Commonwealth immigration accordingly grew rapidly in the late 1950s and early 1960s.

Political sentiment and concern about the changing jobs market led to the Commonwealth Immigrants Acts of 1962 and 1968, which began to place restrictions on primary immigration from the Commonwealth. These restrictions have been gradually tightened over time, although large numbers have continued to come to the UK despite this, under different headings such as family reunion and political asylum. Many also come on temporary visas as students or tourists and may stay for longer periods. Furthermore, membership of the European Economic Community, later the European Union, led to substantial inflows of workers from Europe, on which few restrictions could be placed. And the relative openness of the UK to foreign investment has encouraged the inflow of entrepreneurs, Russian oligarchs and highly skilled employees from the US and many other countries worldwide.

The UK therefore became a country of substantial annual net immigration, a situation which proved unpopular with the general public (and ultimately contributed to the Referendum decision to leave the EU). In trying to restrict immigration, governments placed much of the burden of control on employers, whose freedom to recruit has been increasingly restricted.

The Asylum and Immigration Act 1996 created a new offence of employing a person who is prohibited from working, and successive legislation, orders and government 'advice' have forced employers to adopt elaborate procedures (including minimum advertising time for certain vacancies, and passport and other checks on job applicants) to ensure that they do not inadvertently breach the law. The government now places an annual cap on those coming to work here from outside the European Union and a rudimentary 'points-based system' determines who is allowed to take up jobs. Since 2010 employer obligations – and penalties (including prison sentences) for breach of these obligations – have sharply increased. A new annual levy on employers who take on skilled workers from outside the EU was already planned to come into action in 2017: following Brexit the scope of this measure may be extended.

Conclusion

This brief historical excursion has demonstrated that the view that employment regulation is a relatively new phenomenon is mistaken. Its forms and motivation have changed, but there has long been a belief that governments should intervene in one way or another. If the economists' theoretical arguments about 'market failure' are one line of argument supporting government intervention, the ancient lineage of such intervention is another.

Today's employment regulation is on an unprecedented scale and covers matters which would not have crossed the minds of earlier generations of politicians and activists. But the impulse to interfere with the labour market is certainly not some new aberration.

4 EMPLOYMENT REGULATION IN THE UK TODAY: EXTENSIVE AND COSTLY

From this historical excursion we now return to the present day, and an outline of the current extent of regulation in the UK's labour market. It is impossible to capture in a limited space the whole range of regulations with which UK businesses now have to comply when they employ people. Interested readers can find many legal texts which go into the details of UK employment law. Table 1 can only give a brief overview of some of the main areas of cross-economy regulation: as will be indicated later, considerable further regulation deals with specific industries and occupations. The information in the table is correct to the best of my knowledge at the time of writing (November 2016), but is indicative only and should not be relied on for legal purposes.

This regulation will be examined in more detail in later chapters. Enforcement occurs through a number of different mechanisms. Health and safety issues are handled through the Health and Safety Executive, which can inspect premises, issue notices or initiate prosecutions. Breaches of Minimum Wage laws are pursued by HM Revenue and Customs. A specialist regulator such as the Gangmasters and Labour Abuse Authority has enforcement powers, including arrest. The government has appointed a Director of Labour Market Enforcement to coordinate these different responsibilities. In the main, though, individuals must pursue claims themselves against employers through the courts, or in most cases, the employment tribunal system.

Tribunals

Employment tribunals began life in 1964 as industrial tribunals, set up to consider appeals by businesses against long-forgotten training levies which operated in the 1960s.[1] Their jurisdiction was extended to hear individual employees' cases under the Redundancy Payments Act of 1965. The Donovan Commission recommended that they be given a wider brief to provide a cheap and informal way of resolving a range of employment disputes without unions resorting to strikes. Gradually, tribunals acquired more and more areas of jurisdiction[2] and moved from informality towards increasing use of legal representation. This trend was emphasised as unions began to realise that tribunals offered a way to achieving their objectives through test cases and what amounted to class actions over matters such as equal pay.

Tribunals involve a legally qualified Chair and two lay representatives,[3] one chosen for experience of employing people, and one with experience from the employee side, usually as a trade union official. This structure reflects corporatist ideas which were common when the tribunal system was set up: the 'two sides of industry' working together with the state. Nowadays, critics complain that the system over-represents large firms and trade unions in a world where the labour market, and types of employment, have changed considerably.

---

1 Firms which could show that they were spending significantly on certain types of training were exempt from the levies. As usually happens with this sort of impost, big companies were able to avoid paying levies while smaller businesses had to pay up.

2 An outline of the development of tribunals is provided in Shackleton (2002).

3 In some circumstances, however, mainly concerning preliminary arguments, the Chair can sit alone.

Table 1   Main areas of current UK labour market regulation

Area	Key elements
Distinction between 'employees' and non-contracted workers (including self-employed)	Employee status involves a contract setting out conditions, rights, responsibilities, duties. Some employment rights differ between employees and non-contract workers.
Written statements	Employees must have certain information about their employment in writing, including pay details. Failure to provide this information can lead to limited compensation by tribunals.
Unlawful deduction of wages	No qualifying period, no maximum award.
Breach of contract	No qualifying period. Tribunal maximum award £25,000. High Court – no limit.
Unfair dismissal	Employees can only be dismissed for five 'fair' reasons: misconduct, capability, redundancy, illegality or 'some other substantial reason'. Employer must have a fair procedure including appeals, otherwise dismissal is automatically unfair. Applies after two years' employment. Compensatory award capped (currently £78,962). Employees cannot be dismissed for union membership, striking if a legitimate ballot has been held, or whistleblowing.
Redundancy	Occurs when a business closes or requirement for particular type of employee has reduced. Two-year qualifying period for statutory redundancy pay linked to age and length of service: upper limit £14,370. Employers must follow a formal procedure and in the case of 20 or more simultaneous redundancies there must be prior consultation with unions or employee representatives.
Discrimination	Treating people unequally on grounds of age, disability, gender, sexual orientation, race, religion or belief, marriage or civil partnership, pregnancy and maternity, gender reassignment. No qualifying period (legislation applies to recruitment process too). No limits to compensation.
Equal pay	If paid less than appropriate comparator, may claim – including back pay. No qualifying period, no maximum award. Can be backdated for up to six years. Mandatory pay audits, formerly a punitive measure for organisations in serious breach of legislation, are now required for all with more than 250 employees.
Maternity leave and pay	Right to 26 weeks leave, two weeks of which are compulsory. Can take up to 26 weeks additional leave. Right to return to same job or similar. No qualifying period. Statutory maternity pay up to 39 weeks.
Adoption leave and pay	Right to 26 weeks, can take up to 26 additional. Statutory maternity pay up to 39 weeks. Qualifying period 26 weeks continuous service. Surrogacy also included.

Continued

Area	Key elements
Paternity leave and pay	Two consecutive weeks per pregnancy (statutory paternity pay). Additional leave minimum two, maximum 26 weeks. Qualifying period 26 consecutive weeks prior to 15th week before birth.
Shared parental leave	Partners may share the maximum leave to which mothers are entitled. Grandparents now also allowed to share in leave.
Other parental leave	Unpaid, caring for child, up to 18 weeks. Qualifying service one year.
Time off for dependants	Reasonable time off (unpaid) to look after dependant for injury, unexpected incidents, death. No qualifying period.
Flexible working	An employee with 26 weeks' continuous service can request flexible working arrangements. Can be refused on grounds of additional costs, inability to replace, detrimental impact on performance. One request per 12 months. Some compensation payable for procedural irregularities up to £3,830.
Various rights to paid time off work	Union activities, public duties, safety representative duties, employee representatives, occupational pension scheme trustees, antenatal care – no limits to compensation. Right to job search for redundant employees – maximum of 40 per cent of pay.
Consultation	Employees have a legal right to be informed and consulted about issues at work if the company or organisation has 50 or more employees. Employees of large multinational companies based in the UK and with a presence elsewhere in Europe have a right to ask for a European Works Council to be set up.
Right to request time off for study/training	Those continuously employed for 26 weeks can request time off for study or training related to employee's performance at work. Failure to follow procedural requirements can lead to compensation up to £3,830. For young people (for which time must be paid), no limits to compensation.
Training and Apprenticeship Levies	The Construction Industry Training Board and the Engineering Construction Training Board have the right to impose training levies on all but the smallest firms, both employers and labour-only subcontractors. There is also a levy on film production expenditure for training purposes. From April 2017 all employers with a pay bill of at least £3 million will pay a 0.5 per cent levy to support apprenticeships.
Working time	Maximum 48 hours per week (over 17 week reference period); specified rest periods; 5.6 weeks paid annual leave (pro-rata entitlements for part-time workers). Restrictions on night-time working. Specific further rules apply in particular areas, e.g. transport. Enforcement via Health and Safety Executive. Compensation capped.

Continued

Area	Key elements
Sunday working	In England and Wales (Scotland has no restrictions) large stores (>280 square metres) can only open for six consecutive hours on Sundays, and must close Christmas Day and Easter Sunday. Employees have a right to opt out of Sunday working under certain conditions.
Statutory sick pay	No qualifying period. Paid to those with earnings over National Insurance threshold. Set each year (currently £88.45).
National Minimum Wage (NMW) and National Living Wage (NLW).	NMW set in October each year, on advice of Low Pay Commission. Main rate for under-25s (currently £6.95), two youth rates and an apprentice rate. Enforced by HMRC. New NLW of £7.20 for all 25 and over.
Health and safety	General requirement to provide a safe environment, provide training, publish written health and safety policy (if 5 or more employees), form a safety committee if requested. Enforced through Health and Safety Executive, which can issue prohibition/improvement notices or institute court cases.
Child employment	Minimum age for part-time work 13. Children not permitted to work in factories, industrial sites, pubs, betting shops. Extra restrictions during term time. Some local authorities require employment permits and may impose additional restrictions. For work in TV, theatre, etc., a performance licence is required. 16- and 17-year-olds in employment must engage in some part-time education/training.
Immigration	Employers must ensure any potential employees have evidence of entitlement to work in this country. Civil penalty up to £20,000 per worker. It is a criminal offence to knowingly employ overseas nationals aged 16 or over without authorisation, punishable by up to two years in prison. From April 2017, businesses must pay an annual charge of £1,000 for every skilled worker brought in from outside the European Union.
Trade unions	Employers may be obliged to recognise unions. Unions apply to Central Arbitration Committee for statutory recognition for bargaining purposes in businesses with over 21 employees. This may be granted on evidence of existing membership and/or a ballot. Unions following proper procedures in relation to balloting and notice of industrial action are immune from action for breach of contract. They have a right to be consulted over a range of matters including health and safety and collective redundancies.

Continued

Area	Key elements
Administration of income tax, national insurance, tax credits, statutory sickness pay, maternity/ paternity pay, etc.	Employers are obliged to administer and report on a variety of statutory payments and make appropriate returns of income tax and national insurance. 'Real time information' requirements now mean employers must send details electronically to HMRC every time a payment is made; this is ultimately required from all employers, although micro-businesses have been permitted delayed implementation.
Temporary contracts	A succession of temporary contracts for 4 years establishes a permanent contract.
Temporary agency work	Agencies cannot charge fees to employees. After 12 weeks agency employees must be treated equally with permanent workers.
Gangmasters	Gangmasters and Labour Abuse Authority (formerly Gangmasters Licensing Authority) regulates businesses supplying agricultural and related workers. It now has powers to investigate 'modern slavery'.
Pensions	Employers have to provide workers with a workplace pension and automatically enrol eligible workers; employer must make a contribution (this is being rolled out gradually, with larger employers first, but will eventually cover all employers). Where employer has an occupational scheme, members can nominate representatives.
Occupational regulation	Around 130 professions or trades, accounting for at least 13 per cent of workforce employment, involve legal requirements for practitioners to be licensed and/ or possess qualifications and/or work experience.
Disclosure and barring	DBS checks required for a wide range of employment which involves working with children (e.g. teaching, childcare, school transport, healthcare, sports), young people or vulnerable adults.

Sources: Various, including https://www.gov.uk/browse/employing-people/contracts (accessed 22 February 2016); http://www.legislation.gov.uk/uksi/2016/288/made (accessed 25 March 2016); https://www.gov.uk/training-study-work-your-rights/appealing-the-decision (accessed 25 March 2016).

Notes: Compensation and pay rates typically change every year. The rates shown are current at November 2016. Some employment rights differ between employees and (non-contract) workers.

Tribunals which find in favour of a complainant can award compensation and costs, require reinstatement in unfair dismissal cases (though this power is rarely used), and (since April 2014) fine employers for breach of employment rights.

Those wishing to make a claim to a tribunal must first discuss the issue with a representative of ACAS (the Advisory, Conciliation and Arbitration Service).[4] ACAS (another corporatist body) was set up in its current form in the 1970s to help resolve industrial disputes between unions and managements. It still has this role (it was involved in over 850 disputes in 2013–14), but for many years its main function has been to help conciliate between individuals and their employers. From April 2014 this has become compulsory: the tribunal system will not accept claims unless they have first been discussed with an ACAS conciliator. ACAS will try to bring employer and employee together to resolve an issue. If it is not successful after a month, it will issue a Certificate allowing a claim to proceed.

The growth of employment legislation, often involving vague and imprecise matters of interpretation and subjectivity, produced more and more business for tribunals, and the number of cases accepted grew considerably if erratically[5] over many years, as Figure 2 shows. In recent years the bulk of claims have concerned unfair dismissal, unauthorised pay deductions, breach of contract (about half of claims) and discrimination, equal pay and working time (about a third of claims).

However, there was a dramatic drop in the number of claims after July 2013, when charges for bringing a claim were introduced for the first time.[6] This seems to have led to a fall of around 70 per cent in the number of claims in a full year. If these claims were frivolous attempts to 'take a punt' on getting some compensation from an employer who would want to avoid the cost of a

---

4   See http://www.acas.org.uk/media/pdf/h/o/Early-Conciliation-explained.pdf (accessed 22 April 2015).

5   There is some inherent cyclicality; for instance, unfair dismissal applications have tended to rise as total dismissals rise in recessions.

6   Fees for claims for unpaid wages, redundancy payments, etc., cost £160 and £230 if the claim goes to a hearing. For more complex claims such as unfair dismissal or discrimination the cost is £250 and £950. Fees for appeals are steeper. However, as these are means-tested, many claimants do not pay.

Figure 2   Claims accepted by employment tribunals

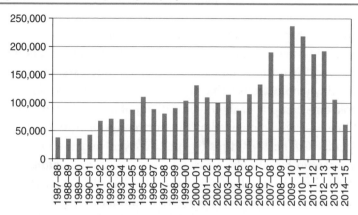

Source: Employment Tribunals Service, Ministry of Justice.

tribunal hearing, their reduction is a good thing. However, there are concerns that some legitimate small claims (for example, for employers not paying what they owe employees) may have been deterred by the charges. Even where such claims are successfully pursued, it appears that substantial numbers of employers do not pay up, as the House of Commons Justice Committee has documented.[7]

The reduction in overall claim numbers does not, however, mean that employers' fear of tribunals has disappeared. There still seem to be a similar number of major claims which raise concerns for all employers – not just those directly involved – who struggle to interpret and comply with employment law.

More will be said on this later, but a couple of recent cases illustrate what employers say is the most worrying issue about tribunals, the uncertainty created by judgements which reinterpret or extend the law beyond what Parliament probably

---

7   http://www.publications.parliament.uk/pa/cm201617/cmselect/cmjust/167/16702 .htm (accessed 27 July 2016).

intended. In one, an employment tribunal in Bedford judged Tesco to have indirectly discriminated against two Muslim employees by restricting access to an on-site prayer room at one of its distribution depots.[8] This prayer room had been in operation for several years, but management decided that it should be kept locked when not in use, that those using the room should sign a book, and that prayer should be individual rather than in groups.

The case was supported by the Northamptonshire Rights and Equality Council (paid for by the taxpayer) and the men were represented by one of its caseworkers. The complainants were awarded undisclosed compensation for injury to their feelings. There is of course no legal obligation to offer a prayer room, although employers have been encouraged to offer them by business groups and government. Clearly, however, businesses will have to tread warily in future (religious discrimination claims have been running at about 1,000 a year) and it is possible that this judgement will discourage some companies from offering prayer facilities. It may discourage others, sadly, from employing some Muslim workers. While blatant cases of discrimination will attract legal sanction, subtler employer preferences are impossible to police, particularly in smaller firms.

Another case also concerns the protection given to beliefs in employment law. This protection, originally intended to benefit religious believers, has been extended by case law to a wider range of 'beliefs'. In this particular case, an employee of GMB, the trade union, was dismissed for various misdemeanours, which may have included organising a picket at the Houses of Parliament and trying to discourage Labour MPs from crossing it. Whatever the rights and wrongs of his dismissal (parts of his case were rejected), the tribunal held that he had been discriminated against because of his militant political beliefs. Judge Nigel

8   See http://www.dailymail.co.uk/news/article-2442448/Muslim-Tesco-workers -win-discrimination-case-bosses-locked-prayer-room.html (accessed 2 March 2015).

Mahoney found that 'left-wing democratic socialism is a philosophical belief for the purposes of the Equality Act 2010'.[9] Importantly, the emphasis on the difficulties faced by employers should not lead us to ignore problems created for employees by the ambiguity of much employment law and the stress and strain caused by the lengthy and over-formal procedures adopted by the Tribunal system (Kirk et al. 2015).

Costs of regulatory compliance

Even where the law is clear, there are substantial resource costs to conscientious employers of complying with regulatory requirements. In addition to the direct costs of mandates (such as higher wage costs as a result of minimum wage legislation, or extra staffing to cover longer holidays and parental leave), Hasseldine et al. (2006) point to procedural costs of hiring and firing; costs of complying with health and safety and workers' rights through consultation with works councils, health and safety committees and trade unions; statistical reporting of employment-related data and administering employment-related tax (including tax credits), national insurance and pensions; and recording and administering maternity and paternity leave, caring leave, sick leave and flexible working arrangements. To this list we could now add new obligations such as pension auto-enrolment, migration status checks, extra disclosure and barring (DBS) checks, and the development of records for the new Apprenticeship Levy. There are, of course, also continuing training costs associated with regulations, not only for those with direct responsibility for overseeing implementation, but also for ordinary members of staff, who need to be aware of possibly breaching general obligations in relation to, for example, discrimination law.

---

9 See http://www.clarkslegal.com/Legal_Updates/Read/GMB_discriminated _against_union_member_because_of_his_left_wing_socialist_beliefs (accessed 2 March 2015).

It is impossible to put a precise monetary value on these compliance costs, but it is useful to get some idea of the rough order of magnitude of one aspect – the aggrandisement of the 'human resource management' function in businesses. Provisional figures from the April 2015 Annual Survey of Hours and Earnings (ASHE) show there were 107,000 'human resource managers and directors' earning a mean gross weekly wage of £935.[9] In addition there were 141,000 'human resources and industrial relations officers' with mean gross weekly earnings of £540, and 25,000 in 'human resource administrative occupations', on £327 a week. The cost of this alone would have to be over £10 billion per year. Add in the cost of pension contributions, other administrative support and part of the time of payroll staff, and the total cost of the HR function in the UK economy must currently be in excess of £15 billion per annum. In addition to the specialist HR function, a sizeable chunk of the time of general and other functional managers is necessarily taken up with compliance issues. It might be a very conservative estimate to suggest that 5 per cent of senior managers' time is taken up with HR issues, but that would add at least another annual £5 billion.

Some of this expense would, of course, be necessary even in the absence of extensive employment regulation; staff recruitment and training, for example, is something to which businesses will always have to devote resources. However, the growth of UK membership of the major professional body, the Chartered Institute of Personnel and Development, over the last 35 years[10] suggests that there has been a considerable enhancement of the HR function accompanying the growth of regulation.

These costs will fall disproportionately on smaller businesses that lack specialist human resource management skills, which may have to be hired in at considerable expense. They are likely

---

10 The Institute of Personnel Management (now the Chartered Institute of Personnel and Development) had 12,000 members in 1979: in 2015 the CIPD had around 140,000 members.

to deter employment expansion, particularly for those micro-enterprises with no employees. The step towards taking on the first employee involves a harsh entry for would-be businesspeople into a world which was not designed with their needs in mind.[11] This differential impact of regulations is doubly concerning because there is evidence (Urwin 2011) that small businesses with fewer than 25 workers employ larger proportions of disadvantaged employees – young people, those with no formal qualifications, those with language difficulties, and those without a continuous work record – than large enterprises with more than 500 employees.

Business respondents in one inquiry (Hasseldine et al. 2006) believed that it was not possible to comply fully with all regulatory requirements. They cited the volume and complexity of rules, the frequency of change and the high level of subjectivity involved. This is because many regulations require judgements to be formed about what is 'reasonable', for instance, in relation to changing workload, adjustments to deal with disability or the acceptability of flexible working; such judgements can be, and frequently are, contested. By contrast, environmental regulations (even though they can be costly and irksome themselves) 'were considered to be better enforced because they are very specific and thus easier to measure and comply with than the more subjective nature of many employment-related requirements' (ibid.: 4).

Similar concerns were raised in a consultation carried out by the Department for Business, Innovation and Skills (2012). Employers were sometimes said to be deterred from hiring new employees for fear of being taken to an employment tribunal should business requirements change and the employees become redundant. The threat of tribunals was also held to be an inhibiting factor in relation to the management of underperforming staff,

---

11 Disproportionate compliance costs are also a strong disincentive to households to formalise employment relationships with cleaners, gardeners, nannies and other domestic employees.

and companies produced an excessive amount of paperwork to help counter this threat.

This reminds us that the costs associated with even relatively narrow areas of employment regulation are difficult to measure. Occasionally, figures surface in the media. For example, the British Chambers of Commerce (BCC) reported in 2011 that the Working Time Directive would cost British business a recurring £1.5 billion a year. But such figures are not necessarily any more reliable than those produced by the government when introducing a regulation. All new measures nowadays are accompanied by an 'Impact Assessment',[12] a formalised procedure which attempts to assess the positive and negative impacts of policy proposals. However, governments can never know the real costs of what they propose, as these costs are essentially subjective.[13] Where precautionary compliance is concerned, attitudes to risk and experience of handling regulations differ considerably from individual to individual and from business to business, leading to different procedures and different costs falling on enterprises. As we shall see, British regulators are often accused of 'gold plating' rules coming from the European Union. In a similar way, organisations may 'gold plate' regulations by attempting to minimise risk. Their decisions may be influenced by HR managers and consultants (for whom extra procedures and exhaustive training generate increased income and influence) and by unions which, particularly in the public sector, make threatening noises.

---

12 All OECD countries now use Impact Assessments. The UK's Department for Business, Innovation and Skills, responsible for most employment legislation, publishes summary versions of its IAs. They can be found at https://www.gov.uk/government/publications?departments%5B%5D=department-for-business-innovation-skills&publication_type=impact-assessments (accessed 29 March 2016).

13 There is a theoretical case, based on the concept of 'opportunity cost', for saying that all costs are subjective (Buchanan and Thirlby 1981).

A recent example occurred when in 2014 the government gave employment tribunals the power to require an 'equal pay audit' (reporting in detail on gender pay gaps within the organisation) from employers which had been found against in an equal pay claim. Ironically, this proposal emerged from a group set up to consider deregulation; but the result was that many companies voluntarily[14] decided to organise such an audit in order to be prepared for any possible claim against them in the future. They were probably sensible. Eventually, the government decided to implement powers available in the Equality Act 2010 and imposed mandatory audits on all organisations employing more than 250 people from March 2016.

But who really bears the cost?

A further and much more fundamental issue is the question of who ultimately bears the cost of employment regulation. The complaints of businesspeople against excessive regulation, while understandable and often justified, concentrate on the short-run impact of a measure on their bottom line: this is what is picked up, for example, in the BCC figures for the cost of the Working Time Directive. But the impact of a measure does not fall exclusively on the owners of a business in the medium to long term. Its impact is rather like the effect of a tax on the consumption of a product; the business may pay the government the monetary value of the tax, but its incidence – who bears the burden – is less clear. The same applies to a regulatory measure, which has been called a 'stealth tax'.

Take a mandated benefit, a government requirement to offer some benefit to employees. A hypothetical example

---

14 'Voluntary' action is often seen as preferable to compulsion. But where this voluntary action is undertaken because of perceived threats, and the action itself is of doubtful benefit, this voluntarism is not necessarily a good thing. Pay audits, as we shall see, are likely to produce misleading results and lead to actions with undesirable consequences.

might be a requirement to give all workers free annual visits to a health spa. The cost of this 'tax' might appear to be borne by the employer. This is how the public would tend to see it. However, in the long term the extra cost would reduce profits and might lead the firm to switch resources to another use. Firms will therefore try to pass on the cost in higher prices (or, equivalently, lower quality at the same price) to the consumer. This is likely to lead to some fall in the quantity demanded of the product or service, and thus output and employment. In a competitive environment, where international competition for traded goods means that the scope for price increases is limited, what is more likely to happen is that the cost of the benefit is shifted to the workers themselves. Figure 3 (from Summers 1989) illustrates this.

Initially, the demand curve for this type of labour is D1 and the supply curve is S1. The wage rate is W1 and employment is Q1. The mandate is introduced and this raises the cost of hiring labour. The demand curve shifts to the left as it is less profitable to employ a given amount of labour at any given wage rate. The mandate's cost per unit of labour is shown by the vertical distance between demand curve D1 and the new demand curve, D2. The supply curve will also shift if the employee values the mandated benefit, because at any particular wage rate the job is now marginally more attractive. The vertical distance between supply curve S1 and supply curve S2 represents the employee's valuation of the benefit.

The diagram illustrates one possible outcome, which is that where employees value the mandate less than it costs the employer to provide (this can often happen when governments impose mandates which reflect the choices of activists rather than the employees themselves, or where compliance costs such as registration and training are very heavy). In this case the wage

Figure 3   The impact of a mandated benefit

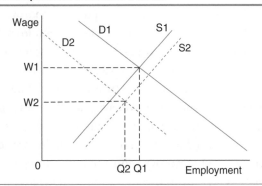

rate tends to fall (from W1 to W2),[15] but not to the full extent of the cost of providing the benefit. Part of the cost is borne by the employer, and thus profit-maximising employment falls from Q1 to Q2.

If, however, the employee were to value the benefit at exactly what it costs to provide, the wage would fall to the full extent of the cost. As the employer would then bear none of the cost, it would be just as profitable to the employer to employ the same amount of labour. Demand would be unchanged and employment would remain constant. Employees would be just as 'well off' as before, only now part of their remuneration would be in the form of the benefit rather than cash.[16]

A final possibility is that employees value the benefit at *more* than it costs the employer to provide, which might arise if the

---

15 In a dynamic context, where wages are shifting all the time as demand and supply change and variations occur in the general price level, the wage change may not be overt or recognised by the employees. It is rather a *reduction of the wage rate from what it otherwise would have been.* This is the 'stealth tax' effect.

16 Summers argues, though, that this might be better than providing the benefit out of taxation, as taxes produce labour market distortions while this situation leaves employment and output unchanged.

provision of the benefit was subject to considerable economies of scale. In such a case we get the odd prediction that wages would fall by more than the cost of the mandate and employment would actually increase. This is unlikely to arise in practice, because the employer would already have had an incentive to provide the benefit without being required to by law: it would be cheaper to provide the benefit and pay lower wages. Of course, many non-pay benefits are in fact provided by employers on precisely such grounds:[17] examples include private health insurance, maternity pay in excess of statutory requirements, childcare vouchers, season ticket loans, car allowances, reduced prices on company products and gym membership.

All three of these scenarios suggest that the equilibrium wage will fall. However, if the existing wage rate is very low, and there is a minimum wage rate, wages will not be able to fall, putting all the burden of adjustment on employment.[18]

This simple example shows that there are quite fundamental problems in assessing the real cost of an employment regulation and in considering the burden of this cost. Rather than falling on profits, the cost of a mandate normally falls on some combination of consumers (in the form of higher prices or lower quality), employees (in the form of wage reductions and/or job losses) and potential employees (who cannot find jobs as employment opportunities dry up).

Moreover, these costs may take considerable time to work out. A firm may continue to operate in the short to medium term in a heavily regulated environment, but in the longer term it may

---

17 Although the tax treatment of these benefits also plays a part in making them cheaper to provide.

18 There is a theoretical possibility that employee productivity is boosted by improved morale consequent on the introduction of the mandated benefit – say, through a reduction in labour turnover or reduced absenteeism – and this could in principle mitigate the employment effect. This is a version of the *efficiency wage hypothesis* noted in Chapter 7.

switch technologies to produce using less labour, and may shift resources to producing in other countries, while investors in new businesses may also look elsewhere. Another knock-on effect, then, is that the government's tax take eventually falls.

Political discussion of employment regulation very largely ignores this as politicians assume (or perhaps pretend) that employers bear the cost of ever-more-generous mandates. This is why we should be suspicious of attempts to quantify the costs to the economy of employment regulation. I have no doubt that these are considerable, but they are not accurately reflected in either business estimates or government Impact Assessments.

One element which can never be quantified, even in the crude fashion of Impact Assessments, is the cumulative effect of repeated changes in the regulatory environment on business confidence and willingness to invest and take on employees. It is likely that this is particularly strong on smaller firms, and may be one of the reasons why more micro-businesses do not grow larger.

Conclusion

In this chapter I have outlined the extent of UK employment regulation. In addition to the costs directly associated with legal obligations and mandated benefits, substantial real resources are used to implement regulation, with many employees being diverted to non-productive tasks in order to ensure compliance. The true extent of these costs is difficult to measure.

But something which clearly comes over from analysis of employment regulation, as we shall see repeatedly in more detail later, is that costs of regulation are widely dispersed, falling on consumers, employees, potential employees and the taxpayer rather than being borne entirely or even mainly by employers and shareholders. This important observation is something which is rarely spelt out in political debate.

5 THE EUROPEAN UNION DIMENSION

Whatever burden regulation imposes on the UK labour market has only in part been the consequence of political choices made by our own governments. Many regulatory initiatives have come from the European Union. This chapter outlines those elements of regulation originating from Europe, and suggests reasons why the European Commission's regulatory drive has been strong. However, I argue that those who expect Brexit to lead quickly to substantial deregulation[1] underestimate the extent to which the Commission's past initiatives have been – and will probably continue to be – supported by our own politicians.

The EU's reach[2]

In 1973, when the UK joined the European Economic Community (later the European Union), this only involved committing the country to fairly limited elements of employment regulation – most notably the principle of equal pay for men and women, embodied in Article 119 of the Treaty of Rome. As equal pay was already the law in the UK, this might not be thought important, but

---

1   A view held by those on the left as well as those on the right. The TUC warned before the referendum that remaining in the EU was essential to protect workers' rights, which would otherwise be under threat from the Conservatives. See https://www.tuc.org.uk/sites/default/files/UK%20employment%20rights%20and%20the%20EU.pdf (accessed 12 July 2016).

2   A fuller discussion of the development of EU competence in this area can be found in HM Government (2014).

it became clear over time that the European interpretation of the principle was stricter than the original UK legislation. The 1975 Equal Pay Directive and a subsequent European Court of Justice ruling established that it is not just equal pay for the same work which was covered by the European interpretation of equality legislation, but also 'work to which equal value is attributed'.

The implications of this directive were still resounding 40 years later, with employers obliged to make comparisons between apparently very dissimilar jobs which men and women had undertaken.[3] Moreover, what is meant by 'pay' was broadened to include occupational pensions, and two European rulings in 1994 established that the exclusion of part-time workers from employers' schemes was illegal because females were more likely to work part-time than men.

The European Commission's ability to propose employment regulation was limited until the 1990s, although some intervention was possible under health and safety powers. In 1989, however, the Charter of Fundamental Social Rights of Workers set out considerable new areas of European 'competence'. This Charter became part of the Maastricht Treaty. John Major's government opted out of what became known as the 'Social Chapter' of this treaty, but Tony Blair's New Labour signed the UK up to the full programme in the Treaty of Amsterdam. Broader European influence[4] on UK employment regulation was further entrenched

---

3   One recent case has concerned Birmingham City Council, estimated to owe more than £1 billion in back pay following a legal ruling. Thousands of female council workers, such as carers, cleaners and cooks, came forward with claims after it was ruled they had been discriminated against compared with male road workers, street sweepers and bin men, who had picked up extra pay through regular overtime and other bonuses. See *Birmingham Post*, 3 May 2014, 'Council is "stalling" on equal pay settlements', http://www.birminghampost.co.uk/news/local-news/birmingham-city-council-stall ing-equal-7066029, and 25 June 2015, '"Staff died" waiting for Council Pay update', http://www.birminghampost.co.uk/news/regional-affairs/staff-died-waiting-city -council-9521937 (both accessed 15 September 2015).

4   The European Convention on Human Rights predates the European Community, being agreed in 1950. Although it is outside the European Union structures, it strongly influences many aspects of EU law.

by the Human Rights Act of 1998, which incorporated the European Convention on Human Rights into UK law.

Labour became more reticent, however, when signing the 2007 Treaty of Lisbon. Together with Poland, it secured an exemption from a further extension of EU powers over employment matters. The Lisbon Treaty's new Charter of Fundamental Rights included 54 provisions over a wide range of matters, including such employment-related elements as the right to strike, the right to collective bargaining, the right to fair working conditions and protection against dismissal.

Although the UK's opt-out was regarded at the time as watertight, there were occasional concerns that European Court rulings might lead to these rights being extended to the UK. Whether or not these concerns were justified, it was already the case that many areas of UK employment regulation were now required by our European obligations and could not be unilaterally reformed or scrapped while we remained members of the EU.

Such areas included the controversial freedom of movement between member states; restrictions on working hours; holiday leave; parental leave; pro-rata payments for part-time workers; information and consultation requirements (including European Works Councils for large multinationals); consultation over collective redundancies; equal conditions for permanent and agency workers; maintaining conditions for workers transferred between undertakings; and the outlawing of discrimination not just between men and women, but on grounds of ethnic origin, religion, sexual orientation, disability and age.

It is easier to point to areas where there is *not* a common European approach. One is minimum wages, where there is no compulsion for EU members.[5] Another is unfair dismissal, an important UK concept which does not have exact counterparts in

---

5 Although Jean-Claude Juncker, the President of the European Commission, is among those who have advocated that a compulsory minimum wage be set by each national authority: http://www.euractiv.com/sections/social-europe-jobs/juncker

most other European countries.[6] A third is collective bargaining, where there are no trans-European requirements.

In this chapter I sketch the contours of European labour law and its intellectual background, drawing a contrast with UK traditions. I go on, however, to emphasise the strong domestic taste for interference in labour markets, which means that our exit from the European Union, while increasing the *potential* for deregulation, may make much less difference than has often been supposed by either right or left.

European law and the labour market

Our European obligations have arisen primarily from *Treaties* (for instance, the free movement of labour) and from *Directives* (for instance, limitations on working time). The latter are proposed by the European Commission and must be adopted by the Council of Ministers and the European Parliament in order to come into force. They lay down end results to be achieved in every member state. National governments must adapt their laws to meet these goals, but are free to decide how to do so. A time limit is set for a directive to be 'transposed', as the eurojargon has it, into domestic law.

Table 2 lists some of the most important employment directives. The table shows the most recent relevant directives, which consolidate and add to earlier directives. The development of European labour law has moved in one direction only, to greater transnational regulation. The process has never gone into reverse. Indeed, it is difficult to see quite how it could be reversed

---

  -calls-minimum-wage-all-eu-countries-303484 (accessed 22 July 2014). See also Schulten (2010).

6 'Unfair dismissal' is a form of Employment Protection Legislation that lays down conditions under which contracts can legitimately be terminated. It now only applies to people who have been employed for two years, and is one of the less strict EPL regimes in the European Union (OECD 2013: Chapter 2).

significantly without a fundamental change in approach. Each new member of the EU has had to sign up to the whole existing package, the principle of the *acquis communautaire*. There is no obvious constitutional mechanism to unpick existing directives, although it has been argued that a member state's parliament could in principle alter the way in which it has transposed directives, removing any 'gold plating' (discussed later in this chapter) accreted in the process of transposition (Sack 2013). This procedural rigidity is one of the problems which hindered David Cameron's ill-fated attempt to renegotiate the terms of the UK's relationship with the EU.

Another point worth noting from Table 2 is that several directives (indicated by an asterisk) were developed under 'Framework Agreements' involving what Brussels terms 'European social dialogue'. That is, their content was agreed following discussion between 'social partners'. For instance, the directive on Fixed Term Work resulted from discussions between three bodies: the private sector UNICE[7] (*Union des confédérations de l'industrie et des employeurs d'Europe*), CEEP (*Centre européen des entreprises à participation publique et des entreprises d'intérêt économique general,* a body representing public sector employers) and ETUC (the European Trade Union Confederation). This corporatist dialogue under-represents the interests of smaller businesses and unorganised workers (including the self-employed and unemployed).

In addition to directives, there are *Regulations*. These are the most direct form of EU law, as once passed (either jointly by the EU Council and the European Parliament or by the Commission alone) they have immediate legal force in every member state. For example, Regulation (EEC) 1408/71 covers the application of social security schemes to people moving between member states. It requires that persons residing in the territory of a member state enjoy the same benefits as the nationals of that state,

---

7   Since rebranded as 'BusinessEurope'.

a provision that has been highly controversial – not just in the UK – as mobility between EU members with very different living standards has increased in recent years. Some minor concessions on the application of this regulation were one of the elements in David Cameron's package of reforms agreed with the EU before the referendum. Regulations have also been used to mandate sectoral provisions relating to directives, for instance, to set specific limitations on working time in road transport, railways, civil aviation and seafaring.

There are also *Decisions*, which can come from the EU Council or the Commission, and relate to specific cases. They require individuals or authorities to do something (or else stop doing something).

Finally, the *European Court of Justice* also has the power to adjudicate in cases of employment law which come before it, and its rulings have been very important in defining, for example, the scope of European legislation on age discrimination and the interpretation of the Working Time Directive. ECJ decisions cannot directly overturn domestic laws, but have obliged UK governments to alter legislation to make it compatible with EU law. The limitless scope of the ECJ's powers was one of the key issues in the referendum debate.

A recent example of a ruling which seems to have led to alterations in UK law is the ECJ Advocate-General's opinion[8] that obesity can amount to a 'protected characteristic', and thus make obese individuals a protected group in terms of discrimination

---

8   The verdict concerned the case of a grossly overweight Danish childminder who was sacked because it was claimed that he could no longer fulfil his duties: among other things it was said that he needed help to tie children's shoelaces. See 'Obesity can be a disability, EU Court rules', *The Guardian*, 18 December 2014: http://www.theguardian.com/society/2014/dec/18/obesity-can-be-disability-eu-court-rules (accessed 15 September 2015). Following this, a Northern Ireland employment tribunal has judged someone who was being mocked for being overweight to have been discriminated against: http://www.personneltoday.com/hr/obesity-discrimination-first-uk-tribunal-finds-obese-worker-eligible-for-disability-protection/ (accessed 15 November 2016).

Table 2 Key EU employment directives

Area	Main features	Most recent Directive #
Equal pay	Forbids all gender discrimination in relation to pay, broadly defined.	2006/54/EC
Equal treatment in employment and occupation	Requires equal treatment in employment and membership of certain organisations: no discrimination by gender, age, disability, religion, belief or sexual orientation.	2006/54/EC
Collective redundancies	Requires employers to consult staff representatives and provide information about reasons for redundancy, criteria for selection, etc.	98/59/EC
Transfer of undertakings	Aims to safeguard employment rights, requires consultation with employees when business ownership is transferred.	2001/23/EC
Protection of employees in event of insolvency	Aims to guarantee payment of employees if employer becomes insolvent.	2008/94/EC
Obligation to inform employees of applicable working conditions	Employees must have job specification, information about pay, leave arrangements, etc.	91/533/EEC
Pregnant workers	Mandates 14 weeks maternity leave, protected employment, avoidance of exposure to risks, time off for antenatal care, etc.	92/85/EC
Posting of workers	Employers' obligations in posting of workers to other member states in the provision of services.	96/7/EC
Working time	Fixes maximum working week, requires rest periods, mandates 4 weeks annual paid leave.	2003/88/EC
European Works Councils	Employers with 1000+ employees in European Economic Area must set up a European Works Council.	2009/38/EC
Parental leave*	Mandates 4 months unpaid time off for each parent of a child aged up to 8.	2010/18/EU
Leave for family reasons*	Rights to unpaid time off for urgent family reasons.	97/75/EC
Part-time working*	Requires comparable treatment to full-time staff on open-ended contracts.	98/23/EC
Fixed-term work*	Fixed-term workers must not be treated less favourably than permanent workers; maximum renewals of short-term contracts mandated.	99/70/EC

Continued

Area	Main features	Most recent Directive #
Temporary agency work*	Requires equal treatment of agency workers in respect of pay, working time and annual leave.	2008/104/EC
Maritime labour standards	Requires ratification of ILO Maritime Labour Convention.	99/95/EC

Latest directive may consolidate earlier directives or Treaty obligations. Equal pay, for example, dates back to the Treaty of Rome in 1957.
*Developed under Framework Agreement.
Sources: http://europa.eu/legislation_summaries/employment_and_social_policy/employment_rights_and_work_organisation/index_en.htm (accessed 26 June 2014); Sack (2013).

legislation. The UK has had no venue for discussing or means of challenging this ruling, which has considerable cost and other implications.

European political economy

I have already outlined in general terms the reasons why governments intervene in labour markets – both the economists' theoretical justifications for intervention and the political pressures which are usually more important. But apart from those pressures operating within the UK, there are special factors that have imparted a bias towards regulation, and often regulation of a particularly inefficient kind, in the wider EU context.

For one thing, emphasis on economic analysis has always had very limited appeal in continental Europe, where economics has had less influence than jurisprudence. Rather than trying to analyse issues of market failure in an otherwise free market model, the European Commission has an open-ended commitment 'to offset the inherent economic and social inequality within the employment relationship' (quoted in Siebert 2015: 47).

Legal traditions dating back to the Romans, and in modern terms built on Napoleonic and Bismarckian ideas about the state's role, emphasise government control and regulation, with ideas about rights awarded by the state rather than the 'freedom from' tradition of common law jurisdictions (Siebert 2006). Political systems support this: in the post-war period leading parties in Western Europe were either social democratic (particularly strong in Northern Europe) or Christian Democrats (emphasising Catholic traditions of social concern). In addition, the expansion of the EU to embrace much of the formerly communist Eastern Europe absorbed a large population with a rather different mindset, but one with long experience, and continuing expectation, of state involvement in the labour market.

Allied to this has been the popularity of systems of proportional representation, which lead to frequent coalitions and inevitable compromise, particularly in those countries, such as Germany, Italy and Spain, which were torn apart in the interwar period by extremes of right and left. In parallel with this was the expectation in many countries that compromise should also prevail in the conduct of employment relations. Hence there has been widespread recognition of, and government support for, collective bargaining,[9] and various forms of worker representation[10] in large private sector businesses in Germany, France, the Netherlands and elsewhere. More generally, there is broad sympathy with the idea of social dialogue between representatives of capital and labour.

Indeed, this preference for compromise and deal-making may have been responsible in the first place for the expansion of EU competence to include employment regulation. The development of the Social Charter in the 1980s can be read as a response to the

---

9   In France, for example, the results of such bargaining extend to all workers in a sector or industry, even though membership of the bargaining unions is often pitifully small.

10 Works Councils and employee representation on supervisory boards.

development of the Single Market. As this was thought (wrongly) mainly to benefit business interests, the expansion of the social dimension was intended to provide quid pro quo benefits to workers. The union side of the social partnership saw increasing international competition as threatening workers (ibid.: 3):

> [T]he expansion of EU labour regulation was born out of a concern that the increased competition resulting from the completion of the single market in 1992 would lead to a race to the bottom in labour standards.

Fear of what is termed 'social dumping' is widespread. The European Commission even has an official definition of this unlovely expression: it describes the practice as a situation 'where foreign service providers can undercut local service providers because their labour standards are lower'.[11] To economists, this looks perilously close to protectionism. And logically, if EU members are not to be allowed to compete over employment regulation, why should they be allowed to compete over wages? Or even over other advantages such as transport links, or better training, or higher levels of capital investment?

Finally, the particular form of governance of the EU, with the Commission (a type of civil service) having such an important role in initiating policy[12] – a role found in no nation state – arguably produces a permanent bias towards interference in labour markets.

Moreover, since the EU's budget is constrained to a fixed proportion of European Union GDP, regulatory solutions to perceived

---

11 http://www.eurofound.europa.eu/areas/industrialrelations/dictionary/definitio
ns/socialdumping.htm (accessed 19 July 2014). The directive on Posting of Workers
is one measure which attempts to limit wage competition.

12 The Commission finances, or helps to finance, a large number of pressure groups
and charities which, according to Snowdon (2013), generate apparent public support for policies it wishes to pursue.

problems inevitably tend to be preferred to financial redistribution. Where economic inequality is an issue, for example, a nation state might favour some income-related benefit targeted at those most in need. A European 'solution' would instead be to mandate employers to provide extended leave, reduced working hours and so forth, even though this might not be the economically most efficient way of helping people,[13] or indeed what the intended 'beneficiaries' necessarily want or value.

But will repatriation of powers over the labour market make very much difference?

Withdrawal from the EU in principle can bring some clear benefits for those advocating greater labour market flexibility. It can, for example, prevent a qualified majority of EU members imposing further employment restrictions on the UK; it removes the necessity for involvement of 'social partners' in labour market matters; it can remove the powers of the European Court of Justice to impose new non-negotiable obligations on British employers.

But just what effect will repatriation of powers over employment have? Open Europe (Booth et al. 2011) calculated the continuing cost of European regulation of labour markets by adding up the costs shown in government Impact Assessments conducted at the time legislation was passed. On this basis it calculated that a 50 per cent cut in the cost of regulation could add £4.3 billion, in 2011 prices, to GDP. On some back-of-the-envelope assumptions about the proportion of such a gain going in productivity increases, it further suggested that the equivalent of 60,000 new jobs could be created.

---

13 A bias also often found among single-issue pressure groups which prefer mandates (for example, employer adjustments to the needs of disabled people) or prohibitions (for example, smoking bans) to transfers and taxes.

Seizing on these estimates, the Fresh Start Project (2012, 2013) noted that the bulk of these gains would come from scrapping the Temporary Agency Workers Directive and the Working Time Directive.[14] It put the repeal of this legislation at the centre of its own proposals for renegotiation of the UK's European employment commitments.

Reviewing and, where necessary, repealing 40 years of EU-influenced employment law is no easy task. Even if legislation and Orders in Council in these areas can be unpicked relatively easily, possibly through use of 'Henry VIII powers' (see Howe 2016), it is simplistic to assume that repealing the relevant legislation would necessarily release significant resources in the short term. For the costs which Fresh Start and other analysts identify arise through having to develop new procedures (for example, to record working time), taking on extra workers, altering contracts and shift arrangements and so forth. Companies would find it costly to reverse such changes. Few might initially choose to do so given that it would mean disruption and cause friction with employees.

Over time new entrants may take advantage of relaxed regulation, and existing firms gradually alter their practices, but such innovation could take years to emerge, and might anyway be overtaken by other labour market changes and new patterns of work (for example, the spread of self-employment and working from home – which, incidentally, may already have mitigated some of the original costs of European regulation).

But in any case, given the continuing (indeed, growing) enthusiasm of UK politicians for regulation, would a domestic review process really lead to significant change? Note the words of Lord Mandelson, admittedly while he was a European Commissioner:

---

14 According to Open Europe, two thirds of the costs of European employment regulation are associated with these two directives.

> Before you accuse Brussels of excessive regulatory zeal, remember that a greater part of the burden on business comes from national measures which go beyond what is required by European legislation.[15]

Mandelson was probably correct in his assessment.[16] It is indeed possible that European directives complained about in public were secretly welcomed by UK administrations. Some certainly seem to have been 'gold-plated': that is, the transposing legislation has added to directive requirements in various ways, so that regulation goes beyond what is mandated by the EU. Gold-plating, according to Tebbit (2009), can occur when the government extends the scope of its implementing legislation beyond what is required by a directive, when it fails to take advantage of exemptions allowed by a directive, when it introduces penalties for employers in its implementing legislation that go beyond the penalties required by a directive, or when it introduces its transposing legislation earlier than required.

One example is the Working Time Directive's requirement for 4 weeks' annual holiday; after the directive came into force, the Labour government increased this to 5.6 weeks (Department for Business, Innovation and Skills 2014: 8). Similarly, the Coalition government added significantly to the parental leave requirements of the 2010 directive. Sack (2013) provides other examples.

In any case, the recent imposition of pension auto-enrolment, the Conservative government's National Living Wage, its Apprenticeship Levy and compulsory pay audits cannot be blamed on the EU. If even centre-right UK politicians are unenthusiastic for a large-scale reduction in employment regulation, the Labour

---

15 http://europa.eu/rapid/press-release_SPEECH-07-365_en.htm (accessed 13 July 2014).

16 Though, as Vaughne Miller (House of Commons Library 2010) shows in his lengthy examination of the issue, it is no easy task to put a figure on the proportion of legislation directly resulting from Brussels.

Party, the Liberal Democrats, the Scottish Nationalists and the Green Party all want to see further expansions of employment law.

Conclusion

This chapter has set out the areas in which European Union membership has obliged us to have a considerable degree of employment regulation. It has pointed to the way in which ECJ judgements have forced further obligations on the UK which were not anticipated at the time directives or regulations were originally agreed. However, I have also pointed out that 'gold-plating' of EU rules, and the continuing push of domestic policy, rather weakens the arguments of those who see Brussels as the main source of excessive employment regulation.

Though recovery of powers over employment law may be a *necessary* condition for major deregulation of the UK labour market, it is very far from being *sufficient*. Those arguing for greater labour market freedom need to change the thinking of our own politicians, and indeed the current beliefs of much of the general public. Brexit will bring many changes to this country, but it is unlikely of itself to lead to major deregulation of employment.

PART 3

EMPLOYMENT REGULATION IN DETAIL

6 PROTECTING WORKERS, FAMILIES AND CONSUMERS?

We begin more detailed examination of employment regulation with a look at measures ostensibly designed to protect people from physical or moral harm – by contrast with measures intended to redistribute income, to give greater job security, to redress perceived unfairness and so on. The rationale for intervention is that the unregulated labour market provides insufficient protection, for reasons touched on in Chapter 2.

This is the area of employment regulation where there is possibly the greatest consensus on the need for government involvement of some sort. Indeed, even a classical liberal such as John Stuart Mill argued a century and a half ago that 'the only purpose for which power can be rightfully exercised over any member of a civilized community, against his will is to prevent harm to others' (Mill 2006: 16). The problem is that in practice government intervention is rarely as effective or as benign as its advocates suggest.

Health and safety at work

This is a wider issue than can be treated fully here, as it concerns much more than the labour market. Nevertheless some observations about health and safety as an aspect of employment regulation are clearly necessary. As outlined earlier, workplace safety legislation dates back to the early nineteenth century. The present form of regulation comes from the 1974 Health and Safety at

Work Act, which consolidated earlier legislation and set up the Health and Safety Executive (HSE).

The 1974 Act sets out 'reasonably practical' duties which employers have towards employees and the general public, and employees have towards each other. The Management of Health and Safety at Work Regulations (1999) make these responsibilities more explicit. They require employers of more than five people to carry out periodic risk assessments of potential hazards associated with their workplace, to implement measures which the risk assessment identifies as necessary to reduce or eliminate identified hazards, to appoint competent individuals to assist in carrying out these measures, to work with other businesses operating on the same site, to set up emergency procedures and to provide clear health and safety information and training to employees. Employers are obliged to consult with employees over health and safety matters, and where unions are recognised for bargaining purposes this usually involves an obligation to operate a health and safety committee with union representation.

What is the case for regulation in this area? After all, in a free market decisions on acceptable degrees of risk at work are potentially negotiable between employers and employees. In particular, the theory of *compensating differentials* holds that jobs having relatively unpleasant characteristics must (other things being equal) offer higher wages than otherwise similar jobs in order to attract workers, with the equilibrium wage premium being just enough to compensate workers for having to put up with the unpleasantness.[1] There is evidence (Marin and Psacharopoulos 1982; De Simone and Schumacher 2004; Gertler et al. 2005; Grazier 2007) that pay does indeed reflect risk, with more dangerous jobs carrying just such a pay premium.

---

1 Conversely, people are often prepared to accept low pay in a job which gives them great inherent satisfaction, such as working for a charitable organisation whose goals they support, or particularly pleasant working surroundings, or the opportunity to work at home.

There is also, however, evidence that individuals' attitudes to risk vary considerably, with some individuals being prepared to take much greater risks than others. It is just as well they do. Without some individuals being willing to take more risks than the rest of us, we would have no test pilots, astronauts, firefighters, soldiers, oil rig workers or trapeze artists.

It can be argued (Taylor 2010) that regulation is needed where market power, essentially some form of monopsony, gives employers the ability to exploit employees who have to accept dangerous conditions because they have no alternative. Another possibility, touched on earlier, is that we may have a situation of asymmetric information about the hazards associated with a work task. If the employer knows that a process is dangerous, but the worker doesn't, then people may accept jobs at wages which do not reflect their valuation of risk.[2]

While these dangers are real possibilities, increasing competition in labour markets suggests that over time the possibility of monopsonistic exploitation must have diminished,[3] while the increased dissemination of information on the internet and through the actions of trade unions and other pressure groups should make asymmetry of information less of a problem. Over time, then, we might have expected to see a reduction in the pace of regulation of workplace safety, if not in its absolute level. This does not seem to have happened. Despite the UK being one of the safest places to work in Europe, regulation is perceived to have grown significantly in recent years.

Perhaps health and safety are 'normal' goods, and thus just something we want more of as we become better off over time.

---

2   Such a situation could be argued to override the principle of *volenti non fit injuria* (injury can't be done to someone who voluntarily accepts a risk), which held sway in English law until the 1890s.

3   Except perhaps in the case of illegal migrants who cannot speak English and work for gangmasters such as those responsible for the tragic deaths of Chinese shellfish-pickers in Morecambe Bay in 2004.

And as there are coordination problems in large societies, many expect the government to take the lead.

But if health and safety legislation imposes a uniformly low level of risk on all jobs, it may prevent bargains being struck which would benefit employers, employees and the general public. For, in the limit, extreme levels of required safety could prevent almost any employment taking place.[4] As so often in economics, we need to think about a balance between benefits and costs – in this case the benefits, in terms of lives saved or injuries prevented, versus the loss of output and employment.

As Nobel prizewinner Daniel Kahneman (2011: 351) has argued:

> Intensive aversion to trading increased risk for some other advantage plays out on a grand scale in the laws and regulations governing risk. This trend is especially strong in Europe, where the precautionary principle, which prohibits any action that might cause harm, is a widely accepted doctrine.

He points out that excessive adherence to the precautionary principle would have prevented the development of many areas of medicine, aircraft, nuclear power, X-rays and so on.

One problem is 'mission creep', with matters such as stress at work now being part of the remit of health and safety as a result of union and political pressure.[5] Indeed, more generally, 'health' issues seem now to be more prominent than traditional safety concerns. These issues are much more debatable, and less clear-cut, than those covered by historic factory legislation.

---

4   Even voluntary events can be deterred by health and safety fears. Taylor (2010) refers to the Voluntary Arts Network's guide to health and safety for outdoor community events, which runs to over 200 pages. If organisers do not adhere to such guidance, they may be held liable in the event of an accident and will not be able to secure insurance.

5   Including pressures from the European Commission, from where about two thirds of health and safety legislation is alleged to have come in recent years (Lofstedt 2011).

Redefinition of traditional responsibilities also plays a part; for instance, the well-publicised examples of police officers being warned to avoid pursuing suspects in dangerous situations or other public employees being discouraged from attempts to rescue people without trained personnel and safety equipment being available. Trade union influence through health and safety committees may be a factor in this redefining of responsibilities.

Another problem – common also in other areas of employment law – is that it is not so much the formal rules that matter as how they are perceived. Taylor (2010) went against the common business view of excessive regulation by making a case that health and safety legislation is in reality rather limited, and the inspection regime has been relatively light (with the number of HSE inspections having fallen sharply in recent years). However, in his view a 'culture of over-compliance' (ibid.: 6) has developed.

This is partly the consequence of the inevitable imprecision of legislation, which enjoins 'reasonably practical' measures to avoid danger. The cost of insurance and fear of paying compensation (especially since the proliferation of no win–no fee lawyers has reduced the cost of litigation against employers) has arguably made businesses err on the side of caution in interpreting this obligation. Such a tendency may have increased since the Corporate Manslaughter and Corporate Homicide Act 2007: legal judgements have also made clear that individual board members can be liable for health and safety lapses.

Taylor's arguments were buttressed by the findings of the Lofstedt Review (2011) of UK health and safety laws. Lofstedt concluded that the problem lay not so much with excessive legislation but rather with the way in which the law is interpreted. He pointed to one problem, which was the sometimes conflicting views taken by the HSE and local authorities. Another issue was the influence of 'third parties that promote the generation of unnecessary paperwork' and promoted 'activities that go above and beyond the regulatory requirements' (ibid.: 2).

Such 'third parties' include members of the specialist health-and-safety profession. In the last twenty years the membership of the Institution of Occupational Safety and Health has grown from 6,000 to around 36,000, while some 1,500 specialist health and safety firms offer consultancy and training services to businesses. It does not require excessive cynicism to suggest that such firms are unlikely to advise their clients to reduce their worries over health and safety.

Lofstedt drew attention to what he saw as excessively detailed[6] risk assessments which are often prepared. The burden of producing these documents falls disproportionately on small businesses. Lancaster et al. (2003) estimated that small firms spent almost six times more per employee than large firms on these assessments, while more generally the Health and Safety Executive (2004) found that small enterprises received fewer communications from HSE and were much more likely than large firms to regard regulation as burdensome.

The Lofstedt Review made some sensible suggestions about streamlining regulation, directing enforcement towards businesses where there are greater safety risks, reducing employer exposure to civil liability, and excluding the self-employed from most regulation. Some of his suggestions were adopted by the Coalition government (for instance, in the Social Action, Responsibility and Heroism Act 2015), though it is too early to say whether they have had much impact.

The UK has the one of the lowest fatality rates at work in the EU, its accident rate is less than half the EU average, and employees report fewer work-related health problems than any European

---

6   All very well, but what is 'excessively detailed'? A recent judgement of the Supreme Court found that an employer of home carers was responsible for an employee who slipped on an icy path when visiting a client. Such a (surely fairly remote?) possibility should have been covered by a risk assessment, so the employer was liable ('Employer's duty to home carer travelling between clients', *The Times*, 29 February 2016).

country except Ireland (Shackleton 2012; BIS 2015). Now that we are leaving the EU, we might be bolder in looking at deregulation in this area.

Working time regulations

I pointed out earlier that a major element in the early factory legislation of the nineteeth century was legal restrictions on working hours. Many of these restrictions were repealed under the Conservative administrations of the 1980s and early 1990s. However, the EU Working Time Directive, promulgated in 1993 and adopted by the UK in 1998, reintroduced regulation in this area. The directive limits working hours per week (normally to 48) and mandates minimum rest periods, maximum lengths of night shifts and minimum paid holidays. More detailed EU rules apply to areas such as road, rail and air transport. These requirements have since been augmented by further EU regulations, legal interpretations by employment tribunals and the European Court of Justice, together with additional domestic legislation.[7]

The UK is often assumed to be exceptionally prone to a 'long hours culture', but this is not the case. Average working hours in the UK fell by 3 per cent over the last decade. Although they are higher than in some European countries, they are considerably below those found in the US, Canada, Australia and New Zealand, as Table 3 demonstrates. And we have a smaller share of those in employment who work long (over 40) hours per week than countries such as Italy and Germany, or indeed the G7 as a whole.[8]

---

7 As noted earlier, the minimum paid holiday leave laid down in the Working Time Directive is 4 weeks, but in 2007 domestic legislation increased it to 5.6 weeks.

8 The proportions shown will vary according to the importance of different industries and occupations in the employment patterns of different economies, so nothing much should be read into these figures. They serve simply to refute some standard misconceptions.

Table 3   Hours worked, selected countries 2014

	Average annual hours actually worked per worker	Percentage of total employees usually working more than 40 hours a week
Australia	1,664	44.3
Canada	1,703	50.2
France	1,473	27.5
Germany	1,366	48.9
Ireland	1,821	33.8
Italy	1,719	52.1
Netherlands	1,420	28.4
New Zealand	1,762	65.5
Spain	1,698	59.6
Switzerland	1,568	62.0
UK	1,677	45.3
US	1,789	75.5
G7 average	n.a.	60.6
OECD average	1,770	63.5

Source: OECD.

The economic rationale for intervention over working time is, as with health and safety legislation more broadly, that there may be asymmetric or otherwise imperfect information which leads employees to choose to work longer hours than they would want if in full knowledge of the effect on their health – particularly where employers have some market power and employee choice is limited. As noted in the previous section, there are doubts about how important these concerns should be in modern conditions.

When the Working Time Directive was first introduced in 1993, it was presented as purely a health and safety measure as the European Community at that time did not have any competence

Table 4   Full-time employees usually working more than
           48 hours a week by occupation, Q4 2013

Occupation	Numbers	As % of all FT employees
Managers, directors and senior officials	724,000	34.5
Professional occupations	994,000	22.8
Process, plant and machine operatives	314,000	22.6
Skilled trade occupations	360,000	19.6
Associate professional and technical occupations	478,000	16.0
Elementary occupations	186,000	12.1
Caring, leisure and other service occupations	124,000	8.5
Sales and customer service occupations	76,000	7.1
Administrative and secretarial occupations	89,000	4.3

Source: BIS (2014).

in social and employment matters.[9] However, an additional element nowadays is the belief that there are externalities associated with the damage to family life of excessive hours of work. The empirical basis for this claim is shaky, for the evidence is that long hours are in the main voluntary (BIS 2015). As Table 4 shows, among those working the longest hours are professionals, managers and highly skilled workers[10] who are strongly committed to their careers. It appears that these are often highly paid workers (ibid.: 77).

The EU has allowed UK employees voluntarily to opt out of the 48-hour maximum in some circumstances, although this

---

9   David Hunt, at that time the UK Employment Secretary, denounced it as a 'flagrant abuse' of Community rules to allow a social measure to be characterised as a health and safety issue.

10   The data on hours worked by these groups are usually self-reported in the Labour Force Survey. Among those apparently working very long hours are academics, though they usually have considerably more autonomy over the hours they put in than most employees.

concession has been under attack both domestically and from other European countries. The sector most likely (40 per cent of workplaces) to have opt-out agreements from the 48-hour maximum working week is the 'other business services' sector, which includes non-financial professional occupations such as lawyers (ibid.: 41), who do not come high up on most people's list of potentially exploited workers. The evidence seems to suggest, too, that people tend to work long hours for relatively short periods rather than it being a permanent feature of their working life (ibid.: 7).

Arguments for regulating working time seem to imply that everybody has similar preferences over work and leisure choices. But this is not the case: attitudes to work, tolerance for long hours, and need or preference for extra money, for example, differ throughout the population. Those who would prefer to work longer hours, either because they would choose extra money over extra hours watching television or because they are absorbed in their work, are prevented from doing so by restrictions on working time. When the French introduced the 35-hour week it was resented by many blue-collar workers as it restricted their earnings opportunities (Estavo and Sa 2006). Similarly, the Department for Business, Innovation and Skills (2014: 7) found that 'the vast majority of long-hours workers would not like to work fewer than 48 hours per week if it meant less pay'. Although much is made of the alleged need for 'work–life balance', regulation of working hours means in practice a paternalistic imposition of a particular view of how time should be spent. It does not fully take into account, for example, the way in which preferred hours vary over the life cycle in response to family and other commitments. At certain stages of their lives, people want to work more, to bring in more income or to enhance their future promotion prospects.

Moreover, the degree to which working hours regulation can be enforced differs through the population. Its impact is much greater on production workers, for example, than on senior executives or many professionals such as academics or creatives.

Employees in these groups have an element of their working time predetermined, but otherwise decide for themselves how much time they spend on their careers. There are also variations in the ability of different occupations to engage in 'moonlighting' – working for more than one employer as a means of evading limits on hours worked.[11] And there are no working time limits on the growing numbers of self-employed.

Restrictions on working time can be expected to have increased employment costs, though it is possible that there may be some offset from higher productivity during shorter hours, particularly in the longer term when capital can be substituted for labour in many processes. To the extent that productivity increases occur, though, they undermine the argument sometimes made for restricting hours in order to create extra jobs during periods of high unemployment. Estavao and Sa (2006: 15), reporting on the introduction of the French 35-hour week, conclude that

> our results cast serious doubts on whether the reduction in hours benefited French employees. Overall, our evaluation of the effects of the 35-hour workweek law is negative. It failed to raise aggregate employment and increased job turnover. Evidence from dual-job holdings, transitions from large to small firms, and subjective measures of satisfaction with hours of work consistently suggest that a significant share of the workforce was constrained by the workweek reduction.

As is often the case with employment regulation, the implications are difficult to anticipate and evaluate when the law is unclear and employment tribunal and European Court judgements have led to new interpretations. For example, European Court rulings

---

11 In 2015 there were around 1.2 million workers officially recorded as having at least two jobs, up from 1.05 million in 2007. This may be an understatement as HM Revenue and Customs believes that many second jobs are not recorded (O'Connor 2015).

in 2000 (the SiMAP case) and 2003 (Jaeger) established that time on-call was counted as working time, with major implications for hospitals and other public services. Two 2009 judgements established that workers coming back from sick leave could then immediately go on holiday leave which they continued to accrue while ill, while in late 2014 the cost of entitlement to holiday pay was increased by an Employment Appeal Tribunal judgement that it should include sales commission which would have been earned if an employee had been working. The danger of such unanticipated changes in legal interpretation have probably led employers, as suggested earlier, to go beyond what they are legally required to do – adding further to the costs of such interventions. This is certainly one important area where exit from the EU should lead UK policy-makers to rethink the basis for regulation.

'Family-friendly' policies

The work–life balance arguments deployed in support of working time regulation are also brought out in support of an increasing range of 'family-friendly' policies. Balancing the demands of family life (including the care of children, the elderly and disabled family members) with the imperatives of the workplace has always been a difficult task. Attempts to cope with this conundrum have historically tended to rely on a rigid gender-based division of labour. In the nineteenth and early twentieth centuries this was associated with trade union demands for a 'family wage'; the male breadwinner should be entitled to a wage enabling him to keep his family in reasonable comfort while his wife stayed at home to provide care and carry out domestic chores. The corollary of this was the exclusion of married women from large sections of the workforce – a policy reinforced by some employers, including the government, requiring women to resign from jobs on marriage and imposing different pay rates for men and women.

In the second half of the twentieth century this approach came increasingly to be seen as anachronistic and inappropriate. One reason was the influence of feminist ideas. As importantly, higher levels of educational achievement by women led them into a wider range of better-paying and interesting jobs which they were reluctant to leave following marriage and childbirth; their employers also became more reluctant to see them go. Other factors included the gradual break-up of close extended-family structures as people moved away from their place of birth; increased divorce rates, and later the rise of the lone-parent family; the spread of labour-saving home technology such as washing machines, vacuum cleaners, fridges and freezers; and the growth of paid childcare.

To a degree, the labour market adjusted to these changes with a wider choice of working arrangements (such as part-time or school-term-only jobs) being voluntarily offered to women. However, there have also, particularly in recent decades, been major legislative interventions to make work more 'family friendly'.

Maternity (and paternity) leave

Mandated maternity leave has been available in the UK for some women for many years. From 1978 those who had worked for two years full time or five years part time with an employer were entitled to a limited period of maternity leave. Following a European directive, this right was extended in 1993 to all in work, whether full time or part time, irrespective of length of service. Further extensions of leave arrangements were made in 1999, while in 2001 paternity leave[12] was introduced. Minor adjustments have been introduced more recently.

---

12 Currently, up to 26 weeks. Same-sex partners are now entitled to request similar leave. From April 2015 parents have been able to share the mother's entitlement to leave between them, though only a small minority of new fathers has so far taken up

Currently, female employees are entitled to 52 weeks' maternity leave (two weeks of which are compulsory; four weeks if you work in a factory), with pay for 39 weeks, albeit at different rates as leave continues.[13] This is one of the longest periods of leave entitlement in the OECD, although some countries allow longer extensions in some circumstances. During this period the mother remains an employee and retains entitlement to some of the benefits of employment, such as the accumulation of holiday leave. Her job must be kept open for her return: if the job disappears as a result of reorganisation in her absence, a job of similar standing and remuneration must be offered.

What reasons are offered to justify this type of regulation? The wellbeing of children has often been mentioned, particularly with respect to the period around birth, as a reason for intervention. Promoting the mother's health and reducing stress have also been highlighted. But much has also been made of economic arguments. It has been claimed that childcare leave with jobs safeguarded makes it more likely that women will accept jobs if they intend to become pregnant, more likely that they will return to work after childbirth, and more likely that they will return to the same or similar job. In the past women returners are said to have had often felt they had to give up their existing jobs and accept less well-paid work. Legislation is argued to benefit them directly, but it also potentially keeps them on a career track, so that over time more women remain in the workforce, at higher rates of pay, thus boosting taxes and reducing benefits paid out. Moreover the pay gap between women and men (see Chapter 8) might be expected to diminish over time as a consequence. Politicians have also argued that employers gain from this arrangement as it means they are more likely to retain the services of valuable employees.

---

this option. In October 2015 it was announced that working grandparents are also to be allowed to share paid leave.

13 Similar arrangements now also apply for adoptions. Note that entitlement to Statutory Maternity Pay is subject to various qualifications.

However, these 'externalities' are not guaranteed. Critics have pointed out that longer periods out of the workforce could perversely weaken future labour market attachment and thus lifetime earnings. It could also conceivably deter employers from hiring women of childbearing age or lead to their paying lower wages through the mechanism outlined in Chapter 4. Indeed, early work on mandated maternity benefits in the US (Gruber 1994) suggested that such mandates did indeed lower women's pay.

More recent empirical work has been carried out which sheds further light on these issues. For example, Schönberg and Ludsteck (2014) examined the effects of five major expansions in maternity leave coverage in Germany. Four out of five of these measures had only a small positive effect on women's employment rates and incomes six years after childbirth, while one measure to extend maternity benefits beyond the period of job protection actually worsened women's long-term labour market prospects. The authors conclude (ibid.: 5) that overall 'the reforms did not succeed in promoting employment continuity or in improving the position of women in the labour market after childbirth'.

A larger review (Thévenon and Solaz 2013) of 30 OECD countries over the period 1970–2010 also provides some insights. The authors find extensions of paid leave to have a small but positive influence on female employment rates, although this effect disappears when women spend more than two years on maternity leave (which can happen, for instance, if women have pregnancies in rapid succession). However, they find that the gender pay gap is *not* reduced as entitlement to paid leave is extended. What may happen is that as increased leave entitlement is taken up, women spend longer out of the workforce and thus tend to lose out on promotions and pay increases.

Moreover, despite being able to return to the same job, many women still choose to change to less-demanding (and less well-paid) jobs on returning to work. One study (Connolly and Gregory 2008) found that as many as 29 per cent of female managers in the UK shed their managerial roles on returning to work. Although this is seen by some as a waste of talent, from the point of view of women with new family responsibilities it may make sense: a job with more flexible hours, shorter travelling time and the opportunity to work at home and so forth may now be more attractive than their previous one even if less well-paid.[14]

As for employers, any benefits from a continuing relationship with valuable employees need to be seen alongside the costs which maternity (and paternity) leave may impose. If a new member of staff has to be appointed on a temporary basis to cover for the absent employee, this inevitably involves some extra recruitment, training and administrative costs,[15] which may be repeated if the temporary worker moves on as a result of finding a permanent post, or if the absent employee extends their leave. These costs may again fall disproportionately on small businesses, which are less likely to have cover available within the firm. Some businesses may trip up though failure to follow correct procedures, for instance, in applying for statutory maternity pay or in fully informing temporary employees of the nature of their contract.

A particular concern for employers in trying to make cover arrangements is that they are forbidden to ask mothers when they are coming back to work, or indeed if they are coming back to work at all. The employer has to assume that the employee will return when her leave expires unless informed to the contrary.

Parental leave and flexible working

Employees with at least one year's service and who have children under five are entitled to 18 weeks of unpaid leave up to each

---

14 Remember that the theory of compensating differentials suggests that pay is not the only determinant of employment choice.

15 Some costs may also fall on users of services, a point often neglected: locum doctors, substitute lecturers and supply teachers, for example, may give a poorer service than established staff.

child's fifth birthday.[16] A maximum of four weeks' absence in each year is permitted subject to 21 days notice, though employers can postpone this leave for up to six months for business reasons.

A more important issue is the right to request 'flexible working arrangements'. Under the regulations introduced in 2002, an employee with 26 weeks' continuous employment can request a change in hours of work (for instance, a switch from full time to part time or a job share), a change in working hours (for example, term-time-only working, earlier or later starting or finishing times, or 'compressed weeks', where people work 35 hours spread over four days rather than five, or some portion of time to be spent working at home.

This provision was originally introduced to cater for parents, and covered those with children under the age of 18. Coverage was extended in 2007 to carers looking after, for example, a husband, wife or partner or a close adult relative living at the same address. Following a consultation exercise, the coalition government extended the right to request flexible working to all employees. This is an interesting example of how regulation increases the demand for further regulation. We start from a plausible and widely supported case for new parents to adjust hours, to a situation where anybody is entitled to seek changes to their contractual arrangements, for whatever reason.

Advocates of the right to request flexible arrangements claim that agreeing to proposals increases employee satisfaction, loyalty and motivation, and enables organisations to retain employees who might otherwise have left. Much is made of the fact that 90 per cent of applications are accepted. This is taken as evidence that employers can make adjustments at little cost. But this cannot be assumed: it may be that the employer wishes to avoid the confrontations and unpleasantness which often accompany refusals. It seems likely that there *are* additional costs, for example,

---

16   Parents of disabled children have the right to leave for a longer period.

recruiting an extra part-timer to cover for someone who wishes to reduce or stagger hours. These costs may be absorbed in the short run by employers but could once more be particularly significant for small firms.

Furthermore, as suggested in Chapter 4, in the longer term the burden of all these measures is likely to switch to employees and potential employees, through slower wage and/or employment growth. This hypothesis is supported by work done by Heywood et al. (2005). These authors use data from the Workplace Employment Relations Survey to demonstrate that there are real costs to employers of family-friendly practices and that 'much of the cost appears to be borne by the workers that the practices are designed to assist'.

Sunday working

Another type of regulation, with a long and venerable history, is that surrounding Sunday working. Originally basing their case firmly on religious grounds, more recently Christian churches have recognised that Britain is now a multicultural society where other religions (Islam and Judaism in particular) have large numbers of adherents, while growing numbers of people profess no religion at all. The defenders of restrictions on Sunday working now tend to refer to Sunday being a 'family' day, though the reality of twenty-first century Britain is that growing numbers of people live alone and see their families infrequently.

The peculiar laws surrounding Sunday opening are the result of legislative compromise, as are the conditions which surround Sunday working in general. They include complicated rules about opting out from Sunday work and a prohibition on discriminating against workers who refuse Sunday working. Probably the most significant constraint on Sunday working has been the restriction on the opening hours of large retail stores in England and

Wales.[17] Those larger than 280 square metres can currently only open for six hours on Sunday, and must close on Easter Sunday and Christmas Day. The rules were suspended for eight weeks during the 2012 Olympics and Paralympics, and there has been pressure to change the law permanently. It has always seemed odd to force Tesco and Sainsbury's to close their big out-of-town stores when there are no restrictions on their smaller outlets, which now dominate suburban streets, and when an increasing part of their business, and that of their competitors, is conducted 24/7 online.

Evidence from earlier reforms suggests deregulation would probably lead to a modest increase in employment. But an attempt by the government to give local authorities the power to relax restrictions was defeated in the House of Commons in March 2016 in bizarre circumstances, with the Scottish Nationalists voting alongside Labour and Conservative rebels.[18] Despite there being no national restrictions on Sunday trading in Scotland, the SNP felt justified in intervening in the business of England and Wales to prevent any contagion undermining higher rates of pay paid to Sunday workers in Scotland. Potential extra jobs in England and Wales were thus sacrificed to protect the pay of Scottish workers, a clear example of the way in which regulation protects some groups at the expense of others.

Employment of children

One group of the workforce which is particularly tightly regulated is young people below school leaving age. Considering that

---

17 There are no general restrictions on Sunday trading in Scotland, although in the Western Isles (where the Free Church of Scotland still has a strong following) all shops are closed on Sundays. In Northern Ireland slightly different rules apply, aimed at maximising church attendance: large shops can only open from 1 p.m. to 6 p.m.

18 http://www.bbc.co.uk/news/uk-politics-35768674 (accessed 12 April 2016).

at any one time up to a million schoolchildren may[19] have paid part-time jobs, remarkably little is known about them. The Labour Force Survey, which provides so much useful information about the UK's working-age population, does not ask questions about the labour market activity of children under 16 in the households it covers. It probably should.

We do know, however, that the number of 16–17-year-olds working while studying has fallen sharply – from 42 per cent in 1997 to 18 per cent in 2014 (Conlon et al. 2015), so it is likely that the numbers of younger children working have fallen too. Certainly anecdotal evidence suggests that numbers have been falling as a result of such factors as increased parental affluence, growing demands of school examinations (sometimes reinforced by the negative attitude of teachers to children's employment), parental fear of sexual abuse, and a decline in the availability of traditional 'children's work' such as milk and newspaper rounds. But regulation is an important factor.

The ILO, the UN and the EU have all for many years had codes which in principle forbid child labour. This reflects a revulsion against the employment of children for long hours and in dangerous conditions which was prevalent in most countries in the early nineteenth century, and is still found today in many parts of the developing world. In economic terms young children are nowadays deemed to be unable to consent to work, presumably on the grounds that they cannot form a balanced view of its costs (for example, potential damage to health) and benefits, or may not be able to assert their preferences against those of their parents. The banning of work is the logical corollary of mandated education.[20]

---

19 Based on small occasional classroom samples, grossed up to the population age group.

20 This is not the place to discuss the issue in detail, but there are libertarian arguments against mandated education of any kind. There are less radical arguments which suggest that schooling should be confined to a shorter period (the UK is at

In the EU's case, the minimum age for employment is set as the school leaving age (as this varies between member states, the default is 15). However, it is recognised that there are legitimate 'derogations' to allow schoolchildren to receive training or work experience.

In the UK the relevant primary legislation dates back to the Children and Young Persons Act of 1933 (when, incidentally, the school leaving age was 14).

The current legal position in England (slightly different rules apply in other parts of the UK) is full of detailed prohibitions. You must be at least 14[21] in most paid employment, which must be 'light' work. Examples of permitted work in official guidance include newspaper delivery (with recommended weights of bags), hairdressing, office work, shop work including shelf stacking, and some agricultural or horticultural work. You cannot work in manufacturing, construction, transport or other 'industrial' work – classified in an old-fashioned manner so that, for instance, you cannot do clerical work in an industrial sector such as transport (unless in a family firm) but you can do similar work in, say, an advertising agency. You cannot work in an amusement arcade but you can work on a fairground stall.

The position is complicated because the 1933 Act gave local authorities discretion to institute their own bye-laws, meaning that there are significant variations between areas. In some local authorities children can deliver milk, in others they cannot. Work in street trading is forbidden in some areas, permitted elsewhere. Young people can serve alcohol when waiting on table in some towns, but not in others. Most importantly, some areas require employers to have permits to employ children, while others do

---

the upper end of years of compulsory education) or perhaps should be judged on outcome – reaching some agreed minimum standard, rather than having to spend a given number of years in education.

21 Though there are some exceptions where 13-year-olds can work, while theatrical performances have separate rules of their own.

not. Moreover, even in areas where permits are legally required, it is estimated that only about 15 per cent of employed children are covered by such permits (McKechnie et al. 2011).

There are further complications about the hours which you are permitted to work. All work must be done between 7 a.m. and 7 p.m. On a school day you can only work for 2 hours. On a non-school day you can only work up to 5 hours if you are under 15, or 8 hours if you are 15 or over. There are mandated breaks of 1 hour which apply if you are working more than 4 hours. You cannot work more than 12 hours a week in term time. Outside term time an under-15 can work 25 hours a week, while a 15-year-old can work up to 35 hours; however, this only applies to full weeks, so if term ends on a Tuesday that is treated as a term-time week. No child is allowed to work more than 2 hours on a Sunday. Different working hours rules apply to children on unpaid work experience – and so on.

Given all this mind-blowing complexity, it is not surprising that 'it is generally accepted that the majority of child employees work illegally' (McKechnie et al. 2011: 12). Few employers – or anyone else for that matter – seem to have anything approaching a full understanding of the rules which cover child employment.

There are arguments for a more positive attitude towards child employment even in poor economies (Kis-Katos and Schulze 2005). In developed economies we might take the view that general health and safety and other forms of employment regulation protect children to a considerable degree, and emphasise instead that early employment experience can be invaluable for giving children insight into the world of work, improved self-discipline and self-esteem, and in some cases allowing them access to goods and services which their parents could not afford to give them. State-sponsored 'work experience' for schoolchildren (compulsory until 2012) is usually a poor substitute for a real job.

In his review of employment law for the Conservative–Liberal Democrat coalition, Adrian Beecroft (Department for Business,

Innovation and Skills 2012) argued that the employment rules for children could be greatly simplified and the permit system scrapped. Nothing came of this. The pressures currently seem to be in the opposite direction. The European Committee on Social Rights (part of the Council of Europe, not the EU) has recently argued that some paper rounds may breach the European Social Charter, and that young people may be working too many hours during school holidays.[22] At home, a House of Commons Committee has proposed to ban under-18s from working as catwalk models.[23]

Politicians might be better advised to take inspiration from New Zealand where, by contrast with most developed countries, a much more permissive attitude has been taken to child employment – which seems to be more widespread than in Britain. A good deal of evidence has been accumulated that this has no negative consequences. For example, a recent longitudinal study (Iosua et al. 2014) looked at the lasting effects (up to age 32) of schoolchildren's paid work on a range of factors including academic achievement, psychological wellbeing, smoking, drug and alcohol use. Its lead author concluded that 'moderate part-time work is unlikely to be detrimental in countries like New Zealand'.

It seems likely that the same applies in the UK. There is certainly evidence that 16–17-year-olds may gain in terms of career prospects from part-time work (Conlon et al. 2015: 5):

> Those combining work with full-time education are 4–6 percentage points less likely to be NEET [Not in Education, Employment or Training] five years later than those just in education. They are also likely to earn more than those just in full-time education, with a premium of 12–15 per cent.

22 Paper rounds 'may breach European law', says watchdog: http://www.bbc.co.uk/news/education-35430053 (accessed 2 March 2016).

23 Under-18 models may be banned from catwalk: http://www.bbc.co.uk/news/health-35596475 (accessed 3 March 2016).

Occupational regulation

The forms of regulation discussed so far in this chapter are ostensibly intended to protect employees and improve their working conditions. However, another form of employment regulation is primarily rationalised as a means of protecting consumers and the general public. Apart from regulations which apply across the workforce, governments in developed economies typically regulate a wide range of specific occupations where it is believed consumers, service users and the general public might be at risk in some way. Writing in 2010, Humphris et al. (2011) estimated that over 13 per cent of the UK workforce now required a government licence in order to practice their occupation. This was more than double the percentage 12 years previously (Bryson and Kleiner 2010). Such jobs predictably include professionals such as doctors, solicitors and financial advisors, but also a range of less-skilled roles including driving instructors, security guards and dental hygienists.

An international perspective is provided in Table 5, where countries across the EU are compared using the EU's Single Market Regulated Professions Database to determine jobs which are regulated in some way. This is a broader definition which includes *licensing* (where it is unlawful to practise without a licence, which is typically associated with educational qualifications and/or training), but also includes *registration* (where practitioners are legally required to be listed, but which does not involve any qualification requirements and *certification* (where the government gives formal recognition to a qualification and legal protection for use of a title, but does not require such certification for employment).[24]

---

24 Individuals can also be *accredited* by a purely private body such as a professional association (in the UK accountancy is an example). Although governments play no role in demanding such a qualification, possession of accreditation can be an important labour market advantage. Thus associations may possess some power to influence entry into a field, which they could abuse if, for instance, they deliberately kept examination pass rates low to prevent competition from new entrants.

Table 5   Regulated occupations in the EU27*

Country	Number of regulated professions*	Percentage of employed who are in regulated fields
Estonia	14	3
Latvia	16	3–6
Lithuania	27	6–7
Sweden	38	11–14
Bulgaria	39	4–15
Luxembourg	48	11–20
Romania	48	10–11
Ireland	57	8–11
Cyprus	62	9–30
Finland	63	10–15
Hungary	75	14–23
Malta	75	11–14
Belgium	78	16–26
Portugal	85	7–21
Germany	86	4–31
Italy	86	6–27
Netherlands	87	10–16
Denmark	90	13–43
France	90	13–20
Greece	98	8–26
Slovak Republic	109	12–23
Spain	112	8–26
UK	131	11–21
Slovenia	135	11–22
Austria	151	15–29
Poland	162	14–27
Czech Republic	215	17–39
EU27		9–24

*Using EU Single Market Regulated Professions Database, including licensing, accreditation and certification. No data for Croatia.
Source: Koumenta et al. (2014).

The first column of Table 5 shows that the number of regulated occupational areas varies considerably across the EU. Perhaps surprisingly in view of the UK's reputation as a country with comparatively little regulation, on this indicator it appears to be at the more heavily regulated end of the spectrum (see also Kleiner 2015). This may in part be explained by the sectoral composition of UK employment (for example, finance and professional business services play a big role in UK employment, and their many different types of practitioners are now highly regulated), and in part also by the amount of time for which the UK has been regulating professions. Countries such as Latvia, Lithuania and Estonia did not have a comparable tradition of professional regulation under communism.

The second column of the table gives estimates of the percentage employed in regulated occupations. These figures derive from the European Labour Force Survey. In most cases a range is shown. This is because the number of individuals whose employment is regulated is not known, but it is known into which broad occupational category they would fall. So the numbers in each broad occupational category provide upper and lower limits on the numbers who may be regulated. The overall figures for the EU27 indicate that between 9 per cent and 24 per cent of workers are in regulated fields. This appears to be markedly lower than the corresponding figure for the US, where more information is available. Kleiner and Krueger (2010) suggest around 30 per cent of US employees are subject to occupational licensing.

The economic arguments for licensing are usually based on asymmetric information problems: in many fields, medicine being perhaps the paradigm case,[25] the producer usually knows more than the consumer. Unscrupulous practitioners could exploit gullible consumers, making them pay for worthless services, or in extreme cases endangering their health and property. A

---

25 But see Friedman (1963: 149–60) for a powerful argument against medical licensure.

system of government licensing signals an attested level of competence and integrity, and reduces search costs for individuals looking for an acceptable level of service. It clearly acts as a deterrent to malpractice, as the penalty of taking the licence away will destroy the practitioner's livelihood.

However, practitioner membership bodies can and do offer the same kind of service without government intervention; the accountancy bodies mentioned earlier are an example. Milton Friedman (1963) argued that such accreditation was a good 'half-way house' that offers consumers a degree of protection against unscrupulous producers without the need for government regulation, which he abhorred. However, as Bryson and Kleiner (2010) point out, this may not be a stable situation. Private organisations have an incentive to limit entry, force up wages and raise costs to the consumer; to assist in this, many are perversely happy to solicit support from governments. As Friedman pointed out more than fifty years ago, 'the pressure on the legislature to license an occupation rarely comes from members of the public ... the pressure ... comes from members of the occupation itself' (Friedman 1963: 140). As always, concentrated producer interests are better able to organise to push for such support than diverse consumers, each of whom has only a limited concern with the service provided. Governments are short of in-house expertise and, having decided to regulate, come to rely on producers to staff regulatory bodies – giving rise to the problem of 'regulatory capture'.

Carpenter et al. (2015) have documented how far occupational regulation has proceeded in the US, with even relatively low-skilled occupations such as barbers,[26] florists, manicurists, home entertainment installers and bartenders being licensed in at least some states.

---

26 Timmons and Thornton (2010) find that aspects of licensing of barbers may have raised barbers' earnings by between 11 and 22 per cent in the US.

The difference in requirements between US states provides a natural experiment to determine the effect of regulation. Licensing of opticians in only around half of the states does not seem to be associated with different quality of service, though prices are higher in regulated states. In the case of interior designers, Carpenter and his colleagues observe (ibid.: 24) that

> only three states and the District of Columbia license interior designers, but that occupation is the most difficult to enter in those states. It seems implausible that interior design poses a health and safety risk in these four jurisdictions that is absent everywhere else (or that there is risk severe enough to warrant requiring would-be designers to complete six years of education and training).

We do not have quite such egregious examples of occupational exclusivity in the UK as in the US, but the persistent attempt of British teachers' unions to exclude from the profession those without a formal teaching qualification, for example, may not be dissimilar in intention and consequence.

Often regulation comes about as a knee-jerk reaction to a scandal of some sort, but vested interests quickly kick in. As a result of the tabloid newspaper phone-hacking scandal, which involved some private investigators, Theresa May, then Home Secretary, required all such investigators to be registered, trained and subject to a code of practice. She was egged on by the Association of British Investigators, an existing trade body.

Occupational licensing and regulation raise wages[27] and reduce employment without demonstrable benefit to consumers, as Bryson and Kleiner (2010) conclude. This is bad for the public

---

27 Kleiner (2015: 69) suggests that there is a wage premium in regulated occupations of around 13 per cent; ironically, he points out, this is similar to the premium calculated for trade union–engineered 'closed shop' arrangements, which are now illegal.

in a narrowly economic sense, but it can also be 'a serious infringement on the freedom of individuals to pursue activities of their own choice' (Friedman 1963: 142).

Conclusion

I have attempted to show in this chapter that there is a wide and growing range of employment restrictions aimed at protecting employees, their families and consumers from various sorts of harm. These interventions are often inefficient. They may not succeed in their officially stated aims, but serve sectional interests rather than the wider public. Once instituted, they are very difficult to remove. Potential losers from reform are, as always, more vociferous than gainers who are mostly unaware of the costs they collectively bear from regulation. These costs are popularly assumed to fall on employers when their true incidence lies elsewhere.

Furthermore, in restricting entry into some areas unnecessarily, some forms of regulation can also be an illegitimate infringement on liberty. Voters need to be much more suspicious of politicians bearing gifts which promise to protect people from perceived danger.

7 OTHER PEOPLE'S PAY (1)

Other people's pay is something politicians seem to find endlessly irritating. As we saw in Chapter 3, King Hammurabi was trying to enforce particular pay rates in Babylon nearly 4,000 years ago. The twentieth century saw many attempts to regulate pay: most ended badly. In the Soviet Union and its satellites, the government attempted to impose pay structures which conformed to its political priorities, and also to a misplaced emphasis on a reading of Marx's version of the labour theory of value. This meant, for example, higher pay for 'productive' workers, who made things, than for service workers involved in what Marx called 'the distribution of surplus value'. The predictable consequences were shortages of labour in some areas (secretaries in Moscow, for example) and excess supplies elsewhere. This in turn led planners to controls on migration between areas and direction of labour. In the worst scenario this could mean forced labour in Siberian gulags, or, less harshly, direction of East German university graduates to their first jobs.

In the UK, despite experience of the direction of labour during the exceptional circumstances of both world wars, conditions were more benign. We did, however, have a prolonged series of experiments in the 1960s and 1970s with attempts to control wage inflation through incomes policies.[1] These policies aimed

---

1   There had been limited attempts at controlling wages in the late 1940s and again in the late 1950s, but the 1960s and 1970s saw activity on an unprecedented scale. There was a blizzard of White Papers on pay policy: one in 1962 (Conservative); three

to restrict average pay increases to the rate of growth of labour productivity (always a slippery concept, like many macroeconomic variables). Many groups of workers claimed to be exceptional cases, requiring their pay to rise faster than the 'norm'; unsurprisingly, few if any offered themselves as deserving less. Where workers had union muscle behind them, they often won a larger increase. Even without this, employers facing an employee shortage, or wanting a quiet life, would often collude in devices such as regrading staff, uncovenanted bonuses, local hours adjustments and so forth: 'wage drift' was ubiquitous. Incomes policies were unsuccessful in containing pay inflation except for very short periods.

The fundamental reason for this was that inflation was essentially caused by monetary expansion feeding demand, rather than 'wage push'. But the experience of these years also shows just how easily central government diktats on pay (even when backed up by considerable sanctions) could be undermined by private initiatives beyond our rulers' control. As one author put it, 'all that was required to evade the policy was an exercise in ingenuity' (Richardson 1991: 440).

Most of today's politicians were in nappies when the powers of government over wages were exposed as the Emperor's New Clothes, but they should reflect that the 'ingenuity' shown by a previous generation of employers and employees is still present today. We no longer attempt to control average pay to combat inflation, but our rulers are again obsessed with wage-setting, albeit for different reasons.

---

in 1965 (Labour); one each in 1967, 1968 and 1969 (Labour); one in 1972 and another in 1973 – plus a Green Paper also in 1973 (all Conservative); and further papers in 1975, 1976 and 1978 under Labour's Social Contract. There was also frequent institutional innovation as governments attempted to implement their policies of wage restraint. Thus we had a National Incomes Commission in 1962, a National Board for Prices and Incomes (1965), a Commission for Industry and Manpower (1969), an Office of Manpower Economics (1970) and a Pay Board and Prices Commission (1973).

Does this reflect shifting public attitudes? In the past it might have been considered impolite to ask or write about how much an individual earns. But the new normal is for everyone to have an opinion on how much everyone else should be paid. Such disparate commentators as *The Guardian*'s Polly Toynbee and Conservative MEP Daniel Hannan have suggested that our tax returns should be publicly available. This nosiness feeds into debates surrounding minimum wage policies, income inequality and various earning 'gaps' between groups of employees.

Pay is becoming increasingly politicised, and not just in terms of those things politicians currently control (whether it be public sector pay or minimum wage rates). Politicians pass instant judgement on everything from how restaurant tips are handled to how much 'top talent' at the BBC is paid. These off-the-cuff pronouncements can sometimes be leading indicators for future legislation.

In this chapter I examine two issues which are very much part of today's political agenda: wage-setting for the low-paid and compulsory private pensions. The next chapter covers two other concerns: top pay and the gender pay gap.

The National Minimum Wage and the National Living Wage

Most developed countries impose minimum wage rates: the first to do so was New Zealand, as long ago as 1896. The UK's National Minimum Wage (NMW) – an hourly wage floor – was introduced by Tony Blair's New Labour. It was a marked change from the past. Although we have seen that minimum wages were set in specific low-paid trades from the first decade of the twentieth century until the early 1990s, there had never been a national minimum – historically anathema to the trade union movement.

Though initially opposed by the Conservatives, the NMW is now accepted by all political parties. An independent Low Pay Commission (LPC) was created to set it, with representation for

Figure 4 The National Minimum Wage (£ per hour) over time

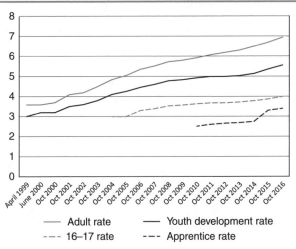

Source: Low Pay Commission.

trade unions and employers, together with a strong academic component. This body advises the government on different NMW rates for adults, 18–20-year-olds (the 'development rate'), 16–17-year-olds, and for apprentices under 19. The rates are usually proposed early in the year, for operation from the following October. Figure 4 shows how they have evolved over time.

The initial terms of reference for the LPC required it to recommend levels for minimum wage rates 'that will help as many low-paid workers as possible without any significant adverse impact on employment or the economy'.[2] This was important, as it flagged up explicit concern with employment and not just with living standards. The Commission's recommendations, based firmly on evidence about demand and supply conditions in the labour market, have therefore been fairly conservative. They have usually been accepted by successive administrations.

2   https://www.gov.uk/government/organisations/low-pay-commission/about/terms-of-reference (accessed 28 June 2016).

Figure 5   Adult National Minimum Wage rate as
            percentage of median hourly earnings*

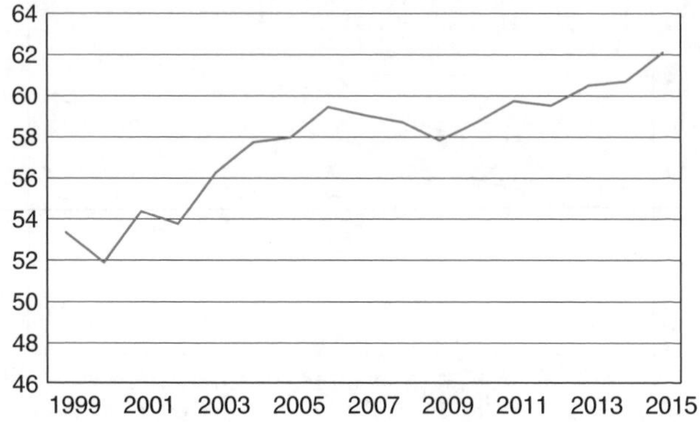

*Using Labour Force Survey data.

As Figure 4 shows, the 'adult'[3] minimum wage has risen continually in money terms, although some of the other rates have
increased only fitfully. The under-25 adult rate currently (November 2016) stands at £6.95 an hour. Despite fluctuations over the
period (after 2007 it fell back in real terms, but has since recovered) the NMW has also increased in value over time. Between
1999 and 2016 the adult rate grew by over a third in real terms.[4]

It has also risen significantly as a proportion of median hourly earnings (its 'bite'), as Figure 5 illustrates.[5] Moreover, this has

3   Although the age of adulthood changed slightly, all adults were paid the same
    NMW until April 2016 when the National Living Wage came into force for over-25s.

4   Calculated using the Consumer Price Index measure of inflation: in RPI terms real
    growth was slower.

5   Figure 5 uses Labour Force Survey (LFS) data rather than Annual Survey of Hourly
    Earnings (ASHE) data. The LFS data (from households) are believed to underesti-
    mate hourly earnings, partly because of proxy responses. ASHE figures (based on
    employer-provided data) are probably more accurate, but there have been several
    changes to the methodology over the period covered here. The figures used here
    exaggerate the bite of the NMW, but indicate the trend reasonably well.

been achieved against a background of rising employment, only temporarily halted during the post-2008 recession.

The apparent success of the NMW in boosting pay at the bottom of the earnings distribution without significant job losses has emboldened those who wish to see pay rise faster, notably the Living Wage Campaign. This campaign, spearheaded by the Living Wage Foundation (see Box 1), has called for a much higher level of minimum pay based on an assessment of acceptable living standards. The Living Wage Foundation encourages employers to sign up to paying its target Living Wage: those doing so are accredited and can display the Foundation's logo on their premises and in their marketing.

Responding to this mood, the Conservative government returned at the last general election has changed the nature of minimum wage setting. George Osborne announced in his July 2015 budget that a new 'National Living Wage' (NLW) of £7.20 an hour for over-25s would be implemented from April 2016; furthermore, it was intended that this would rise to over £9 by 2020 – the aim being to hit a target of 60 per cent of the ASHE measure of median earnings from then onwards. As a result, it is estimated that by 2020 about 3.7 million workers (13.7 per cent of all employees) will have their pay determined by a government-set minimum. As it is likely that those earning slightly above the minimum levels – for instance, those supervising small groups of minimum-wage workers – will have pay raised to maintain differentials, up to six million workers in total may be affected (Low Pay Commission 2016: 85).

The effects of minimum wages: theory and evidence

Traditional 'blackboard' economics suggests that a wage floor set above the market-determined level will necessarily mean that fewer labour-hours are demanded, while workers will wish to supply more hours. In this framework, gains to those receiving

Box 1   The Living Wage Foundation

The Living Wage Foundation, a coalition of church leaders, trade unionists, poverty campaigners and sympathetic businesspeople, encourages employers to pay an hourly wage calculated to give a full-time worker an income sufficient to reach a decent standard of living.

At the end of 2016, while the NMW stood at £6.95 per hour and the NLW at £7.20, the Living Wage Campaign was advocating a rate of £9.75 an hour in London and £8.45 an hour outside the capital. The figures are updated annually.

The Living Wage targets are calculated by two different bodies. In London, GLA Economics, a body under the auspices of the London Mayor, sets the figure. The outside-London target is produced by the Centre for Research in Social Policy at Loughborough University. These bodies, using both expert opinion and focus groups, set a figure (based on a number of stylised households with different patterns of work and family commitments), which is said to suffice for an adequate level of warmth and shelter, a healthy diet and a reasonable level of social integration. In London, this needs-based approach is complemented with an analysis of those earning less than 60 per cent of median income for each household type. In both cases a weighted average Living Wage is produced reflecting the mix of households in the population.

This figure, unlike the National Minimum Wage, is set without reference to an employer's ability to pay: it is a purely voluntary target. A number of major private sector employers have signed up to it, proudly proclaiming that they pay all their workers at or above the Living Wage – although few are employers of large numbers of low-paid workers. Some local authorities, particularly those controlled by Labour, have also joined the campaign.

higher pay have therefore to be weighed against losses of hours or employment opportunities to other individuals.

While this is still an important first step in reasoning, we should remember that in practice the returns from jobs involve elements other than basic pay, such as provision of training, attractive working conditions, overtime at premium rates, pension schemes, staff discounts and other fringe benefits. Faced with the introduction of (or an increase in) a minimum wage, employers can adjust these conditions rather than cut employment. The advent of the National Living Wage has been marked by a number of stories in the media which illustrate this: firms such as B&Q and Waitrose have been accused of lowering premium pay for weekends and other 'unsocial hours', while Caffè Nero staff seem to have lost the perk of free paninis. So even if relatively few jobs or working hours are initially lost, those gaining from pay increases may lose out in other ways.

More optimistically, it has sometimes been argued that the 'shock' effect of minimum wages can induce previously lethargic employers to search for ways of increasing labour productivity, allowing them in the longer term to maintain or even increase employment. In such circumstances there need be no obvious losers from the minimum wage. This is certainly possible if the increased productivity comes from improved organisation and the reduction of what economists call 'X-inefficiency' (Leibenstein 1966), or perhaps because of investment in training. On the other hand, if productivity increases come from a switch to investment in labour-saving technology, such as self-check-outs in supermarkets, the longer-run impact of the minimum wage might be to generate larger reductions in employment than is the case in the short run.

Some economists, however, believe that labour markets simply do not work as blackboard economics suggests. Sir John Hicks (1932) long ago pointed out that the standard model in effect assumes perfect competition in the labour market. If, however, there is a monopsony – a single buyer of labour – profit maximisation leads firms to pay less than the value of the marginal product of labour and employ fewer labour-hours than would be the case under competition. The implication is that, given monopsony in the labour market, government imposition of a modest minimum wage can theoretically lead both to an increase in pay per hour *and* an increase in hours of employment. In these circumstances workers gain unequivocally from the minimum wage, at the expense of previously exploitative employers.

But unambiguous examples of monopsony – such as the 'company town' where everyone works for the same employer – are vanishingly rare in the modern world. Most low-paid sectors, such as hospitality and catering,[6] are surely highly competitive when we look at conventional indicators such as numbers of competing employers and freedom to enter or leave the industry. But maybe employer market power is more subtle: some economists, notably Alan Manning (2003), claim that all employment situations have an element of monopsony. Manning argues that employees have imperfect information and this, coupled with the costs of switching jobs, always gives the current employer a degree of market power over workers. To counter this, however, others point out that that existing employees have some limited countervailing market power in relation to their employer, because it would be costly for the employer to dismiss them and recruit replacements (Kuhn 2004).

Theory, then, does not seem to get us very far. Does empirical evidence shed any light? Two decades ago David Card and Alan Krueger (1994) startled economists with their findings on the effect of minimum wage increases in New Jersey restaurants. They claimed that these wage hikes had not in practice caused reductions in employment: indeed they may actually have been

---

6　The adult minimum wage in accommodation and food services is over 80 per cent of median hourly earnings.

associated with employment increases relative to a neighbouring state where no such pay increase had occurred.

However, their analysis was based on telephone surveys of employers. Later analysis using payroll data (Neumark and Wascher 1995) found a conflicting result: the minimum wage increase *had* reduced employment after all.

Battle over these and many other studies has raged backwards and forwards ever since. Nevertheless, a broad consensus view of the academic literature seems to have emerged. This is that minimum wage laws have a small but significant negative effect on overall employment levels, with the effect being greater for young adults (Williams and Mills 2001; Neumark and Wascher 2004) and in recessions (Dolton and Bondibene 2012).

Economists understand labour markets rather better today as a result of improvements in data and econometric methods. They now stress the *dynamics* of the labour market (Meer and West 2013), pointing out that even if the labour market is in some sort of 'equilibrium', firms will always be simultaneously gaining and losing workers as people move in and out of jobs for a variety of reasons. Adjustments to the introduction of a minimum wage take time and are not altogether predictable. There are costs associated with firing workers – redundancy payments, loss of expertise from the firm and psychological costs to managers who dislike unpleasant scenes. So a gradual reduction in hiring, rather than sacking existing workers, is the favoured means of reducing the payroll. Indeed, work using Canadian data (Brochu and Green 2013) suggests that in some cases firing rates may even *fall* when minimum wages rise, as cuts in hiring take the strain of employment reductions.

The effect of this on the actual level of employment may be that there are significant lags in adjustment, perhaps through natural wastage as workers leave voluntarily (Neumark and Wascher 2007). The argument that the impact of minimum wages takes time to work through is supported by the work of Aaronson et al. (2016) on the US restaurant industry. The novelty of their approach is to demonstrate that, though existing firms may not reduce employment by much when wages rise, as firms leave the industry, new entrants which replace them employ less labour.

These lags make it difficult to measure the consequences of introducing, or changing the level of, a minimum wage floor. For if it takes time for the effects to work out,[7] they can be masked by other changes which are taking place, for example, shifts in demand (positive or negative) for goods and services produced by low-paid labour.

It's also important to recognise that, in the sort of low-paid job where minimum wages are paid, hours worked may fall rather than employment (Stewart and Swaffield 2008). This is confirmed by HM Treasury analysis which showed that since 2007, the growth of *weekly* wages for NMW wage workers had tended to be below the growth in the *hourly* rate (BIS 2015). There is some evidence that hours worked by young people fell as a result of minimum wage increases during the recession (Bryan et al. 2012).

Policy

This all suggests that introducing or raising a modest minimum wage may not produce marked or even detectable reductions in employment in the short run – though this cannot be taken to suggest that big increases in wage levels can be engineered without eventual reductions in jobs, hours worked or a combination of the two. Minimum wage increases are therefore a trade-off, between raising pay for those fortunate enough to keep their jobs and hours against the potential reduction in labour demand. Any reduction in demand will hit young and unskilled workers, particularly those from minority groups, hardest. It is also likely

---

7 The studies by Aaronson et al. suggests that, while the short-run elasticity of demand for minimum-wage labour is only 0.1, it is 0.4 in the long run. This latter elasticity is used by the Office of Budget Responsibility (OBR 2015: 204–6) in its modelling of the NLW.

Figure 6   Adult minimum wage as % of median hourly earnings by region/nation (April 2015)

Source: ONS.

to have a bigger impact in some parts of the country than others. Figure 6 shows that the 'bite' of the National Minimum Wage is considerably deeper in Northern Ireland and the East Midlands than in London. This led Gordon Brown briefly to consider regionalising the minimum wage.

Though the NMW has increased significantly both in real terms and relative to median earnings since its introduction, the Low Pay Commission has been aware of the jobs–pay trade-off and its remit explicitly called for it to take into account the impact on the labour market. This is not the case with the new National Living Wage, which is likely to have a significant impact on jobs, particularly since there will probably be knock-on effects on the pay of other workers as firms attempt to maintain pay differentials.[8] At the time of the announcement of the NLW, the Office of Budget

---

8   Evidence of this has begun to emerge in the most recent report of the Low Pay Commission. See https://www.gov.uk/government/uploads/system/uploads/att achment_data/file/575634/10583-LPC-National_Living_Wage_WEB.pdf, page 74 (accessed 23 December 2016).

Responsibility expected it to lead, even assuming continued favourable macroeconomic conditions, to a loss of 60,000 jobs and a reduction of four million hours of work a week by 2020 (OBR 2015: 204). If there is another recession, the situation could be worse.

Apart from increased risks to jobs and hours at projected wage rates, the National Living Wage is leading to growing politicisation of low pay. The basic NMW, initially controversial, had settled down into something which was relatively uncontentious between the parties. But the NLW has become subject to competitive bidding-up. The Living Wage Campaign thinks it is only a halfway house and still wants to see its own higher rate widely adopted: Jeremy Corbyn has proposed that big businesses which don't pay this higher rate should not be allowed to pay dividends to shareholders. While this particular threat is unworkable, other proposals will surely follow: if millions of people have pay determined directly by the government, their votes are up for auction. It would be unsurprising to see the NLW drift closer over time to the Living Wage Campaign's target figure. If this happens there would surely be substantial job losses, as there would be if there was a move towards extending the higher NLW rate to all workers, and not just the over-25s. This is the Living Wage Campaign's position: employers who have signed up to the Living Wage already pay all their low-paid workers, whether over 25 or not, the same rate. Several politicians and union leaders have endorsed this position.

By linking the NLW to 60 per cent of median earnings, George Osborne aimed to provide flexibility if the economy were to hit a recession or a period of income stagnation. But given the precedent for political determination of the wage, it seems unlikely a Chancellor (unable to blame the Low Pay Commission) will in future announce nominal cuts or freezes to wage rates to such a large proportion of workers should median earnings falter.

Another aspect of the politicisation of pay is the demonisation of businesses which attempt to mitigate the effects of compulsory pay increases. While still Chancellor, George Osborne warned companies of the reputational dangers from cutting staff perks to compensate for the higher cost of the NLW, while another minister, Nick Boles, promised 'to use the full force of our office ... to put pressure on those companies to live up not only to the legal obligations ... but to their moral obligations'.[9]

This adds to the problems associated with government pay-setting. While previously governments have publicly shamed[10] those failing to pay the NMW, employers now seem to have acquired additional moral obligations going beyond the law. It is unclear who exactly politicians think should bear the burden of higher minimum pay. Apart from the nebulous idea of increasing productivity (which we have seen is anyway quite likely to lead to job losses), the cost can only be borne by consumers paying more, shareholders getting reduced dividends, cuts in other elements of the remuneration package or taxpayers paying more for home carers or hospital cleaners. In competitive markets, especially those facing foreign competition, there is a limit to what can be passed on to the consumer. Lower dividends will in the long run lead to reduced investment or withdrawal from businesses employing large amounts of low-skilled labour. And higher public spending is difficult in a time of retrenchment.

By labelling the new rate as a National 'Living' Wage, moreover, the government has entrenched the Living Wage Campaign's philosophy that businesses should set pay not according to the work you do, your productivity or broad market conditions, but to compensate you for your cost of living. This could have damaging long-term consequences.

---

9 http://www.bbc.co.uk/news/business-36082247 (accessed 29 June 2016).

10 Perhaps unfairly. The government has regularly published lists of offenders, but many seem to be small businesses which misunderstand the complicated rules on minimum wages relating to, for example, piece rates, registration of apprentices, training costs, travel between appointments, accommodation disregards and withholding of pay.

In all this, we should remind ourselves that 'Living Wage' is a misnomer. Three fifths of those earning less than the Living Wage Campaign's targets work part-time: they cannot reach a minimum living standard through their wages alone. In many cases, however, this may not matter. A large proportion of low-paid part-time workers are young people who have family and other support.

Even full acceptance of the Living Wage Campaign's hourly rate targets would not be very effective in combating poverty. It obviously could not help the unemployed. But in addition the Institute for Fiscal Studies (2014) has calculated that, of those families in which someone earns less than the LWC's targets, only 6 per cent are in the bottom 10 per cent of the family income distribution. By contrast 44 per cent are in the top half of the income distribution, with 5 per cent in the top decile. Many of the low paid may be, for example, young people living with better-off parents, students who will get better-paid jobs later in their career or part-time employees living with spouses with full-time jobs. Few adult workers who are sole family earners remain for long periods on very low pay levels. Such individuals and their families are a real concern, but they are better supported through improved training opportunities and, where necessary, in-work benefits.

Pensions auto-enrolment

Pension arrangements are not obviously relevant to a discussion of employment regulation. However, pension contributions paid by employers can be thought of as a form of deferred pay,[11] and as such can be briefly considered here. They are also an example of

---

11 The reasoning which led to the important 1982 European Court of Justice judgement that access to pensions was within the scope of equal pay legislation.

a mandated benefit where the costs are to a considerable degree passed on to the employee.

UK pensions are, it is probably fair to say, in something of a mess. The growing share of the population made up of older people, and their increasing longevity, place a considerable and arguably unsustainable burden on the taxpayer. In the current fiscal climate, a substantial increase in state pensions is not plausible. Until relatively recently, a high proportion of employees were enrolled in defined benefit or final salary occupational pension schemes. These were seriously undermined by changing pension regulations and tax changes, and by changes in employment patterns and industrial structures.[12] Most private sector employers have closed their schemes to new entrants: final-salary-based schemes are increasingly the preserve of public sector workers, and even here reforms are being made to reduce pension entitlements.

For many years, governments have sought to encourage individuals to save in defined contribution schemes, in which members build up 'pension pots' for retirement. Such schemes transfer the risk to individuals: the pension which individuals can obtain depend on investment returns on the underlying assets of the scheme and on annuity rates. They have not proved very popular in the past, partly because of poor returns and high administrative costs and partly because many households have used other savings media such as ISAs and, very importantly, owner-occupied housing.

Politicians have taken the view that people, especially lower earners, are going to have to save more if they wish to enjoy a comfortable retirement. Since 2012 employers must make arrangements for automatically enrolling employees into a workplace pension scheme if they are aged between 22 and state

---

12 Between 1997 and 2014 the proportion of employees in defined benefit schemes fell from 46 to 29 per cent.

pension age and earn more than £10,000 a year. Apart from the cost of nominating such a scheme and administering contributions, they must also make a contribution, initially 2 per cent of earnings[13] to the pension fund.

Auto-enrolment seems to be boosting membership of pension schemes as intended. However, critics have pointed out that the high administrative costs of schemes mean that most low earners will gain poor returns from their scheme membership, and without substantial injections of their own savings will not obtain a significant additional pension. It is also likely, once again, that employer costs will be passed on to the employee through smaller wage increases than would have been possible otherwise. So it is far from clear that low earners will be net gainers from auto-enrolment.

Furthermore, it is possible that small employers, who will face disproportionate costs, may alter employment patterns in ways which may disadvantage workers: by, for example, employing part-timers earning less than the threshold, rather than full-time workers who would have to be enrolled. Micro-employers may be tempted to switch employment to the informal economy.

One example where concern has been expressed is families employing nannies: to set up pension arrangements for one person, who may not remain with the family for more than a year or two, is an excessive requirement.[14] Families may switch to employing nannies indirectly through agencies, which may reduce nannies' net earnings. They may switch to nanny-sharing arrangements which allow nannies to become self-employed but

---

13 The process has been rolled out slowly, starting with larger firms. Individuals can opt out of entering schemes, but must not be placed under any pressure or inducement by the employer to do so.

14 There appear to be some 33 responsibilities which all employers face, breaches of which carry the threat of fines and even imprisonment. http://www.thepensions regulator.gov.uk/docs/detailed-guidance-5.pdf (accessed 21 May 2015).

may increase their workload. Or they will be tempted to pay in cash and thus avoid all other employment obligations and taxes.[15]

Conclusions

Each of these policies is a badly designed way of trying to improve the lot of poorer people. Many of those who gain from the NMW and the National Living Wage are not poor, while those who do not have or cannot get jobs are not benefited. Wage floors always have the potential to impose significant collateral damage, including damage to those at whom the policies are targeted – and it looks as though such damage is likely over time as the bite of the NLW increases. The government is being drawn into a situation where a large and growing section of the labour force will have its wages directly determined by politicians, a situation which does not augur well. If possible, the initiative for recommending NLW and NMW rates[16] should be shifted back to the Low Pay Commission. In any case, there are more targeted ways of achieving poverty reduction, for example, through better-designed tax and in-work benefits, which do not threaten jobs and or take pay decisions away from employers.

As for auto-enrolment in pension schemes, it seems unlikely that the lowest earners will get any significant benefit from being in membership while small businesses and households may be deterred from offering employment, at least in the legitimate economy.

---

15 'The black market for cash-in-hand nannies who don't go through payroll will definitely grow,' said Sarah-Jane Butler, director of childcare agency Parental Choice. 'A lot of parents may reduce the salary of the nanny or do half pay on the books and half cash in hand.' http://citywire.co.uk/new-model-adviser/news/auto-enrolment-could-spark-black-market-for-nannies/a816111 (accessed 20 May 2015).

16 We probably also ought to reduce the number of different rates now set.

8 OTHER PEOPLE'S PAY (2)

If low pay and pensions are hot political issues, so is the pay of those at the upper end of the earnings distribution and the disparity in pay between men and women. This chapter discusses these issues.

My concern here is pay inequality, not income or wealth inequality, however much political discussion mixes up these concepts. Box 2 briefly explains what is meant by income and wealth inequality. The pattern of income and wealth distribution at any particular time is often thought by many people to be 'unfair', a moral or political judgement. Economists have little advice to offer about the basis for this judgement, except to remind fellow citizens that some modicum of income inequality is probably necessary to motivate economic activity – and that forcible redistribution of wealth has had a very poor record in the past both in terms of economic consequences and human rights abuses. They can also usefully debunk some of the claims that income and wealth inequality are synonymous with widespread poverty (Niemietz 2012) or that such inequality is a main or proximate cause of such social ills as crime, drug abuse, health problems, obesity and so on.[1] More positively, wealth inequality also has a positive role in that it maintains independent fortunes, which can be (and are) used in such causes as philanthropy, medical

---

1 The argument that inequality is the source of very many social evils was most forcefully put by Wilkinson and Pickett (2009). The statistical and analytical basis of their claims was, however, seriously undermined by Snowdon (2010).

research, and innovative forms of investment. While government spending can also do this, independent wealth offers competition rather than state monopoly, and can pursue worthwhile projects which are not high among government priorities.

If we now focus on earnings from employment, economists have rather more to say. Pay differentials are seen as an essential means of allocating and reallocating labour. As pointed out in Chapter 2, shifts in the demand for labour or shifts in the supply of skills and aptitude will lead to changes in relative wages which induce changes in the pattern of employment. In the long run pay will reflect such factors as the human capital people possess, with more highly skilled people earning more to reflect the costs (monetary and opportunities forgone) of their education and training, plus a range of other factors such as the degree of trust and responsibility involved and the pleasantness or unpleasantness of the conditions under which work is carried out. In the case of individuals possessing rare talents – exceptional footballers and entertainers – which cannot be replicated by standard education and training, their pay is simply demand-driven. The pay of such performers is largely a scarcity payment or *economic rent.*

This analysis is a commonplace among economists and, in outline, is broadly accepted as a rationale for pre-tax earnings even if people believe that, for example, highly paid sports or film stars should be paying higher taxes.

High pay

However, although the overall pay distribution has, after a widening in the 1980s, remained relatively stable recently, pay at the very top has increased sharply. The increase in the share going to very high earners has not been to the top 10 per cent, nor even the top 1 per cent, but something like the top 0.1 per cent (Bourne and Snowdon 2016). This phenomenon, not confined to the UK, has taken place against a background of static or declining pay

Box 2   Income and wealth inequality

Income inequality is most usefully discussed at the household level, and is concerned with all types of income. Wages and salaries are only a part of household income: there are also property income, dividends and tax-funded benefits. Comparisons are usually made after tax. The evidence seems to be that UK household income inequality, relatively high by international standards, rose in the 1980s, then flattened out and actually fell during the recent recession (Snowdon 2015).

Household income distribution measures, such as the Gini coefficient, can change for a variety of reasons including the rates of taxes and benefits, unemployment levels, profit rates and rates of interest, number and ages of children, and changes in marriage and cohabitation rates and patterns. Some of these influences are little understood by the general public. One is 'assortative mating', the tendency of people to marry or partner people of similar economic status. One study of the US between 1960 and 2005 (Greenwood et al. 2014) shows that, as college graduation and women's labour force participation rose, more and more college graduates were marrying other graduates. If matching in 2005 between husbands and wives had been random (with graduates marrying non-graduates in similar proportion to their incidence in the population), instead of the pattern observed in Census Bureau data, income inequality would have been lower: the Gini coefficient would have been 0.34, rather than the actual 0.43. Assortative mating has probably been at least as significant in the UK.

Another unremarked issue is patterns of migration. Immigrants are disproportionately from the top (think Canadian bankers) and bottom (fruit pickers) of the income distribution, while emigrants are rather differently distributed. Over time changes in household population brought about by migration can have a marked effect on overall income distribution.

Wealth inequality is typically much more unequal than that of income. Conventional measures of wealth, such as the Office of National Statistics' Wealth and Assets Survey, cover real estate (predominantly owner-occupied housing), physical assets such as artworks, financial assets such as company shares, and private pensions. As wealth such as this is accumulated over lifetimes, older people usually possess far more assets than younger people. It is also important to note that many people have negative wealth, i.e. they have substantial debts (including student loans, large mortgages or negative equity, and consumer debt), whereas people do not have negative income. Long-term changes in the measured wealth distribution can occur for many reasons, including changes in the rate of return on different assets (in the UK, house price inflation is a major factor), changing family size, changing divorce rates, changes in life expectancy, tax rates (particularly inheritance tax) and so on. In the UK, as in a number of other countries, wealth inequality appears to have increased over time, but with the increase being concentrated in the very top wealth owners. The top end of the wealth distribution is dominated by financial assets and housing, which can both fluctuate dramatically in value in the short run.

The data necessarily omit the value of human capital, an asset which cannot be sold in a free society despite the fact that it is a major source of future income. Newly trained doctors, for example, have very considerable future earning power just as if they had stocks and shares worth millions of pounds – even though they may currently have no measured assets and indeed have negative measured wealth because they are paying off student loans. Another problem is state pensions, both those owed to former government employees and state retirement pensions. These are not usually counted in wealth, although as government commitments to pay regular incomes they are far more reliable sources of future income than most financial assets.

Measured inequality of wealth distribution in the UK is not particularly high by international standards. Intriguingly, Sweden, which, as is widely known, has a markedly more equal pattern of *income* distribution than the UK has a much more unequal *wealth* distribution. According to Sanandaji (2015) the UK's wealth distribution has a Gini coefficient of 0.66 while that of Sweden is 0.89, higher even than the US.

for many workers since the recession (although the position of the lowest paid may have improved), which explains much of the political context.

The rise in the pay of IT entrepreneurs, top entertainers, authors and sportspeople can be explained largely in terms of increased international mobility and changes in technology and media ownership which have focused consumer attention on a smaller number of performers with worldwide recognition (Rosen 1981; Frank and Cook 1995). There is no apparent political drive to try to change this situation; any policy attention has focused on blocking loopholes in the tax system[2] so that high earners pay more taxes.

---

2 Loopholes are often created by governments attempting to support some crowd-pleasing objective, such as investment in particular industries. This then inevitably creates difficulties in deciding what is legitimate tax-minimising investment, as celebrity investors in a scheme to finance films discovered in 2014. http://www.taxation.co.uk/taxation/Articles/2014/08/12/329151/down-hole (accessed 17 March 2015). The hapless investors then face obloquy, and in some cases financial ruin.

Where attention has focused is instead on the pay of company executives, bankers, and public sector and not-for-profit organisations. Here some economic analysis has been used.

CEO compensation

Most attention has focused on the pay of top business executives. The High Pay Centre – a UK pressure group of academics, business consultants and journalists – produces regular reports on the subject. In August 2015 it reckoned[3] that FTSE-100 chief executives were being paid on average 183 times as much as the median full-time UK employee, up from 160 times in 2010. Many were being paid a far larger multiple.

As long ago as the 1930s, economists drew attention to the divorce between ownership (dispersed shareholders) and control (salaried management) in large corporations (Berle and Means 1932; Marris 1998). This separation is said to enable management to pursue policies which are not necessarily in the interests of the shareholders – including over-generous pay for incumbent executives. In modern economics this is seen as an example of a more general principal–agent problem (Jensen and Meckling 1976). Economists have argued that the solution in the case of business firms is to devise remuneration systems tying executive reward to the profits or share price of the company (Jensen and Murphy 1990). The influence of these ideas, particularly in the US and the UK, has been considerable: hence the growth of pay packages which incorporate large performance-linked elements such as bonuses and share options.

But designing performance-related pay schemes is difficult at all levels of an organisation, as individuals will adapt their behaviour to maximise their performance on the criteria which

---

3   http://highpaycentre.org/files/State_of_Pay_Aug_2015.pdf (accessed 29 June 2016).

determine their pay and neglect performance in other areas. At the top of a company these difficulties are compounded. If executives are in a position to manipulate information about company performance, they may be tempted to do so.[4] There is now a substantial literature (Conyon 2006) on the factors which determine an appropriate pay structure for executives.

There is evidence that, despite claims to the contrary, FTSE-100 performance is usually reflected to some extent in chief executive pay. For example, Bell and Van Reenen (2012) find that a 10 per cent increase in firm value is associated with an increase of 3 per cent in CEO pay. Perhaps more importantly, declining firm performance is followed by CEO pay cuts and significantly more CEO firings. Of course, other factors also play a part, as they do in the determination of any pay. The role of chief executive in a large corporation requires skills and experience which few possess; it is also demanding work with long hours and much travel. Individuals have to be resilient and totally focused on the firm.[5]

Furthermore, pay has risen over time for many of the same reasons as the pay of entertainers and sportspeople have risen. Just as with footballers and rock stars, there is now an international market for top executives,[6] and pay is driven up by competition for the best performers. As firms have grown larger as a result of globalisation, top executive pay has risen accordingly. One study (Gabaix and Landier 2008) finds that the sixfold increase in US CEO pay between 1980 and 2003 can be fully explained

---

4   For instance, Tesco seems to have deliberately overstated its profits in the first half of the 2014–15 financial year by demanding promotion payments from suppliers and delaying bill settlements. See http://www.bbc.co.uk/news/business-29735685 (accessed 29 June 2015).

5   See 'Executives battle burnout in world that's "always on"', *The Times*, 30 November 2015.

6   40 per cent of FTSE-100 chief executives in 2015 were born abroad. See http://www .telegraph.co.uk/finance/markets/ftse100/11613102/Forty-per-cent-of-top-UK -bosses-born-abroad.html (accessed 4 June 2016).

statistically by the increase in market capitalisation of large corporations in this period.

The point is that a top executive who makes even a small improvement in the profitability of a very large company is worth a great deal of money to his or her employers. An incoming CEO can make a big difference to a firm, and a competitive market reflects this. When Tidjane Thiam, the Chief Executive of Prudential, announced in March 2015 that he was moving to Credit Suisse, Prudential's shares fell by 3.1 per cent (a fall in value of £1.3 billion) while Credit Suisse's shares rose by 7.8 per cent (£2 billion). Evidence suggests that the impact of CEOs on share prices has been growing over time.[7] Such highly regarded individuals must be paid generously if they are to be attracted to a company or retained, just as footballers Cristiano Ronaldo or Gareth Bale are able to command high pay for their services.[8]

Critics of high pay point to cases where executives whose businesses have done badly nevertheless receive generous payoffs, seeing this as a 'reward for failure'. Perhaps so, but it is probably inevitable in some cases. For one thing, 'failure' in business arises from many different causes: the chief executive may not always be to blame, but nevertheless a change in management may make sense from a shareholder perspective. Payoffs are thus often necessary to prevent damaging litigation by a boss who has been dismissed. The very similar cases of dismissed football managers and coaches is rarely discussed in this context, but it is worth thinking about. In 2008 Chelsea spent £23 million paying off the contracts of two managers (José Mourinho and Avram Grant) and five coaches.

---

7   A recent study of 240 sudden and unexpected CEO deaths shows that market reactions to these events in US public firms increased markedly between 1950 and 2009 (Quigley et al., forthcoming).

8   There is, interestingly, no popular demand for controlling the pay of footballers or entertainers, many of whom earn far more than all but a handful of company executives.

Reforms

Not all CEOs are superstars, though. Critics may have a point if less-than-stellar executives have pay set by remuneration committees which operate without adequate scrutiny and are not genuinely independent from the incumbent management.[9] Concern about this has been around for many years, and led first to the Greenbury Report (1995), which recommended that each board should have a remuneration committee which excludes executive directors, and that pay should be linked to long-term performance measures. Subsequent reports and reviews have gradually produced a Corporate Governance Code which is binding on listed companies. On executive pay the latest iteration of the code (Financial Reporting Council 2014: 21) says that:

> There should be a formal and transparent procedure for developing policy on executive remuneration and for fixing the remuneration packages of individual directors. No director should be involved in deciding his or her own remuneration.

The code suggests that pay should be sufficient to attract, retain and motivate directors of the quality required to run the company successfully, but companies should avoid spending more than is necessary. Comparisons with other companies should be used with caution. A significant proportion of executive directors' remuneration should be structured so as to link rewards to corporate and individual performance. These performance-related elements should be 'stretching and rigorously applied' (ibid.: 20).

---

9   It is claimed that, with dispersed shareholding, it is very difficult for shareholders to exercise control over management, and that this justifies government intervention. This, however, ignores the way in which large institutional shareholders such as pension funds can exert pressure on management should they choose to do so. It is also worth remembering that the UK has an active market for corporate control, so managers who act against shareholders' interests can face a hostile takeover.

Changes to company law brought in by the coalition require much greater transparency in the reporting of all elements of pay. The Enterprise and Regulatory Reform Act 2013 requires UK-listed companies to publish a 'single figure' for the total pay awarded for the top executive's position.[10] Most companies also provide data going back to 2010 for comparative purposes (they will eventually have to provide such information for the previous ten years). Regulation now also requires that a company's remuneration policy be approved by more than 50 per cent of shareholders.

These changes appear to have had little impact on slowing the growth of pay: top executive salaries have continued to drift up in the UK as they have done in other countries with different systems of corporate governance. Some indicators suggest top executive pay in Germany has overtaken that in the UK, despite having a system of corporate governance – widely praised by the left in the UK – involving stakeholder representation in a two-tier board system.[11]

More radical proposals have accordingly been developed by pressure groups such as the High Pay Centre. They include setting a maximum pay ratio between CEOs and average-paid workers; mandating worker representation on company boards and remuneration committees; and legally binding targets for reducing pay inequality within firms. Interest has been shown in these ideas by the Labour Party, which has set up an 'executive pay commission' to recommend detailed proposals. Jeremy Corbyn has floated support for restrictions on the ratio of CEO pay to that of the lowest paid, but so crude an indicator is unlikely to find wider support. For one thing, such a rule would imply that CEOs in some fields – banking, for instance, where even the lowest level of employees are well paid – could be paid much more

---

10 A theoretically difficult thing to do, as it involves assessing the value of future income streams and the risk associated with assets.

11 See http://www.thecsuite.co.uk/CEO/index.php/people-management/167-ceo-pay-in-germany-and-uk-454354 (accessed 29 June 2016).

than those in others such as retailing, where shelf-stackers may be on the national minimum wage. And, in a dynamic context, there would be an incentive for bosses to shed low-paid workers either through automating low-skilled jobs or outsourcing work – neither of which would necessarily benefit the less well off.

Perhaps more surprisingly, Prime Minister Theresa May has also shown strong interest in this area, and she wants to see representatives of both employees and consumers on listed companies' boards in the near future, while shareholders are given tighter control on CEO pay. Further interference with board membership dilutes property rights and it is difficult to see what positive contribution employees (for which in most cases we should probably read trade union nominees) and consumers (more organised pressure groups) would make to the effective running of businesses. It is only too plausible to envisage scenarios where these 'representatives' oppose attempts by management to restructure businesses to face new imperatives.[12] As for the sop of more shareholder control over pay – vetoes on executive salaries – shareholders arguably already possess such power, should they choose to use it.

One area where tighter restrictions have already been implemented is that of bankers' pay. It is widely believed, although probably mistakenly,[13] that inappropriate and excessively generous pay structures, especially the use of bonuses, were an important element in the failings of the banking system leading to the crash. Regulators both in the UK and at the EU level have stepped in with new rules.

---

12 Evidence from Germany, where this sort of co-determination has existed for many years, suggests that employee representatives often resist restructuring efforts. One study suggests that this can cost firms about a quarter of shareholder value (Gorton and Schmid 2000).

13 See the Turner Review (Financial Services Authority 2009), which saw inadequate approaches to capital requirements, accounting and liquidity as more important factors than pay structures.

In the UK the Prudential Regulation Authority now has power to recover variable pay elements for up to seven years from the date of the award, which raises all sorts of issues about property rights and reasonable use of government power. Meanwhile, the EU restricts bonuses to 100 per cent of bankers' pay, or 200 per cent with shareholder approval – a rule which the UK initially opposed on the grounds that it would lead to increases in the level of fixed pay and thus reduce the element of performance-related remuneration. As suggested earlier, restrictions on pay can usually be circumvented by one means or another. Banks have been getting around bonus restrictions by using 'top-up allowances', which the European Banking Authority (EBA) wants to proscribe. The EBA also wants to spread the restrictions to bank subsidiaries in fields such as fund management and insurance.

The public sector and not-for-profits

Critics of pay regulation fear that businesses will be driven to relocate abroad or reduce investment in the UK. This is certainly a real possibility: many CEOs of UK-listed companies are foreign nationals, over half the shares in UK-listed companies are held by overseas investors and over three quarters of the revenue of FTSE-100 companies is earned abroad. Multinationals like these could certainly choose to be listed in other jurisdictions, or be unlisted, if UK restrictions become too irksome.

At the moment, these possibilities remain theoretical. But the antipathy towards high pay is having an impact in other areas – in local and national government, and in the not-for-profit sector.

Unease about alleged high pay in the public sector led the coalition government to set up an enquiry under Will Hutton, a long-standing critic of high salaries. It was expected to lead to a cap on the ratio of top pay to low pay; a maximum for public sector chief executives of twenty times the pay of the lowest paid was touted. However, his report (Hutton 2011) turned out to be a sensible recognition of the dangers of populist thinking on pay. Hutton pointed out that the extent of high pay in the public sector was greatly exaggerated. He also noted that a ratio-based pay cap could create odd incentives: if it was thought important to raise top pay, a cap could be rendered ineffective either by arbitrarily raising the pay of a handful of low-paid workers – or, more worryingly, by contracting their work out to private businesses. More fundamentally, Hutton argued that 'the UK must take care to avoid making the public sector a fundamentally unattractive place for those with talent and drive' (ibid.: 10).

If strict regulations were avoided by Hutton's conclusions, the climate of opinion has made it very difficult to increase public sector pay across the board, and certainly at the top end. This is a good thing in some ways, for instance, in helping to rein in the fiscal deficit. However, there remains a danger that public sector jobs – many of which are highly challenging, and require top-level candidates with vision and the ability to push change through – may become the preserve of less ambitious and less competent plodders.

This isn't just the case for the public sector, strictly defined. University vice-chancellors are another group whose pay has come under public scrutiny. Running a major university today is a demanding job, requiring managerial skill, fund-raising ability and considerable stamina, usually on top of a strong (though increasingly irrelevant) academic record. Vice-chancellors are also appointed against international competition. Yet their pay is under regular attack from university trade unions and politicians. A nadir was reached when, just before the 2015 general election, Shadow Minister Liam Byrne threatened vice-chancellors opposed to Labour's policy of reducing university fees to £6,000 per year with an enquiry into their pay.[14] A real danger in

---

14 See http://www.timeshighereducation.co.uk/news/academys-fat-cats-too-smart
-to-attack-labours-6000-fees-policy/2016354.article (accessed 29 June 2016).

making top pay a political football is that it will inhibit criticism of politicians.

Charities, too, have come under scrutiny: in 2013–14 there were apparently 31 chief executives earning more than £250,000 per year. A report on the sector called for charities to have a clearer strategy for high pay and a transparent explanation of why their CEOs earn what they do.[15]

While it is understandable that top pay in public sector and non-profit organisations, especially in a time of financial stringency and small average pay increases, is examined critically, the issue must be handled carefully. We should not find ourselves moving without thinking into a position where we seem to require CEOs who are (or worse, pose as) preternaturally altruistic individuals. As Adam Smith observed long ago, 'I have never known much good done by those who affected to trade for the public good'.

The gender pay gap

Another controversial pay issue arises from the difference between male and female earnings. Despite equal pay having been required in the UK since the 1970s, women still earn on average significantly less than men – as in most countries. The size of this 'gender pay gap' causes considerable controversy, and governments have tried to reduce it. Public sector organisations have for some time been required to conduct regular audits of pay in an attempt to narrow the differentials between male and female pay, a requirement recently extended to large private sector firms, while employment tribunal judgements have frequently found both public and private sector employers in breach of equal pay

15 Report of the Inquiry into Charity Senior Executive Pay, April 2014, http://www.honorarytreasurers.org.uk/docs/Executive_Pay_Report.pdf (accessed 23 March 2015).

law and ended the observed pay disparity, awarding compensation which can be backdated for up to six years.

Measuring the pay gap

Figure 7 shows three measures of the gap. The preferred measure of the Office for National Statistics is median gross hourly earnings, excluding overtime, of full-time workers. The median is used in preference to the mean because a small number of very high earners can pull the mean up sharply. Hourly rather than weekly or annual earnings are used because men tend to work longer hours and do more overtime than women. The comparison is between full-time workers as part-timers are paid on a different basis (and typically paid less per hour). Over the period shown, this gap – the difference in male and female pay, expressed as a percentage of male pay – shrank from over 17 per cent to just under 10 per cent.

The Equality and Human Rights Commission prefers another measure – the pay gap between all male workers and all female workers. As a higher proportion of females works part-time, and part-time work is commoner in lower-paid occupations, this measure of the pay gap is larger. It has also fallen over time, however, from around 28 per cent in 1997 to under 20 per cent in 2015.

The final measure illustrated is the part-time pay gap. Its negative value means a pay gap in favour of women: women working part-time tend to earn more than male part-timers. This is because male part-timers, who are disproportionately young people and semi-retired workers, are mainly employed in unskilled jobs in areas such as retailing, while women part-timers are more evenly spread across all age groups and in a range of jobs which include relatively well-paid work such as medicine and teaching. This clearly alerts us to the fact that differences between male and female pay cannot be attributed in any simple way to employer discrimination.

Pressure from the Equality and Human Rights Commission and lobbying organisations such as the Fawcett Society has led to concern about this issue being translated into policy. In July 2015 David Cameron pledged to 'end the gender pay gap within a generation'.[16] Since then plans have been announced to force larger employers to publish information about their bonuses for men and women as part of their gender pay gap reporting. 'League tables' are to be published ranking the size of company pay gaps. There is a clear direction of travel towards much greater government scrutiny of firms' pay policies.

Why are women paid less than men?

Aggregate pay gaps such as those shown in Figure 7 reflect all manner of potential reasons why one group has lower average pay than another (Longhi and Platt 2008). These include differences in educational and other qualifications,[17] average age, experience, hours worked, concentration in particular industries and occupations, whether in the public or the private sector (women are more likely than men to be employed in the public sector), and so on.

There are also less obvious factors such as time spent commuting: this is associated with higher pay, other things being equal, and men travel greater distances to work. Economists argue that higher pay is necessary to compensate for the costs and time involved in commuting. Other compensating differentials may be associated with, for example, unsocial hours, physical danger[18]

---

16 Press release: Prime minister: My one nation government will close the gender pay gap https://www.gov.uk/government/news/prime-minister-my-one-nation-government-will-close-the-gender-pay-gap (accessed 29 June 2016). Mr Cameron's successor is even more committed to pay equality.

17 Not just the number of GCSEs, A levels or degrees but the subject matter is important: girls and young women disproportionately choose subjects with a lower market value (Morgan and Carrier 2014).

18 Around 96 per cent of all fatal injuries at work occur to men.

Figure 7   UK gender pay gap for median gross hourly earnings (excluding overtime) April 1997 to 2016

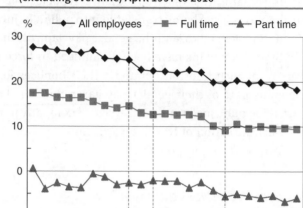

Source: Office for National Statistics.
Note: Changes in the methodology and data source employed mean there are breaks in the series. April 2016 data are provisional.

and working outside or in isolated conditions. Men are more likely than women to be in jobs with some of these characteristics.

Conversely, some jobs with attractive features may induce workers to accept lower pay than they could get elsewhere – a *negative* compensating differential. What counts as an attractive feature may differ between men and women. There is evidence that women are more likely than men to prefer working in public sector or non-profit organisations, jobs which involve working with people, and jobs with an obvious moral dimension. They are less likely than men to value pay strongly over other features of the job. They are thus likely to apply for, and obtain, rather different jobs from those which men go for, as Figure 8 illustrates. Many studies also show that women tend to be happier at work than men. Compensating differentials are an important, often ignored, explanation of much of the pay gap (Shackleton 2008).

Figure 8   Percentage of graduate programme
           recruits who are women, 2015

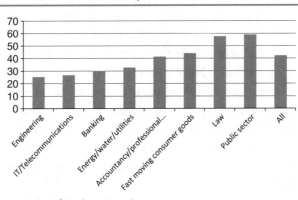

Source: Association of Graduate Recruiters.

There are other ways in which differing male and female behaviour impacts on the pay gap. Niederle and Vesterland (2007)
demonstrate that women are less willing to engage in competitive behaviour than men.[19] Symmetrically, women are more likely
to choose cooperative incentives than men (Kuhn and Villeval
2015). This reduces the number of women willing to work in well-
paid but highly competitive environments such as financial trading. In the same vein, Balcock and Laschever (2003) claim that US
women are less willing than men to negotiate over salaries, partly because they have lower salary expectations than men. Similar
differences in expectations seem to be the case in Britain.[20]

Finally, and very importantly, it is well known that a key element is family commitments, which alter employment patterns and
consequently pay. In the age groups 20–29 and 30–39, women's

---

19 Women in their study are more likely than men to choose a non-competitive piece
    rate rather than take part in a 'tournament' incentive scheme offering potentially
    higher pay.

20 'Female pupils set pay hopes £7000 lower than boys', *Daily Telegraph*, 30 November
    2015.

median earnings in the UK are now higher than men's. This reflects young women's educational achievements, now comfortably outstripping those of young men, plus the later age at which women now have their first child. The pay gap really starts to kick in with the advent of children (Leaker 2008). Women drop out of the workforce to have babies: on return (as noted in a previous chapter) they often switch to part-time work or take jobs with fewer responsibilities. These jobs usually involve less pay and fewer prospects for promotion. Perhaps less obviously, men with children tend to work longer hours and focus more on their careers than single men; this tends to increase the pay gap from the male side.[21]

Attributing gender pay gaps to some unspecified element of discrimination is mistaken, as they largely reflect patterns of behaviour and priorities which differ on average between men and women. Taking 'raw' pay gaps (i.e. without controlling for the various factors determining pay) tells us little about the extent and cause of any disadvantage which women may suffer in particular workplaces. In the public sector, for example, there are huge disparities in the size of the pay gaps in the Ministry of Defence and in Job Centre Plus – similar organisations, of similar size, sharing the official culture of concern over equality issues, together with strong unionisation. It is difficult to believe tightly constrained management behaves very differently in these various parts of the public sector. Rather, the variations represent different patterns of employment, different types of skills and a host of other factors largely beyond the control of government. The danger of the planned league tables for private sector employers is that employers with spuriously large gender pay gaps will be wrongly vilified by single-issue pressure groups. This in turn may, perversely, lead them to adopt behaviours which penalise women (such as

---

21 The extension of paternity leave, and the new possibility of sharing parental leave, is partly intended to reduce this effect.

cutting back on recruitment of younger females or outsourcing low-paid female work) and potentially damage efficiency – but reduce the measured pay gap.

Other pay gaps

Politicians' attention has focused on the gender pay gap; yet there are big variations in pay levels within genders. There are many high-earning women, and many low-earning men, so to concentrate too much on overall male–female differentials is to ignore other dimensions of pay inequality, some of which are at least as significant – and where there is often more evidence of direct discrimination.

There are marked differences in median earnings between many groups within British society. It has long been known, for example, that there are distinct variations in pay between ethnic groups (Metcalf 2009). Most are on average paid less than white British workers, with the exception of people of Indian or Chinese heritage. Male full-time workers of Pakistani heritage earn less than white British women.[22]

People with disabilities do worse than the rest of the working population. Religion is also a factor: in one study (Longhi and Platt 2008) Muslim men had a pay gap of around 17 per cent in relation to Christian men – while Jewish men earned 37 per cent more than Christians. Sexual orientation (Arabsheibani et al. 2005; Drydakis 2014) is also associated with pay differences, with gay men and lesbians earning more than their heterosexual counterparts. There is also evidence of large pay gaps between people rated attractive and those rated unattractive, tall people

---

22 Incidentally, one side effect of narrowing the pay gap between men and women might be to intensify other dimensions of inequality. If as a consequence two-earner white couples saw an increase in their joint income, it would increase the gap between them and one-earner households, which are commoner among those of Pakistani heritage.

and short people, and obese people and those of average weight (Harper 2000; Schick and Steckel 2010).[23]

As with gender pay, these other 'gaps' need to be deconstructed to make any sense. Jewish men, for instance, earn much more than Christians because they are typically much better qualified and are in high-paying professions. Similarly, Indians earn more than white British workers because they are disproportionately professionals – doctors, academics, pharmacists, lawyers. Lesbians tend to cluster in a relatively limited series of jobs, and are more career-oriented on average than heterosexual females (who are more likely to have caring responsibilities).

The point to emphasise is that a pay gap means little in itself without knowing more about the characteristics of the groups concerned: it is a poor guide to policy. Unfortunately, that does not deter politicians, and their responses are often counter-productive.

Conclusions

The classic explanation of how a free labour market allocates people to jobs most effectively sees movements in wages as signalling fluctuations in the demand for and supply of labour.

Attempts to set non-market-clearing wages and salaries, by governments, unions or the febrile 'court of public opinion' are likely to lead to lower productivity as incentives are reduced, as people stay in areas where they are underused, as others are driven out of employment or move abroad.

The market for labour has never been universally popular, but left to itself it works reasonably effectively, certainly rather better than other potential systems. Studies suggest that, while a large proportion of the population think that people at the top are

---

23 There have been proposals to extend anti-discrimination legislation to cover discrimination based on physical attributes.

paid excessively, a much smaller proportion think that the government should do much about it (see, for instance, Orton and Rowlingson 2007). The task of classifying more than 30 million employed people is too difficult, the public's preferences are too inchoate and inconsistent, and the temptations for politicians to meddle to support their own prejudices are too great.

Nor is the task of completely equalising pay between men and women (or between other contrasting groups) any easier to contemplate. Complete gender pay equality would require men and women to have, among other things, identical qualifications, tastes and experiences, to take identical amounts of time out of the workplace, spend identical time in housework, commute the same distances, and be willing to take identical risks. Even if this were thought worthwhile, bringing it about is a task even the most ardent social engineer must blanch at – if they really understood it. Unfortunately, politicians will probably keep trying if there is an easy headline to be achieved and a noisy constituency to be assuaged. We can probably expect ever more intrusive legislation as successive initiatives fail to produce the outcome that lobbyists demand.

9 DISCRIMINATION IN EMPLOYMENT

The last chapter showed that pay gaps exist between men and women, between ethnic groups, between those with different sexual orientations, religion and so on. I argued that a large part of these pay gaps can be explained by economic factors such as human capital, work experience and 'compensating differentials' as well as by individual tastes and characteristics. Nevertheless, there is widespread belief that some at least is explained by discrimination, and this chapter explores the issue in more detail.

In economic terms we can define discrimination as *the differential treatment of individuals whose productivity is identical*, because of ascribed characteristics – those over which the individual has little or no control.

Such differential treatment in the labour market[1] includes pay and other benefits, but also patterns of hiring and firing, promotion, job assignment and treatment at work.

Evidence of discrimination today

As with pay, differentials in patterns of hiring and firing may not in themselves indicate widespread discrimination. What other evidence is there? Discrimination is illegal, and direct evidence

---

1   Discrimination can occur in other contexts too, such as housing, access to finance, policing and so on. These issues are not discussed here.

(for example, job advertisements[2] specifying race, nationality, gender, age and so on) is therefore rare. Particular cases emerge in the courts or employment tribunals where employers (or fellow employees) are heard to make discriminatory remarks or otherwise behave in a clearly discriminatory manner, though such cases are comparatively rare and discrimination cases have a much lower success rate than other types of tribunal claim.

But, although economists are often – with good reason – wary of surveys of subjective impressions, we must recognise that many individuals in disadvantaged groups certainly feel themselves to be discriminated against. In one US survey, 25 per cent of African-Americans, 22 per cent of disabled workers, 21 per cent of Hispanics, 19 per cent of women, 18 per cent of LGBT workers and 11 per cent of Asians felt themselves discriminated against in their jobs.[3] Similar findings can be quoted from most European countries. Among those in self-defined minorities across the EU as a whole, 31 per cent of those with a disability, 23 per cent of those from a minority ethnic group, 12 per cent of LGBT and 12 per cent of religious or other belief group claimed to have experienced discrimination in the previous year.[4] Many more claimed to have witnessed discrimination than those who had experienced it.

More objectively, there is evidence from many 'correspondence' studies. Techniques differ, but a common approach is to submit carefully matched fictitious job applications which do not differ in qualifications or experience, but only in relation to, say, the apparent ethnicity of the 'applicants' as indicated by their names. Evidence from Sweden, France, Great Britain, Denmark,

2 Darity and Mason (1998) produce interesting examples of overtly discriminatory advertisements in the US before the passage of the 1964 Civil Rights Act.

3 http://www.bet.com/news/national/2011/06/09/one-in-four-blacks-say-they-are-discriminated-against-in-the-workplace.html (accessed 14 April 2015).

4 http://ec.europa.eu/public_opinion/archives/ebs/ebs_296_en.pdf (accessed 20 April 2015).

Australia and the US is surveyed in OECD (2008): typically, these studies find that candidates from minority ethnic backgrounds are less likely to be called for interview. Similar findings are not, however, generally reported from correspondence studies which match male and female applications.

Another type of evidence comes from experimentation, such as the introduction of 'blind' auditions for musicians, with candidates performing behind screens: this significantly increased the success rate of women compared with a situation where women were visible when performing (Goldin and Rouse 2000).

So discrimination, though certainly less overt than in the past, does continue. How do economists explain the phenomenon?

Economic analysis of discrimination

Gary Becker

The modern economic analysis of discrimination begins with the groundbreaking work of Gary Becker (1957), who focused on race-based disadvantage. Whereas Marxists and others had seen discrimination as a means by which disadvantaged workers were exploited to boost capitalists' profits, Becker's insight was to see that discrimination in reality could have a cost to the employer and, other things being equal, might actually *reduce* profits.

In his preference-based theory of discrimination, discriminators have a 'taste' for discrimination, leading them to choose white workers over black workers even if whites are more expensive to employ than equally productive blacks; or to choose less productive white workers in preference to black workers if the two types of worker are paid the same. This behaviour is not necessarily 'irrational' in economic terms even though it may be deplored by others who do not share the preference, just as other reprehensible tastes (for smoking, bull-fighting, pornography or whatever) may be deplored but are still amenable to economic analysis. The discriminator need not necessarily have a strong distaste for the group discriminated against; rather he or she may simply prefer the other group for a variety of reasons including family or tribal links. This is sometimes called nepotism.

The key point Becker makes is that indulging a taste for discrimination carries a cost to the employer. If other employers do not share this preference, they will be able to secure an advantage by employing people simply on the basis of their marginal productivity. Over time, discriminating employers will lose out in the competitive struggle to non-discriminators. Indeed, Milton Friedman argued that 'the development of capitalism has been accompanied by a major reduction in the extent to which particular religious, racial, or social groups have operated under special handicaps in respect of their economic activities' (Friedman 1963: 108). He and other Chicago economists argued that widespread and persistent discrimination was often associated with state intervention. The apartheid regime in South Africa and the notorious 'Jim Crow' laws in the American South (which closed many occupations to black workers) are examples where government regulation rather than competitive markets institutionalised discrimination. Governments may also have historically been an important element in discrimination against women by excluding them from certain dangerous or strenuous jobs (see Chapter 3) and, for example, by requiring female civil servants to leave the workforce on marriage.

Some support for the view that competition between firms tends to reduce discrimination is provided by work such as that of Weichselbaumer and Winter-Ebmer (2007). Their cross-country analysis has suggested that increased competition in product markets is associated with lower 'unexplained' (i.e. potentially discriminatory) gender pay gaps.

Belief in the power of markets to eliminate discrimination can be challenged by the argument that imperfect competition is common in labour markets, although as we have seen in earlier chapters this claim is contested. However, more sophisticated analysis (see Donohue 2005) suggests that theoretical models may produce different outcomes depending on the distribution of discriminatory tastes and the size of the group discriminated against. For instance, if most employers are strong discriminators and the discriminated-against group is large, the outcome will be different from a situation where few employers discriminate and there are few in the discriminated-against group. Black (1995), in the context of sex discrimination, introduces job search costs into the picture; in his view the existence of such costs reduces competition and makes it less likely that markets will eradicate discrimination.

Moreover, Becker's work also pointed out that some labour market discrimination may have its source not in the employer's tastes, but in those of customers and fellow workers. An interesting piece of recent evidence of consumer discrimination in the US comes in a study by Ayres et al. (2005), which indicates that African-American cab drivers were tipped approximately a third less than white drivers in a sample of 1,000 rides. It is difficult to see how this type of discrimination would be driven out by competition. However, another example is Doleac and Stein's (2013) study, where an online advertisement for a second-hand iPad attracted fewer bids and lower offers if the illustration showed a black hand holding the tablet rather than a white hand. The interesting thing here is that in areas where there were large numbers of possible buyers, there was less discrimination than in 'thin' markets with very few potential purchasers.

As for fellow workers, an example often quoted is the case of white trade unionists in apartheid South Africa who were a key element in keeping black workers out of jobs. Nearer home, the Transport and General Workers Union was blamed for the all-white recruitment policy on Bristol buses in the 1960s.[5] Largely

---

5   http://www.blackhistorymonth.org.uk/article/section/bhm-heroes/the-bristol-bus-boycott-of-1963/ (accessed 9 May 2016).

male UK unions were also ambivalent in their attitudes to women workers, as Hunt (2012) explains. Of course, the ability of union 'insiders' to discriminate against 'outsiders' arises from their possessing a degree of monopoly power, which in turn often results from privileges granted by the state, as pointed out in Chapter 10.

Statistical discrimination

A second line of analysis was developed more or less simultaneously in the 1970s by Kenneth Arrow (1973) and Ed Phelps (1972). This approach focuses on the existence of incomplete information. Employers do not know much about job applicants, and have to determine whether or not to appoint them on the basis of what little they know. They may, however, have – or think they have – some knowledge about average economically relevant behaviour of different categories of workers. For example, women may be thought more likely to take time off work than men, or young people may be more likely to quit jobs than older workers. Both these behaviours are potentially costly to employers, so on the basis of these stereotypes, they make discriminatory hiring decisions. Men are preferred to women, and older workers to younger workers, other things being equal.

If the stereotypes are incorrect, this may suggest a role for government in disseminating correct information. However, there are also grounds for suggesting that trial and error will lead to better decisions in the long run; in a competitive market, firms which take a risk on employing different types of worker are likely to do better than those who stick to mistaken stereotypes. If, however, these generalisations are on average correct (as the examples in the previous paragraph probably are), following the stereotypes will be a profit-maximising strategy and there is no obvious reason why discriminatory behaviour will be eliminated by competition.

This is a problem because, whatever the average productivity of a group of workers, there will always be a distribution around the mean. Some female workers will take very little time off, some young workers will be highly committed – and they will be penalised by a market which deals in averages. A rational response might be to attempt to signal to the employer that they are the exception to the rule – by, for instance, offering to work for less, or to work a trial period, or to offer some sort of bond. But this is nowadays perceived to be unfair, and government regulation often prevents this form of market-based correction.

Behavioural economics

The approaches outlined so far are developments of orthodox 'neoclassical' economics, where employers, employees and consumers are assumed to have a set of fixed preferences, and they attempt to maximise individual utility and/or profits. These assumptions of rationality have been increasingly challenged by developments in behavioural economics.

Jolls (2012), for example, draws upon the distinction made in the psychological literature between 'System 1' and 'System 2' thinking (see Kahneman 2011). The argument is that people use two cognitive systems to make decisions. We use System 1 to make rapid, intuitive judgements and decisions and System 2 to make more considered choices. Both systems are necessary for successful functioning. We cannot deliberate at length in situations where snap decisions are essential, such as when driving on a busy road, but equally we would be unwise to make major commitments such as buying a house or going to college without carefully weighing things up.

Jolls's contention is that we can often use System 1 inappropriately. She quotes studies using the Implicit Association Test (IAT), which asks individuals to categorise at speed pleasant or unpleasant words or images associated with other categories such as black and white or male and female. Speed of response to pairs of words or images is held to indicate bias: for instance, bias in favour of whites is shown if respondents are quicker to match 'black' and 'unpleasant' than they are to match 'black' and 'pleasant'. Studies using the IAT in the US indicate bias in favour of whites against African-Americans, young against old and heterosexual against gay.

This cognitive bias can be quite unconscious and may conflict with what people say about their tastes and beliefs. Based on their System 2 analysis of the issue, individuals may assert that they are unprejudiced, but many of their unconscious decisions may belie this. Jolls suggests that interventions to make people think more carefully about hiring decisions, say, may be appropriate.

Some large employers have accepted this suggestion to the extent that they remove names from job applications so that decision-makers are not as easily prejudiced. The idea has been taken up by the UK government, with David Cameron[6] having announced in 2015 that the Civil Service and the university admissions system (UCAS) will in future anonymise applications.

How effective this will be remains to be seen. Experience suggests that it is necessary to remove all sorts of information from the application – such as examination results, address, age, hobbies, handwriting – to avoid any possible bias. Even if this succeeds in getting more job or college interviews for disadvantaged groups, this will not necessarily lead to more job offers or places at top universities.[7]

---

6   http://www.theguardian.com/commentisfree/2015/oct/26/david-cameron
    -conservatives-party-of-equality (accessed 10 May 2016).

7   http://www.economist.com/news/business/21677214-anonymising-job
    -applications-eliminate-discrimination-not-easy-no-names-no-bias (accessed
    10 May 2016).

Policy principles

I have already mentioned the development of anti-discrimination legislation in the UK and the EU. Similar laws first developed in the US in the 1960s. Title VII of the 1964 Civil Rights Act is the primary federal law, with most states having similar or more extensive legislation.[8] A major expansion of the scope of this law by the US courts in 1971 was the 'disparate impact' ruling, whereby a practice can be deemed unlawful if, while not ostensibly discriminatory, it has a different impact on, say, white workers and black workers.

Indirect discrimination

The same idea lies behind the idea of 'indirect discrimination' in UK law. This can occur when an organisation's practices, policies or procedures affect different groups of employees in different ways, without the employer being able to provide an objective justification. Such justification needs to demonstrate that the practice is a 'proportionate means of achieving a legitimate aim'.

For example, a requirement that office cleaners or security guards possess five good GCSEs might be held to discriminate indirectly against a minority group where fewer people possess these qualifications. The employer would probably find it hard to convince a tribunal that such qualifications were necessary to secure competent candidates for these jobs. Similarly, a company which regularly held important meetings at a time when some employees (for instance, those with childcare responsibilities) were unable to attend would have to be able to demonstrate why other timings were not possible should an employee who failed to be promoted attribute her failure to this cause.

---

8   Other significant US developments include the Age Discrimination in Employment Act and the Americans with Disabilities Act.

Interference with freedom of contract

While anti-discrimination law is now taken for granted by younger generations, the significance of this relatively recent innovation needs comment. As Donohue (2007) has written, anti-discrimination law represents 'a dramatic rejection of classical liberal notions of freedom of contract'. Although fundamental opposition to the principle of such legislation is now rarely heard in public,[9] a number of important writers have taken a highly critical view. Milton Friedman, for example, opposed the 1964 Civil Rights Act. He pointed out that (Friedman 1963: 111):

> Such legislation clearly involves interference with the freedom of individuals to enter into voluntary contracts with one another. It subjects any such contract to approval or disapproval by the state. Thus it is directly an interference with freedom of the kind we would object to in most other contexts.

Friedman argued that if we agree that the state can place conditions on the type of voluntary contracts which can legitimately be formed, this is a dangerously two-edged intervention. He evoked the 1960s version of a twitterstorm by saying that Hitler's Nuremberg laws (which discriminated against Jews) and the pre-1964 laws in the Southern states imposing restrictions on employment of blacks were both examples which, by prohibiting voluntary contracts, were similar in principle to anti-discrimination law. He also pointed out that, paradoxically, attempts to

---

9   When Nigel Farage, then the United Kingdom Independence Party leader, briefly questioned the continuing need for legislation during the 2015 general election campaign he was quickly denounced by other politicians. http://www.independent .co.uk/news/uk/politics/nigel-farage-sparks-another-race-row-by-calling-for-end -to-out-of-date-legislation-on-discrimination-in-the-workplace-10102133.html (accessed 20 April 2015).

redress inequality (by, for example, employers setting out to hire more African-Americans or more women) would be illegal under the Civil Rights Act. This is the issue of 'affirmative action' which has created many legal tussles in the US in subsequent decades.

Coercion and social engineering

As we have seen, Richard Epstein is a strong advocate of the contract at will, and he has written very critically of the principle underlying US anti-discrimination law from the Civil Rights Act onwards. He argues that, while civil rights originally described liberties and freedom from the oppressive power of the state, they now mean coercing people into activities and contracts which they may not wish to engage in (Epstein 1992: 501–2):

> Civil rights is [a term] that has been ripped from its original libertarian moorings. We are often told that the goal of the civil rights movement is *diversity*. Diversity as it is traditionally understood means that no one should put all his or her eggs into a single basket ... the very term speaks of a toleration of differences and of a willingness to allow other individuals, or other institutions, to go their separate ways when they do not agree with you. With respect to government, diversity speaks of the importance of decentralization in the control of decision-making, and necessarily directs us to limitations on government authority.
>
> Within the modern civil rights discourse, however ... it becomes yet another buzz-word in the campaign for political conformity to a state-imposed ideal. Institutions that do not hire the right number of women or minorities ... should be exposed to government action.... Diversity today amounts to little more than a call for race-conscious and sex-conscious hiring, and in some circumstances even the more extreme position of proportionate representation by race and by sex.

On this side of the Atlantic, one classical liberal writer who criticised the principle of social engineering underlying anti-discrimination laws was the late Kenneth Minogue. He was very conscious of the existence of mutual antipathy amongst populations. He wanted people to think of each other as individuals but argued that anti-discrimination laws encouraged them to think of themselves as part of a disadvantaged group, as victims.[10] He argued that legislation is 'a collective attempt to change the nature of human beings, comparable to making water run uphill' (Minogue 2012: 81) and thus unlikely to succeed. But it was dangerous, as 'the bland surface of anti-discrimination turns out to impose some quite onerous, indeed freedom-threatening, individual responsibilities upon us' (ibid.: 103).

Burden of proof

There is another way in which UK discrimination law raises issues of principle which some may find worrying. Since 2001 (following a European directive embodied into English law by regulation, without full parliamentary scrutiny) the burden of proof in discrimination claims has been reversed. Instead of the employee having to prove that the employer discriminated against him or her, employers have to prove that they didn't discriminate. This reversal of the presumption of innocence was rationalised on the grounds that discrimination was difficult to prove. This is, however, a problem with many laws – including other employment laws where the burden of proof still remains with the employee. As Epstein (1992: 22) points out, assuming guilt before innocence gives rise to increased risk of Type 1 errors ('false positives') even as it reduces that of Type 2 ('false negative') errors. This in turn may encourage employers to settle many cases with negotiated

---

10 In his 2012 book, Minogue suggests that 73 per cent of the UK population fall into one or other protected group as a result of their ethnicity, gender, sexual orientation, age or other characteristics. The proportion is now probably higher.

compensation rather than going to a tribunal hearing, even where they do not think they were in the wrong.

Policy in practice

If few economists are now bold (or foolhardy) enough to break cover and oppose the principle of anti-discrimination laws, several have pointed out the possible empirical downside of such legislation. There is some evidence that anti-discrimination legislation can lead to reduced pay and/or reduced employment for 'protected' groups.

This perverse result is not altogether surprising from a theoretical point of view. While over time anti-discrimination laws can and do lead to changes in attitude, particularly as new generations come along without the same prejudices as their parents, this is a long and uneven process.[11] Moreover, to the extent that employers face real (rather than Becker-style psychic) extra costs – for example, from having to adjust the layout of offices to accommodate staff with disabilities, or from taking on workers with lower average productivity – they can be expected to try to minimise these costs.

Employers may thus react to a requirement to treat equally workers whom they regard as different in rather the same way as they react to the imposition of a minimum wage (Donohue 2007). They will comply, and existing employees may benefit as they are paid more and have better chances of promotion, but rather less of the group may be taken on when employers feel that their freedom of action is reduced.

In a paper reviewing the period before the Federal laws, when some US states prohibited discrimination but others did not, Neumark and Stock (2006) find evidence that anti-discrimination

---

11 For British attitudes towards race over thirty years, see http://www.natcen.ac.uk/media/338779/selfreported-racial-prejudice-datafinal.pdf (accessed 27 April 2015).

legislation reduced employment of women and black workers. In examining the effects of more recent state Age Protection and Age Discrimination laws in the US, Lakey (2008) concludes that 'employers ... react to these laws by failing to hire older men who will be more difficult to fire'.

Acemoglu and Angrist (2001) claim that the Americans with Disabilities Act led to a reduction in the employment of disabled workers. Bambra and Pope (2006) find something similar in the UK: they find that the Disability Discrimination Act had a negative effect on employment rates for individuals with a limiting long-term illness or disability. Those who point out these possible negative effects of regulation are often vilified: for instance, Lord Freud, a junior welfare minister, was forced into a humiliating apology in 2014 when he pointed out that minimum wage laws made it unprofitable to employ some people with disabilities.[12]

Employer discrimination, whether based on irrational prejudice or not, is one – but only one – reason why inequality of outcome, in terms of access to the best or most lucrative jobs, remains evident in most countries. Even after nearly fifty years of legal protection, women are under-represented in key business positions and the highest-paying jobs in the UK, as are males from many minority groups.

But other factors include weaker or less relevant qualifications, which may reflect disadvantage (poor schooling, poor careers advice or poor family background) prior to entering the labour market, which employers can do little directly to redress. Another factor is career choices, which, as we have seen, lead women disproportionately into teaching and caring jobs in the public sector rather than high pay but long hours in the City.

---

12 http://www.telegraph.co.uk/news/politics/david-cameron/11164578/Lord-Freud
-apologises-to-David-Cameron-after-saying-disabled-people-are-not-worth-the
-minimum-wage.html (accessed 10 May 2016).

Affirmative action and positive discrimination

Whether the reason for continuing disparities between groups of the population is discrimination in the sense economists define it, or something more complicated, there is strong political pressure to go beyond anti-discrimination law, to take what Americans have called (since an executive order of President Kennedy prior to the Civil Rights Act) 'affirmative action', or 'positive discrimination' in favour of disadvantaged groups.

In the UK positive discrimination is forbidden, but the 2010 Equality Act does permit something subtly different – 'positive action'. This allows such practices as mentoring people from groups who are under-represented in senior positions. It also allows appointment panels faced with a choice between two equally qualified candidates to choose the one who comes from a disadvantaged group.[13]

Increasing interest is being shown, however, in changing the law to impose quotas as a means of accelerating the progression of under-represented groups into key positions.

Ethnic quotas

Such quotas are common in other countries. In India a certain proportion of jobs is reserved for 'scheduled castes'. In Malaysia there are quotas for *bumiputra*, reserving jobs for people of Malay heritage (as opposed to those of Chinese or Indian origins). The argument here is that historically disadvantaged groups should be given support in the face of strong discrimination and often violent intercommunal strife. A problem with such interventions, though, is that they may benefit better-off members of groups

---

13 This possibility is a minefield, as no two candidates are ever identical in all respects except their ethnicity, gender, sexual orientation or other relevant characteristic. The likelihood that a disgruntled 'losing' candidate will easily accept such an outcome is not high.

which perform badly on average, at the expense of poorer people from groups with a higher average income. This has been one reason why affirmative action in the US in favour of African-Americans has been increasingly challenged by whites and Asians. In the UK, one recent example is consideration being given to having minority quotas for recruitment to the Metropolitan Police. We have had religious quotas for membership of the Northern Ireland police force, and a similar policy was advocated[14] for ethnic minorities in London's Metropolitan Police by Simon Byrne, then Assistant Commissioner, in 2013. The justification here is that community peace – another possible 'externality' – is best served by attempting to manipulate representation of different groups in policing.

The classic study of the effects of police quotas in the US, by Justin McCrary of the University of Michigan, found that affirmative action led over 25 years to an average 14 percentage point gain in the fraction of African-Americans among newly hired officers (McCrary 2007).

But the US experience has not been without real difficulties. Although minority recruitment certainly rose, low levels of quits by existing police officers meant that positive discrimination usually failed to reach target levels quickly and thus quotas, originally thought only to be needed temporarily, remained in place for many years. There were sometimes morale and organisational problems which led to temporary falls in productivity and clearance rates. Rapid changes in city populations meant that quotas needed to be adjusted over time, for instance, as Hispanics and Asians rose in numbers in many cities, and this proved contentious as African-Americans, who had previously benefited, now fell in the pecking order.

Over time the political tide has turned against this type of intervention. In police recruitment and in the comparable area

14 This policy would require a change in the law.

of US university education where similar quotas have been imposed, increasing court challenges by aggrieved candidates have narrowed their scope, and positive discrimination may even be ruled unconstitutional in the near future.

In London there would be particular problems in imposing ethnic quotas. Much has been made of the apparent mismatch between London's population (40 per cent Black and Minority Ethnic in the 2011 census) and its police force which, while having made considerable strides in more diverse recruitment over the last decade, still has only just over 10 per cent BME officers (though 17 per cent among new recruits). This is said to produce problems in policing minority communities who feel alienated from the majority and in the case of black youths seem to suffer excessive numbers of stop-and-search interventions. There is something in this, but it is unclear how simple quotas could address the complexity of London's diversity. Few if any American cities have quite the range of communities to which London is home.[15]

'Black and Minority Ethnic' is a broad statistical category with no real meaning:[16] it is just an administratively convenient way of aggregating data. Just to take some obvious categories, London has large and distinct areas where people of Indian, Black Caribbean, Black African, Bangladeshi, Turkish and Jewish (not usually discussed in this context) heritage are in a clear majority. There are also very large numbers of Pakistani, Chinese, Arab and Polish (again not counted in BME) spread more evenly across the capital, plus many smaller numbers of people from more than a hundred different countries, speaking many different languages. These communities have little in common with each other.

---

15 The pattern of settlement is also changing very rapidly, with large new concentrations of (for example) Somalis, Afghans, Romanians and Bulgarians in recent years implying that target levels of recruitment would have to be adjusted frequently.

16 Its more recent variant BAME (Black, Asian and Minority Ethnic) is a bit better, but not much.

Unless there is to be an attempt to set sub-quotas (a very difficult task indeed[17]), the problems of alienated communities may remain even if positive discrimination takes off; a black policeman in a Chinese community has no obviously greater insight into that community than a white officer. And while persuading some groups to join the Met may be relatively easy, others are likely to prove intractable. Research has shown that London's Indian-origin young people tend to reject policing as a career choice because they aspire to professional status. So do young people from a Chinese background. The currently planned degree-level recruitment scheme may attract some of them, but this would be less attractive to other groups who do much less well in formal education, such as Black Caribbean males. Pakistani Muslims report very strongly negative feelings towards the police on political/religious grounds. Bangladeshi women have an extremely low participation rate in the labour market and many do not speak English. Over half of Black Africans in London are first generation immigrants: 20 per cent have arrived in the last five years, many specifically to work in healthcare, and police work is unlikely to interest them.

Women on company boards

Another area where there are pressures for quotas is on company boards, where women[18] have historically been under-represented. Norway, Spain, the Netherlands and France have had legislation

17 In surveys, individuals can choose how to classify their ethnicity: with increasing intermarriage between groups, children can often lay claim to several categories. If detailed quotas were imposed there might be incentives to alter self-classification in arbitrary ways and, without Nuremberg- or apartheid-style rules, litigation might proliferate.

18 Of course, some ethnic groups have also been under-represented, and there is incipient pressure to have targets for ethnic representation too. http://www.cityam .com/227522/chuka-umunna-and-vince-cable-call-for-an-end-to-all-white-ftse -100-boards (accessed 9 May 2016).

requiring minimum proportions of women on boards of large listed companies for some time, and similar rules came into force in Germany in 2016. The European Commission is seeking to bring in an EU-wide directive that would oblige countries to take steps to establish a process that leads to gender equality among directors. In the UK, following a report by Lord Davies,[19] there are targets for top FTSE-listed companies but as yet no legal compulsion.

The justification offered for quotas for women's representation on boards is primarily on grounds of fairness or equity, and advocates point to the small numbers of women occupying senior positions in business. However, to those who might query the prioritising of equality of outcome rather than equality of opportunity, a further justification is often offered. This is that 'diversity' improves organisational performance in various ways, perhaps by improved knowledge of different groups of consumers, promoting the corporate image, or by bringing new styles of working into boardrooms. One widely quoted study was published by McKinsey, the consultancy. Based on an informal survey of large private sector companies, it found that 'companies with a higher proportion of women on their management committees are also the companies that have the best performance' (McKinsey and Company 2007: 14). Although the findings were of some interest, the sample selection and the lack of controls for other relevant variables mean that, as the authors admit, the results do not in themselves prove the need for diversity. Other more rigorous work, such as the study of a sample of US firms by Adams and Ferreira (2009), while recognising that the relationship is complex, suggests that the overall effect of board gender diversity on firm performance in their data is negative. 'This evidence does not provide support for quota-based policy initiatives. No evidence

---

19 https://www.gov.uk/government/uploads/system/uploads/attachment_data/
file/31480/11-745-women-on-boards.pdf (accessed 26 April 2015).

Box 3   Tradable quotas

An interesting proposal has been put forward (Akyol et al. 2015) to overcome the inefficiencies which may result from imposing employment quotas on businesses. The approach derives from the established principle of traded pollution permits. Suppose the government wishes to increase the proportion of women on company boards. Firms are then required to purchase permits to employ men in board roles. Some businesses will find it very easy to find women, while others will find it much harder. Those employing more women than the target percentage can sell their permits to those with fewer women, who are thus penalised financially. The permit solution can be shown to increase welfare compared with a fixed employment quota, though whether it would be politically acceptable is debatable.

suggests that such policies would improve firm performance on average' (Adams and Ferreira 2009: 309).

A similar conclusion is reached by Ahern and Dittmar (2012) in their study of the impact of the introduction of a law in December 2003 requiring 40 per cent of Norwegian firms' directors be female. The very rapid change in board structure for those companies with few women directors seems to have had a negative effect on company performance. Ahern and Dittmar's results (p. 190)

> are consistent with the hypothesis that boards are chosen to maximize shareholder value and that imposing a severe constraint on the choice of directors leads to economically large declines in value.

It appears from their work that new women directors had significantly less CEO experience and were younger than existing male directors. The expansion of female representation on Norwegian boards has largely been in non-executives,[20] many from civil service or academic backgrounds, rather than coming from women with executive experience in the private sector.

Interestingly, there has been a tendency for some top ASA (the Norwegian equivalent of plc) firms to delist[21] to avoid the legislation – a possibility also presumably open in the UK.

The expanding category of discrimination

Since the early anti-discrimination legislation, what counts as unlawful in the labour market has expanded considerably, and employers' obligations have expanded in line. Discrimination now includes a much wider range of behaviour – not only directly by the employer, but by other employees; employers who do not protect individuals from discriminatory behaviour are themselves legally liable. It has been extended to include harassment at work, which has been illegal in the UK since 1997: the 2010 Equality Act clarified the law to include bullying. Official advice gives such examples as 'spreading malicious rumours, unfair treatment, picking on someone, regularly undermining a competent worker, denying someone's training or promotion opportunities'. Such behaviour can happen 'face-to-face, by letter, by e-mail, by phone'.[22]

---

20 It has also been the case in the UK: the recent growth in the number of women board members in response to the Davies targets has very largely been attributable to non-executives.

21 See http://fortune.com/2014/12/05/women-on-boards-quotas/ (accessed 28 April 2015).

22 See https://www.gov.uk/workplace-bullying-and-harassment (accessed 29 April 2015).

As indicated earlier, the number of potential victims of discriminatory behaviour has grown with the proliferation of 'protected groups', some of which are probably barely understood by many employers, particularly in smaller businesses where HR expertise is absent. Such small businesses may include those from minority ethnic or immigrant backgrounds, where cultural conflicts may create problems.

Those vulnerable to stress, those professing particular beliefs which go well beyond conventional religions, or those contemplating gender reassignment, are all protected categories which many businesspeople may find it difficult to recognise or know how to deal with. They may be augmented by judicial decisions, or by regulations which are not part of primary legislation. I have already mentioned discrimination against the obese becoming unlawful; former Business Secretary Vince Cable was also trying to make caste discrimination illegal under the Coalition.

Critics of the proliferation of anti-discrimination and related laws also point to the subjectivity of many accusations of discriminatory behaviour and harassment. This, and the danger of tribunal financial awards which have no upper limit (unlike, say, cases of unfair dismissal), makes employers very wary of getting things wrong and leads to defensive practices which may go beyond what the law intended. For example, disciplinary codes may penalise staff unreasonably for remarks which were not intended to cause any offence, a tendency which has been exacerbated by the fear of breaching criminal law related to the amorphous but ever-growing concept of 'hate speech'. There are also growing numbers of cases where there are conflicts between the rights of different groups. Several of these involve conflicts between religious sensibilities and those of gay employees.[23]

---

23 For example, in one case an employer sacked a Christian nursery worker for prose-
   lytising a gay fellow employee, only to have a tribunal uphold a case for unfair dismissal. http://www.theguardian.com/law/2015/jun/07/christian-nursery-worker
   -sacked-over-anti-gay-views-wins-tribunal-case (accessed 9 May 2016).

These complexities may lead employers to pay to settle weak or spurious discrimination claims rather than face the legal costs, bad publicity and uncertain outcome of a tribunal hearing.

Conclusion

No reasonable person wishes to see vulnerable groups of people treated in an obviously unfair manner. Some minimum standards of equal treatment are necessary in a civilised society, particularly in the way in which *governments* treat individuals and groups. However, some forms of anti-discrimination laws do not always produce desirable outcomes for those they are intended to benefit. As with any other type of regulation, costs are imposed on employers as a result of anti-discrimination law – and these are passed on to customers and employees in various ways.

At the same time over-zealous interpretations of the principle of equality may lead to favouring individuals simply on the basis of an ascribed characteristic, while threatening free speech and normal social behaviour. The whole area of anti-discrimination law needs a through and dispassionate review, and now that Brexit will allow the UK more discretion in this area, one possible change in the law would be to set an upper limit on financial compensation for discrimination, something currently not permitted by the EU.

10 REGULATING LABOUR SUPPLY: UNIONS, MIGRATION AND APPRENTICESHIPS

This chapter examines some other, possibly less obvious, areas in which government regulation has a significant impact on labour supply, and thus on market outcomes – unions and collective bargaining, immigration policy and apprenticeships.

Trade unions and the economy

Trade union numerical strength has long since passed its zenith in the UK. In 1979, when union membership peaked at 13.3 million, over half of the employed population was in a union. Some 5 million were in 'closed shops', where union membership was a condition of employment. Today there are only 6.4 million union members, about 25 per cent of employees and a smaller fraction of the total workforce.

The Conservative administrations under Margaret Thatcher and John Major severely reduced the power of unions. Yet they retain considerable influence. Employees have a right to join a union and to take time off for carrying out official duties. Under the Employment Relations Act 1999 (one of the few changes Tony Blair's New Labour made to the Thatcher–Major union reforms) businesses with over 21 employees must recognise a union for bargaining purposes if a body called the Central Arbitration Committee (CAC) deems a majority of the relevant group of workers to support it. This may involve a ballot, or the CAC may decide on another basis, for instance, documented evidence of union membership. There are also provisions for *de*recognition, though they have rarely been invoked.

Where unions are recognised, they have a right under European law to be consulted in various contexts.[1] Wages and other conditions of service negotiated by a union are typically applied to all workers in a bargaining unit. Subject to requirements for a secret ballot, unions may call a strike or other form of 'industrial action'[2] in pursuit of a wage claim or grievance, without being liable to legal action for breach of contract. The conditions surrounding the granting of such immunity have been changed from time to time, most recently by the 2016 Trade Union Act, which has increased the period of notice before a strike and erects some extra hurdles (in terms of the proportion of members voting for action) before a strike is called.

Immunity from legal action is clearly a key regulatory intervention by the state, as it prevents employers from obtaining redress when a contract is broken. It was a source of great contention in the nineteenth and early twentieth centuries, as Chapter 3 indicated. For F. A. Hayek (1960: Chapter 18), this immunity gave unions the power to coerce employers and unwilling employees. It enabled them to impose a pattern of wages and other conditions which were economically inefficient, stymied productivity, created unemployment, facilitated high rates of inflation and was ultimately a significant threat to individual liberty. While Hayek had some sympathy for unions as voluntary organisations offering friendly society benefits and helping to channel grievances, in a famous letter to *The Times* in 1977 he argued that 'there is no salvation for Britain until the special

---

1   However, the UK has had an opt-out from the EU's Charter of Fundamental Rights, Article 28 of which would otherwise have allowed the European Court of Justice the right to rule on rights relating to collective bargaining and the strike weapon.

2   Something of a misnomer, as the 'action' usually consists of *not* doing something – bans on overtime, for example.

privileges granted to the trade unions by the Trade Disputes Act of 1906 are revoked'.[3] Other free-market economists, however, have been more sanguine: Milton Friedman (1963), while still a strong critic of unions, thought they had relatively little impact on the economy in the long run. Going beyond this, economists defending unions have constructed a positive case for unionism; most famously Freeman and Medoff (1984) argued that, by giving employees a 'voice' in the workplace, unions may help to reduce employee dissatisfaction and turnover ('exit') – thus indirectly boosting productivity.[4]

Union effects

There is an abundance of empirical evidence on the impact of trade unions in the UK labour market. Union membership is associated with a 'wage premium', which arises through a number of possible mechanisms (Bryson 2007, 2014), such as direct pay bargaining, resistance to wage cuts in periods of recession, and restricting entry and forcing other workers into lower-paid non-union jobs. The size of this premium[5] is not, however, easy to calculate, as we need to control, for example, for the fact that union workers are typically older, better qualified and in larger workplaces than non-union workers – all factors which would influence pay favourably even in a non-union context. We also need to allow for subtleties such as the 'threat effect' of unionism – where employers may boost non-union wages to deter workers from joining unions: this will reduce the apparent impact of union membership.

3   See http://www.margaretthatcher.org/document/114630 (accessed 7 May 2015).

4   However, evidence suggests that, although having a voice may seem to be a positive for productivity, non-union voice mechanisms (consultation) seem to produce better outcomes. See Gomez et al. (2009).

5   Calculated as [(Wu −Wn)/Wn] * 100, where Wu is the union wage rate and Wn the non-union rate.

The evidence from rigorous empirical studies suggests that union members in the UK do in fact obtain a significant premium over non-union members, although this premium has been falling (Bryson 2014). It is stronger for women than for men, and stronger for minority ethnic groups than for white British workers. There are other ways in which union members are advantaged. For instance, they have longer holidays, greater access to family-friendly working arrangements and a higher probability of receiving training (Bryson and Forth 2011). Unions also tend to narrow inter-firm differentials by pressing for standard rates: this has the effect of reducing gender pay gaps in unionised firms.

So there are real benefits of union membership – for members. However, it is likely that these benefits arise to a considerable extent from market power, and are thus gained at the expense of other workers, consumers and taxpayers. If a firm has a monopoly position it can exploit consumers and make excessive profits; unions can sometimes grab a share of these excess profits. More generally though, union 'insiders' may, by forcing up wages, reduce employment opportunities for 'outsiders'.[6] This means the latter either find lower-paying work elsewhere or (particularly if welfare benefits are relatively high in relation to non-union wages) become unemployed. This effect would be mitigated if higher wages were matched by higher productivity, either through the mechanism suggested by Freeman and Medoff, or through a 'shock' effect forcing employers to search more effectively for productivity-enhancing innovations. However, there is no strong evidence for the productivity-enhancing effects of unionisation in the UK (Bryson et al. 2006).

In addition to these workplace effects, UK trade unions influence labour markets in other ways. As mentioned earlier, unions

---

6   One aspect of the inside–outsider distinction is age. Older workers are much more likely to be union members.

nowadays play a very active role in employment tribunals, not only helping individuals with cases, but also organising what are in effect 'class actions' for groups of workers in, for instance, equal pay claims. Unions also act as pressure groups pushing for further employment regulation, for instance in seeking restrictions on zero-hours contracts (see the next chapter) and arguing the case for increases in the minimum wage. As I pointed out in Chapter 3, this is a relatively new phenomenon in the history of the UK trade union movement, which for many years was ideologically opposed to government involvement in the labour market.

Another aspect of trade unionism is its political influence. Several large unions also help fund the Labour Party, both at the national level and through funding individual members of Parliament. Historically, union leadership has often been a voice of moderation within the labour movement, even a conservative force, though in recent years this seems to have changed. Union leaders such as Len McCluskey of Unite, for example, have been key supporters of Jeremy Corbyn and the Labour left.

Unions and the public sector

A particular set of issues is raised by unionism in the public sector. In the private sector, an argument is often made that unions can act as a sort of 'countervailing power' to profit-maximising employers, especially large firms, who would otherwise, it is claimed, be able to exploit workers. As I suggested in Chapter 2, this is a rather weaker argument than is often supposed. It is even less plausible in the case of the public sector, where the employer is ultimately the taxpayer and industrial action is often deliberately aimed at inconveniencing the general public as an indirect means of pressuring the government to 'do something'.

Unionisation rates are much higher in the public sector than in the private sector: in 2015 54 per cent of UK public sector workers were unionised as against just 14 per cent of private sector workers – and in the private sector high unionisation rates are mainly found in what were formerly public sector industries such as utilities and transport.[7]

Public sector pay is on average higher than that in the private sector,[8] though this is partly explained by the characteristics (such as age, experience and qualifications) of public sector employees.

One issue which can lead to serious distortions in the labour market is the prevalence of national bargaining, something unions tenaciously defend. There are some minor increments in pay for working in London, but by and large teachers, nurses and civil servants are paid similar rates wherever they work – despite considerable variations in living costs and in labour market conditions. As a result public sector workers are relatively poorly paid in London and the southeast, but relatively generously paid in the northeast or the southwest. This means that the *public* sector has difficulty in recruiting highly skilled workers in London, but the *private* sector has difficulty recruiting such workers in some regions.

Also problematic is the role that public sector unions may play in holding back productivity growth and improvements in quality, desperately needed in areas such as social services, health, education and transport. Unions resist cuts in services which may be necessary as a result of changing patterns of need as well as fiscal austerity; they also tend to oppose organisational change, innovative methods of service delivery and any attempt to outsource services to private sector providers.[9] It is often

---

7   Railways, where franchise arrangements effectively give companies a monopoly for the duration of the franchise, have been plagued by strikes in recent years.

8   This is more marked if pension provision is also taken into account: relatively generous, but unfunded, public sector pension schemes are often much more attractive than private sector schemes.

9   The most prominent disputes in Spring 2016 concerned opposition to the introduction of a night service on the London underground, the plan to make all schools into academies and the aim to require regular weekend working by junior doctors.

difficult to separate union concern over the pay and conditions of their members from wider political objectives such as resisting (or reversing, in the case of the railways) privatisation.

Public sector unions are much more likely to resort to strike action than private sector unions. While the public sector now accounts for only about 20 per cent of employment, in a typical year well over half of stoppages and 80–90 per cent of days lost will be in the public sector. Staff discipline also tends to be poorer in the public sector, where absenteeism rates are much higher than in private businesses.[10] Public sector workers are also more likely to take out tribunal claims than private sector employees.

All this indicates that trade unions, despite their reduced membership, continue to cause problems for the effective functioning of the labour market. Jeremy Corbyn and other senior Labour Party figures have recently called for reforms to give unions much greater powers:[11] this could be dangerous.

Policy-makers need instead to look again at the basis on which we exempt unions from being sued for breach of contract, and to see if the partial monopoly powers that they use in the public sector can be reduced by ending national bargaining. While knee-jerk reactions to particular disputes do not make for sensible policy, nor does simply shrugging shoulders and allowing unions to use their strengths to slow down necessary economic change.

Immigration controls

Nowadays nobody would seriously argue against mobility within a country – although, as we have seen, Settlement laws in Tudor England sought to restrict mobility, as did restrictions on

---

10 http://www.ons.gov.uk/employmentandlabourmarket/peopleinwork/labour productivity/articles/sicknessabsenceinthelabourmarket/2014-02-25 (accessed 19 July 2016).

11 http://www.theguardian.com/politics/2016/jul/30/jeremy-corbyn-scrap-labour -union-laws-pledge (accessed 15 August 2016).

movement and residence in the Soviet Union and other 'planned' economies. But when it comes to international mobility, matters are rather different. Although public concern about immigration has a long (and sometimes inglorious) history in the UK, it has been heightened in recent years in reaction to a marked increase in net migration into the country and fears about terrorism. Such concern clearly played a role in the EU referendum.

Whereas for many years those leaving and those coming into the country were roughly in balance (indeed in the 1970s emigration usually outstripped immigration), since the mid 1990s there has been substantial net immigration, latterly running at 200,000–300,000 a year according to the Office of National Statistics (Figure 9). These figures are based on responses to the (voluntary) International Passenger Survey, and other sources – for instance, new National Insurance number allocations – and they could be an underestimate.

Free movement of labour within and between countries is something which liberal economists tend to favour. This can be argued as a fundamental freedom, like the freedom to own property and marry whom you wish.[12] It is an ideal which often brings together elements of both the political left and right.

More pragmatically, economically motivated migration is a form of human capital investment where people incur the costs of relocating in order to obtain the benefits of higher income in the future. From the point of view of migrating individuals, this is clearly beneficial and should be given considerable weight. But there are also wider benefits. They arise from workers moving from areas where wages are low, because marginal productivity is low, to areas where marginal productivity is higher, so that total output is increased.[13] This and other dynamic benefits mean that faster growth may be expected.

---

12 For a particularly clear statement of this view, see Legrain (2016).

13 Though note that free movement of capital can in theory have the same effect.

Figure 9   Long-term international migration, UK, 1970 to 2014

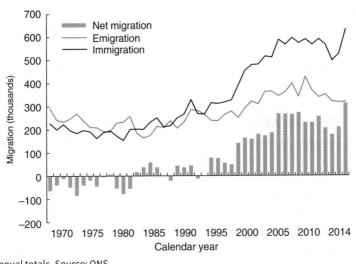

Annual totals. Source: ONS.

In a situation where the demand for certain types of highly skilled labour exceeds the local supply, these wider benefits of labour mobility are emphasised by many commentators. This does, however, depend to some degree on the reason for the shortages of labour. A frequently heard argument, for example, is that the UK's National Health Service would collapse without a constant influx of foreign doctors and nurses. In the short run, perhaps this is true – but the limited domestic supply of health workers is largely the result of the restrictions imposed on training places by government, in collusion with the British medical profession. The rate of return on qualification for UK-trained doctors thus considerably exceeds the norm for graduates, despite the length of training (Conlon and Patrignani 2011: 56), while in recent years there have been approximately ten applicants for every nursing training place. As so often, an apparent 'market failure' turns out to be a consequence of misguided or incompetent government policy.

A case is frequently made against 'excessive' immigration. This can take a number of forms. The extra infrastructure costs – the need for more school and hospital places – are frequently cited, though if incomers pay taxes at the same rate as the indigenous population this need not be a concern in the long run. We would not necessarily see it as a problem if more people from Scotland moved down to the southeast of England. It may be pointed out that some unskilled domestic/native workers may lose out if competition from immigrants drives down wages – although others may gain if skilled immigrants fill shortage jobs and thus enable the economy to grow faster for longer than would otherwise be the case.[14]

It may also be pointed out that much migration arises for reasons other than a desire to work. Some of these motives may be entirely reasonable – political asylum, study or family reunion, perhaps. Others may be less acceptable to domestic taxpayers – such as the use of the National Health Service for expensive treatments unavailable in the migrant's country of origin, or the alleged 'benefit tourism' which concerned David Cameron in his ill-fated negotiations over the terms of the UK's EU membership.

On this latter point, Milton Friedman has often been quoted as believing open borders to be incompatible with welfare states; this has been adduced as an argument for immigration restrictions. It appears, however, that Friedman wanted to scrap welfare states rather than restrict immigration, which he regarded as being hugely beneficial to the US.[15]

If immigrants potentially impose a measurable net cost on sectors of the existing domestic population, this needs to be offset against gains resulting from faster growth. Various official cost–benefit analyses of immigration have been made

14 Borjas (2013) provides a brief discussion of the theoretical possibilities.

15 See http://freestudents.blogspot.co.uk/2008/02/what-milton-friedman-really-said
.html (accessed 3 May 2016).

over the last fifteen years (see, for instance, Home Office 2007). These have usually taken a nuanced view of immigration, emphasising the benefits in terms of faster growth and the fiscal benefits from taxing younger immigrant workers who as yet[16] impose few costs in terms of benefits or healthcare, while recognising that some groups of immigrants impose heavier costs, and bring fewer benefits, than others. Recently, UK politicians have become much more cautious about encouraging immigration as a result of the apparently uncontrollable movement of undocumented migrants into Europe following the Syrian crisis, quoting security concerns as well as the more traditional economic arguments. Whatever the merits of other arguments, there is general agreement that some motives for migration may be completely unacceptable – terrorists or criminal gangs are unwelcome anywhere.

Restrictions

As a result, the UK has had for many years a policy which has attempted, albeit with limited effectiveness, to control the level and pattern of immigration. It has not been able to restrict movement from elsewhere in the EU since free movement of labour, as we have seen, is fundamental to the principles of the EU. Consequently, restrictions on movement from the rest of the world are in principle much tighter. We have had a 'points-based system' for non-EU migrants, loosely similar to that of Australia, since 2008. It was modified by the Coalition government. There are several 'tiers' or categories, where different rules apply. Applications from skilled workers with job offers, for example, receive points for qualifications, type of sponsor and future expected earnings.

---

16 Rowthorn (2014), however, takes a longer-term and more critical view, which touches on the continuing need for net immigration as the current generation of immigrants becomes older. He also touches on the radical cultural changes which high levels of immigration produce, a subject which economists usually steer clear of.

There are quotas for different types of jobs based on official estimates of scarce skills. Critics point out that such quotas are arbitrary: governments cannot forecast employer needs with any precision.[17] Thus employers find they cannot bring in certain types of worker as their quotas have been filled, while other quotas remain underused. What is concerning businesses following the Brexit vote is that applying the same approach to migration from the EU will exacerbate labour supply problems in the future.

Responsibility for ensuring that immigration restrictions are enforced has largely been shifted from the former Border Agency (now UK Visas and Immigration) to employers, who are responsible for ensuring that all the workers they employ have legitimate status. This typically involves employers requiring all new applicants for jobs to produce passports and other documentation when they come for interview, and keeping full records.[18]

Employers complain of the burden these measures place on them, as they are faced with considerable sanctions should one of their employees be found to have breached immigration rules, including fines of up to £20,000 per illegal employee. If you deliberately employ someone you know is not entitled to work, a prison sentence is now also possible. This puts employers in a very difficult position, as the Byron Hamburgers chain learnt recently. After cooperating with the authorities to round up illegal immigrants who had fraudulently obtained work with them, they faced demonstrations, online abuse and calls for a boycott from politicians and activists.[19]

---

17 A lesson which should have been learnt after the failures of 'manpower planning' in the 1960s. See Blaug (1970).

18 Educational institutions have more elaborate procedures and requirements when admitting students.

19 http://www.independent.co.uk/voices/editorials/boycott-byron-burger-illegal -immigrants-arrested-trap-home-office-immigration-rules-a7160746.html (accessed 15 August 2016).

The cost of restrictions obviously falls on immigrants and potential immigrants, but partly on perfectly legitimate employees, too, even over the most trivial matters: while writing this I received an email from a university where I examined a PhD candidate, requiring me to send authenticated documentary evidence of my residential status before my minimal expenses can be paid. It is now standard, when attending a job interview, to be asked to bring your passport and other documentation even if you were born here and have been employed in the UK throughout your adult life.

In many cases jobs also have to be advertised for lengthy periods in a bid to ensure that domestic applicants get a chance to apply before overseas workers are taken on. Since the general election, the Conservative government has further announced that no businesses and recruitment agencies will be permitted to recruit abroad without advertising in the UK.

An alternative

Instead of relying on such administrative restrictions, a market solution was offered by the late Gary Becker (2011). He argued that governments should set a price for entry into the country each year and anyone would be accepted, 'aside from obvious cases such as potential terrorists, criminals and people who are very sick and who would be immediately a big burden to the health system.'

If a fee of, say, £30,000 were charged, Becker claimed, it would ensure that economically active migrants who had a real commitment to the country were most attracted. This is similar to the precedent already established that investors and entrepreneurs can put up money to enter the UK: it would be the same principle extended to employees. This fee could be used to lower other taxes.

Becker argued that his proposal would end any 'free ride' on the health and education systems as they would be paying for the right to enter: 'It will be the young, the skilled and those who have the greatest commitment to the country who will come'. Given the difficulties young people may have in paying such fees, he suggested that a loan system, similar to student loans, could be instituted to support the keen but impecunious.

Another advantage Becker saw in his scheme was that any illegal immigrants who had prospered would be able to pay the fees to convert themselves to legal status. Becker says: 'A country can have its cake and eat it too. The country gets the revenue, and the better sort of immigrants. It seems to me to be a win–win situation'.

There is much in favour of Becker's imaginative suggestion as a second-best solution to free mobility of labour between countries. However, it was originally conceived in the context of the US, where immigration issues are rather different because of the nation's history, culture, permeable borders and vast stock of 'illegals'. The practicalities of the scheme also seem challenging: given the problems which the current student loan system has created, reproducing its elements in an immigration loan system would be unwise. Given the poverty of many existing unskilled immigrants, and the potential demand from many millions who would not currently consider coming to the UK because of the risks involved, it also seems likely that any such loans system would initially be overwhelmed. Perhaps a straightforward 'immigration tax' is more sensible, though this still imposes some administrative burden.

The UK has in fact made a small movement in this direction with the requirement that, from 2017, firms will have to pay an annual charge of £1,000 for each skilled worker from outside the EU. Note that, although this tax ostensibly falls on the employer unlike Becker's proposed levy, as with other types of regulation we have examined, the burden must ultimately fall largely on the employee in terms of lower pay to compensate the employer for the extra cost.

Incidentally, when introducing the charge, Immigration Minister James Brokenshire justified it in terms of an encouragement to train UK workers. He claimed that the charge would 'incentivise employers to reduce their reliance on migrant workers and to invest in training and upskilling UK workers'.[20] We now turn to this issue.

The Apprenticeship Levy

The apparent existence of skill shortages among the UK population has plagued British governments for decades. Economists have sometimes queried this, pointing out that in a free market shortages of skills lead to wages rising to bring supply and demand into balance, and that the pattern of pay movements seems to indicate that employers, despite frequent huffing and puffing, are not quite as keen to employ skilled workers as governments think they should be.

Nevertheless, a frequently offered justification for increased immigration, particularly under New Labour, has been that the influx of foreign workers helps to alleviate these putative skill deficits. As the political tide has turned against immigration, it is not surprising that there has been renewed interest in generating higher skills within the domestic workforce. The government is accordingly imposing from April 2017 a compulsory levy on larger employers to provide funding for an enhanced output of apprentices (a target of 3 million new apprenticeships has been set for 2020).[21] Its belief, shared by politicians of all parties, is that apprenticeships are a 'Good Thing'; admiring mention is made of their role in countries such as Germany and Austria. A good apprenticeship system is held to be an important factor in ensuring a highly skilled workforce and thus high levels of productivity.

---

20 https://www.gov.uk/government/news/governments-new-immigration-skills
-charge-to-incentivise-training-of-british-workers (accessed 6 May 2016).

21 Note that training for employment is a devolved responsibility, so this discussion
refers mainly to England rather than the UK as a whole.

Apprenticeships in theory

Apprenticeships have a long history in Britain, as elsewhere in Europe, going back to the twelfth century. A key piece of legislation was the Statute of Artificers and Apprentices (1563), which forbade anyone from practising a trade or craft without first serving a seven-year period as apprentice to a master: these rules were enforced by guilds, with which apprenticeships had to be registered.

They were not always seen as positively as they are today: Adam Smith (in Chapter 10 of the *Wealth of Nations*) sees them as restricting entry into occupations and artificially raising the pay of skilled craftsmen. He argues that the length of apprenticeships bears no relation to the time taken to learn the skills of a trade, but in effect is set to restrict competition[22] and allow masters to exploit their apprentices by paying them less than the value of their output.

Modern economics has usually seen the classic apprenticeship in a more benign light, as a paradigm case of an institution which evolved to finance training for 'general' skills – those which can be used by a variety of employers or on the worker's own account. This is in contrast to 'specific' skills, which are by definition only useful to the firm providing the training.

In Gary Becker's (1964) analysis of human capital acquisition, outlined in Chapter 2, trade apprenticeships are seen as involving a period of low or even negative earnings during training, but with the time-served worker being free to take his or her skills elsewhere at a market rate of pay significantly above the pay of unskilled labour.[23] In this way the cost of the training falls naturally on the worker rather than the employer.

---

22 Where legal protections of formal apprenticeship systems are still strong, as in Germany, they continue to inhibit competition. If Great British Bake Off winner Nadiya Hussain tried to set up a cake shop in Frankfurt, for example, she would probably not be allowed to do so as she is not a time-served *meister* (or is it *meisterin*?)

23 But see Wallis (2007) for an alternative interpretation of the historical development of apprenticeships.

What is the basis for the belief that the UK has a serious 'market failure' in relation to apprenticeships, and that the government must intervene? It is common to cite the argument (see Wolf 2009: 80) that employers who might have funded apprenticeships fear to do so because their fully trained apprentices would be 'poached' by employers who do not provide training themselves. Thus we require compulsion on employers to train or fund training through a levy system.

This ignores the economic logic of apprenticeship, however: that individuals who acquire a general skill which enhances their future earnings power will in principle themselves pay for relevant training. If they do not do so, this is surely where any 'market failure' resides?

There could be a number of reasons for this – for example, young people's ignorance of the advantages of apprenticeship, inadequate information, employers who are unaware of potential apprentices. There may be some limited role for government in mitigating these problems, for instance, by providing some apprenticeship equivalent of the UCAS system for university entry.

More likely, however, there is the question of affordability. Good-quality training is expensive, and young people and/or their families may not have sufficient income or savings to pay these costs upfront. As in the past, part of the cost may be met by accepting lower wages in training, but there are limits to this given the existence of minimum wage legislation, albeit with a lower rate for some apprentices.[24] The alternative is borrowing to cover the cost, but without surety this is very difficult.

Recent policy

The logical government intervention to overcome this problem might be to provide income-contingent loans to apprentices in

---

24 Those aged 16–18 and those over 19 in the first year of an apprenticeship.

the same way as they are provided to undergraduates (Wolf 2009). Indeed, the absence of financial support for apprenticeships may have persuaded too many young people to go into higher education who might have been better suited to a good apprenticeship route.

However, funding of individuals has not been the favoured approach: instead, successive governments have subsidised employer provision. In 2014/15 around £1.6 billion of government money was directly spent on apprenticeships in England.[25]

But this employer support has been provided in a rather odd way. Essentially, a government-funded organisation, the Skills Funding Agency, has contracted with 'providers' (such as FE colleges or other private organisations) to organise a certain number of apprenticeship 'starts'. These providers have then struck deals with employers to take on apprentices, to which the providers have then given (or have subcontracted) off-the-job training to reach agreed qualifications. These have been an 'intermediate' (actually pretty basic, equivalent to one GCSE grade A*–C) apprenticeship to reach NVQ Level 2; an 'advanced' NVQ Level 3 or a 'higher' (Level 4) apprenticeship.

Employers have had little to do in this system; much of the paperwork and assessment of apprentices have been dealt with by providers, and the formal training programme relates to standards laid down by the Skills Funding Agency and other external bodies.

The incentive for providers has until recently been to generate large numbers of low-level apprenticeships, which are short (some only a matter of months), cheap and easy to complete (payments have been made for successful completion). This is what has happened: in 2013/14 two thirds of the 440,000 apprenticeship starts were at the intermediate level (Mirza-Davies 2015a).

---

25 Tax reliefs on training also subsidised apprenticeships in various ways, but it is difficult to get a clear figure of the cost.

Only 2 per cent were at the higher level, which is the level at which the majority of German apprenticeships are pitched. Much of this spending has been a 'deadweight loss', substituting for what firms would have spent anyway. Rather than new apprentice jobs being provided, some employers have simply had their existing employees accredited: in one notorious case in 2010/11 over 20,000 existing Morrison's supermarket workers, 88 per cent of whom were over the age of 25, were enrolled as 'apprentices' (Wolf 2015: 4). This, though an extreme case, was not dramatically out of line given the changing pattern of apprenticeship provision. Whereas in 2003/04 over half or all new apprentices were the traditional age, under 19, by 2013/14 only just over a quarter were in this age group.

Where have apprenticeships been in recent years? Areas where there are claimed to be significant shortages of domestically trained skilled workers (for instance, engineering, ICT and construction, where many skilled immigrants are employed) have accounted for only modest numbers of apprentices, particularly at the higher level. Retail workers have been one of the largest groups, with other major representation coming from hairdressing, elder care and child care and business administration. It is difficult to believe that large numbers of young and not-so-young workers acquiring low-level qualifications in service, particularly personal service, fields, will do much to raise overall productivity.

Against this background, the government has proposed a number of changes (Mirza-Davies 2015b): a new Apprentice Delivery Board to promote apprenticeships, the development of more than 150 new 'employer-led' standards, the elimination of extremely short apprenticeships (the minimum to be a still-fairly-brief one year), and a legal protection of the title 'apprentice'. These things may do some good, though they do sound rather similar to plans made in the past – the 'modern apprenticeships' developments of the 1990s and indeed the whole national vocational qualifications set-up were similarly supposed to be 'employer-led'. The reality is that employers, particularly smaller businesses, cannot spare the time of senior staff to design standards and qualification frameworks. The work inevitably passes to quasi-representative bodies, consultants and educationalists, who are often far removed from the reality of working with young employees.

Likely effects of the levy

The main proposed feature of the new approach, the employer levy, is to be administered by HMRC, and will be based on 0.5 per cent of the employee wage bill above £3 million.

Training levies have a long history and are found in many countries (Dar et al. 2003). We instituted one under Harold Wilson in the 1960s; it staggered on into the 1980s without notable success. In two areas, construction and construction engineering, the statutory training levy still survives today. As construction is one of the industries where there are held to be high levels of domestic skill shortages, it does not serve as a particularly inspiring example.

With the new Apprenticeship Levy each employer will be given a 'digital voucher' corresponding to the value of the levy and will be able to use this to buy off-the-job training for apprentices which it takes on. As many employers will not use all their digital spending power, it is envisaged that the scheme will be redistributive, with the funds from those spending less than the value of the levy being reallocated to those spending more. While this may sound sensible, it is actually very arbitrary. A company employing only medical or legal graduates, for example, cannot usefully start a large number of apprenticeships and so it is likely to face a pointless tax and be cross-subsidising firms in a completely different field. Employer groups have pleaded for greater flexibility in using vouchers to pay for other types of training[26] rather than simply apprenticeships. If we are to have such a levy, this seems reasonable.

Although there will be other forms of support to apprenticeships, the government should make substantial exchequer savings, always welcome at a time of fiscal retrenchment. However, this is at the expense of passing the cost of apprenticeships on to employers, who, of course, will in turn pass the cost on in various ways to consumers, and to employees in terms of job and pay reductions. When the levy was announced, Robert Chote, the chairman of the Office for Budget Responsibility noted that 'the Apprenticeship Levy behaves like a payroll tax, so we assume the costs are passed on into lower profits and – primarily – lower pay'.[27] It may also encourage firms to contract work out to freelancers and subcontractors so as to avoid paying the levy.

The fundamental problem is that enthusiasm for apprenticeships is a bit like a cargo cult: if we have more apprenticeships, it is believed that all sorts of marvellous benefits will result. But there is no clear explanation of how these benefits will arise. It is a hugely unselective approach: while it might be possible to make a case for more apprenticeships in construction or ICT or in various engineering and manufacturing fields where productivity gains are possible from skill improvements, it is difficult to see a case on these grounds for hairdressing or childcare. And the idea of setting a Soviet-style target for the number of apprenticeships is, despite the rhetoric, just an invitation to create yet more enrolments to low-level qualifications. Expensive high-level qualifications cannot possibly be provided in these numbers, even if there was the demand for them – which there isn't.

---

26 http://news.cbi.org.uk/news/radical-rethink-required-for-apprenticeship-levy/ (accessed 15 August 2016).

27 http://www.telegraph.co.uk/finance/autumn-statement/12017108/Autumn-Statement-2015-George-Osborne-hits-businesses-with-sting-in-the-tail-payroll-tax.html (accessed 5 May 2016).

Although much emphasis is placed in these proposals on giving power to employers, the underlying theme is that employers can't really be trusted to make up their own minds about training priorities, let alone making it possible for young people themselves to make unbiased choice between academic and vocational career paths.

Conclusions

In this chapter I have looked at government policies which affect, directly or indirectly, the supply of labour. Restricting supply, whether through allowing trade unions to use their strike powers to protect 'insiders' or by inappropriate controls on migration flows, hold back productivity and economic growth while penalising workers and consumers. These are sensitive areas to tackle, but a government concerned both with efficiency and personal freedoms should do much more to improve policy in these areas. Trade union law should be revisited with a view to greater emphasis on contract law, with exemptions for strike action more narrowly defined, particularly in the public sector. In the heated debate about the post-Brexit environment, policy-makers need to take a more nuanced view of migration flows and resist blanket bans on movement which will damage individuals and the economy.

In the area of promoting the supply of skills, governments over many years have got themselves into a mess with their policies towards apprenticeships. Instead of allowing market forces (including young people's choices) to determine the number of apprentices, they have declared that the market has failed.

Economic theory suggests any such failure is likely to lie in the inability of young people to pay for apprenticeships as they now pay for university study. But instead of following this logic, successive governments have subsidised employers, and the 'providers' who have taken responsibility for promoting apprenticeships. While it is understandable – and sensible – that the current government should wish to remove the burden of paying for apprenticeships from the taxpayer, they would have been better to completely rethink policy rather than landing employers with what amounts to a payroll tax, inevitably passed on in terms of wage and employment reductions rather than absorbed by employers.

11 PROTECTING JOBS?

The 'contract at will' advocated by Richard Epstein and discussed in Chapter 2 is nowadays hedged around with many qualifications even in the US. In most of the developed world, even though employees unilaterally ending their contracts meet few sanctions,[1] employers are faced with considerable legal constraints on their ability to end employment relationships. In this chapter I explain the debate around 'employment protection' legislation (EPL).

Economic rationale

Employees typically value a degree of job security. Finding a new job is costly for them. Search involves time and resources, and information about employment possibilities is often incomplete. What is a 'good' job is essentially subjective, and taking a new post is inevitably risky. So once individuals have a berth which they regard as satisfactory, they often wish to keep it. Recognising that the economic environment may change in a way which cannot be predicted, they normally accept that in some circumstances employment will have to come to an end. But they want to have reasonable notice, and monetary compensation, in order to smooth their transition out of one job and to give the time and resources to find another one.

---

1   But see Hyde (2012) for discussion of situations where employers may try to restrict employee freedom of movement.

In principle, employment contracts can be designed to give employees a reasonable amount of job security without any government intervention. Clearly, the degree of security people wish for depends on their circumstances. A student looking for a holiday job is not seeking a guarantee of permanent employment. A professional with a family to support who has moved to a remote area to take up a post will require a greater degree of job security. Business employers can never guarantee complete security, and even partial security is potentially costly to them. This means, other things being equal, that pay and job security for workers *of a given level of productivity*[2] will tend to be inversely correlated. In the absence of employment protection laws, some employees with similar skills and value to employers might choose to be paid less but have contracts giving more security than others who prefer higher pay to protected jobs.[3]

In this view, private arrangements may appear to be optimal, and the imposition of employment protection legislation can be interpreted as redistributive in intention (giving workers a benefit at the apparent[4] expense of employers), or perhaps as 'rent-seeking' by pressure groups such as trade unions.

However, there are some 'market failure' arguments that can be used to support EPL. One branch of reasoning relates to monopsonistic employers. Just as in the case of the minimum wage discussed in Chapter 7, a profit-maximising monopsony would

---

2   An important qualification. Workers who are particularly valuable to employers may typically enjoy both higher pay and greater job security than less skilled workers.

3   Such explicit contracts would have the force of law, and employers could be held liable for breaching them just as they could be penalised for failing to pay agreed wages. But contracts need not be written down to be effective. In the 1970s an important literature grew up analysing *implicit* contracts; unwritten agreements about the relationship between employment, layoffs and wages in recessions (Azariadis 1975; Baily 1974; Gordon 1974).

4   As argued in Chapter 4 and several times since, the real burden of any regulation falls elsewhere.

be able to impose suboptimal levels of job security in the same way as it can theoretically impose suboptimal wages. However, this argument faces the objection raised previously: monopsony is uncommon in modern labour markets.

Another possibility arises from credibility issues associated with asymmetric information (Deakin 2012). An individual does not know whether to trust a potential employer's commitment to provide continuing work. Litigation to gain compensation in the event of contractual breach may be too costly, insurance against this risk may not be available, and individuals will thus not be prepared to offer to work for less pay as would be necessary in an optimal contract. Against this reasoning it could be argued that employers prepared to offer long-term commitment might be able to develop some form of reputational 'signalling' to reassure potential employees.

A slightly stronger argument for EPL might relate to externality issues, particularly in the case of large-scale dismissals. There may be knock-on effects on the local community, as businesses feel the effect of a sudden decline in demand. With a lot of people seeking new jobs at once, periods of unemployment will ensue, and in modern conditions this will normally involve the payment of benefits and thus a cost to taxpayers. The unemployed individuals concerned may, if their period of worklessness is lengthy, experience depreciation of their skills. There is evidence that they may also suffer from ill-health and depression (Bartley 1994). This in turn has an impact on their families.

But the case for EPL should be set against the concern that the economy needs to be able to reallocate workers from jobs for which demand is falling to those for which demand is rising. Excessive employment protection slows down this process, with detriment to economic growth. It can also have other negative effects, as we shall see.

Employment protection in the UK and elsewhere

Although countries such as France and Germany have had employment protection laws since the inter-war years, in many developed countries rules were first laid down between the 1960s and the 1980s. The International Labour Organisation's 1963 Recommendation 119 set the scene by proposing that 'termination of employment should not take place unless there is a valid reason for such termination connected with the capacity or conduct of the worker or based on the operational requirements of the undertaking, establishment or service' (quoted in Deakin 2012: 331).

The UK, which never automatically signed up to ILO recommendations, was relatively late in legislating for employment protection. The issue had been recognised to some degree by the Contracts of Employment Act 1963, which provided for statutory minimum notice of dismissal, and the Redundancy Payments Act of 1965, by which employers had to pay severance payments to employees who had been with the firm for a minimum qualifying period.

Other than this, however, employee job protection was largely dependent on private contractual arrangements – or on the hit-and-miss of trade union power. It was the disruptive use of union muscle to resist dismissals that led the Donovan Commission to recommend in 1968, and Edward Heath's Conservative government to introduce in the 1971 Industrial Relations Act, the concept of *unfair dismissal.*[5] The concept and its application have been modified several times since its inception. Today, an employee who has worked for the employer for two years,[6] can only be dismissed for five 'fair' reasons. These are misconduct (such

---

5   Not to be confused with 'wrongful dismissal', a common-law concept relating to breach of contract, predating 'unfair dismissal', which is defined in statute.

6   Some types of dismissal are automatically unfair, even if the employee has only just joined an organisation: for instance, dismissal for trade union membership or for requesting flexible working.

as abuse to fellow workers or customers), capability (not being able to do the job either through incompetence or ill-health), redundancy, illegality or 'some other substantial reason' (such as having been sent to prison).

However, these categories are not simple to interpret. For instance, ill-health which is associated with a recognised disability may protect individuals from dismissal, while incompetent workers have to have been offered training or assistance to reach acceptable standards. People must be selected for redundancy for a defensible reason which does not discriminate against any of the 'protected groups' discussed in Chapter 8. People cannot be dismissed for trade union activity or whistleblowing. Moreover, formal procedures must be followed at all stages; if not, the dismissal is *automatically* unfair even if the underlying grounds for termination are fair.[7]

The scope of unfair dismissal has also been extended over time. For example, the Transfer of Undertakings (Protection of Employment) Regulations, originating from an EU directive of 1977 and subsequently developed as a result of further EU initiatives, are intended to maintain employment protection[8] after a business changes hands.

Unfair dismissal has long been one of the main causes of employment tribunal claims, judgements on which have stretched the concept's definition, particularly in relation to 'constructive dismissal'. Under this heading, individuals do not have to have been formally dismissed in order for the employer to be acting

---

7   A case in point: a chef was jailed for biting two police officers during a drunken argument and subsequently dismissed by his employer. However, an employment tribunal awarded him £11,000 for unfair dismissal. It was held that the employer should have gone to the prison to ask for his side of the story before sacking him for gross misconduct. http://www.cbwsolicitors.co.uk/2016/05/hotel-wrong-to-sack -chef-who-bit-police-officer/ (accessed 20 July 2016).

8   TUPE also requires that employee representatives are consulted when a business transfer is undertaken, and that most terms and conditions are maintained even though the contract between the original employer and the employee has ended.

unlawfully. If employees consider that their contractual rights have been ignored by the employer to an extent that continuing in the job is impossible, they can walk out and claim compensation.[9] Examples of 'repudiatory breaches' of contract which have given rise to constructive dismissal include arbitrary pay cuts, suddenly changing the location of work or lack of support over claims of bullying.

In addition to EPL concerned with dismissal of an individual, further rules apply to collective redundancies. Where 100 or more employees are to be dismissed, no dismissal can take place for 45 days,[10] to allow time for employee representatives to consult with management.

These rules, while certainly not negligible in their impact, are considerably less restrictive than those in many other European countries. In France, for example, notification arrangements are much more onerous, redundancy is only recognised as grounds for dismissal if the enterprise is close to bankruptcy, the maximum redundancy payment is much higher than in the UK, and notice periods are much longer.[11]

In Germany, collective redundancies require consultation with works councils and the preparation of a 'social plan'. Candidates for redundancy must be selected on the basis of social criteria: an employee with no family commitments should be chosen before one with children; a younger worker should be chosen before an older worker.[12]

---

9   Although in principle employees could be reinstated after a finding of unfair dismissal, employment tribunals invariably award monetary compensation, normally capped (currently at £78,962).

10 This was reduced from 90 days in a package of minor reforms which came into effect in 2013.

11 See http://www.personneltoday.com/hr/differences-british-french-laws-collective -redundancies/ (accessed 26 March 2015).

12 See http://www.globalworkplaceinsider.com/2014/06/employees-rights-on -redundancy-in-germany/ (accessed 26 March 2015).

In Italy an employee effectively cannot be sacked for incompetence, but only for wilful negligence. The inability of employees to fulfil expectations is regarded as the employer's fault for inappropriate requirements or inadequate training. And although reforms are in process, most successful appeals against dismissal still lead to reinstatement rather than compensation. Italy is believed to be the only country in Europe which doesn't offer the employer a choice between reemploying the employee or paying compensation instead (Melchiorre and Rocca 2013).

Looking more generally, the OECD publishes composite indicators of the extent of Employment Protection Legislation. Recognising the complexity of legislation in this area, the EPL indicators are compiled from a large number of subcomponents including notice periods, severance pay, grounds for dismissal, consultation requirements, procedural formalities and restrictions on temporary contracts.

These indicators confirm the view that employment protection legislation is not as restrictive in the UK as it is in many of the countries shown in Table 6. A further observation is that the UK is one of a number of common-law countries – the others shown here are the US, Canada, Australia, New Zealand and Ireland – whose approach to regulation differs, as was suggested in Chapter 5, from that of most countries in continental Europe.[13]

Some possible effects of EPL

Early discussions of employment protection legislation, building on the analysis of Walter Oi (1962), tended to emphasise the way in which it reallocated employment and unemployment over the business cycle. By making it more expensive to dismiss employees, EPL encouraged firms to hold on to them longer in a business

---

13 Indicators covering wider aspects of employment regulation, such as the World Bank Employment Law Index and the Economic Freedom of the World database, show a similar picture.

Table 6   OECD employment protection indicators, selected countries 2013

	Protection of permanent workers against individual and collective dismissals	Protection of permanent workers against (individual) dismissal	Specific requirements for collective dismissal	Regulation on temporary forms of employment
Australia	1.94	1.57	2.88	1.04
Austria	2.44	2.12	3.25	2.17
Belgium	2.95	2.08	5.13	2.42
Canada	1.51	0.92	2.97	0.21
Czech Republic	2.66	2.87	2.13	2.13
Denmark	2.32	2.10	2.88	1.79
Finland	2.17	2.38	1.63	1.88
France	2.82	2.60	3.38	3.75
Germany	2.98	2.72	3.63	1.75
Greece	2.41	2.07	3.25	2.92
Hungary	2.07	1.45	3.63	2.00
Ireland	2.07	1.50	3.50	1.21
Italy	2.79	2.41	3.75	2.71
Japan	2.09	1.62	3.25	1.25
Netherlands	2.94	2.84	3.19	1.17
New Zealand	1.01	1.41	0.00	0.92
Norway	2.31	2.23	2.50	3.42
Poland	2.39	2.20	2.88	2.33
Portugal	2.69	3.01	1.88	2.33
Slovak Republic	2.26	1.81	3.38	2.42
Slovenia	2.67	2.39	3.38	2.50
Spain	2.28	1.95	3.13	3.17
Sweden	2.52	2.52	2.50	1.17
Switzerland	2.10	1.50	3.63	1.38
UK	1.62	1.12	2.88	0.54
US	1.17	0.49	2.88	0.33

Scale from 0 (least restrictive) to 6 (most restrictive).

downturn. However, firms would be slower to hire workers as the economy recovered. The initial stages of a recovery are always difficult to interpret, and cautious firms might be unwilling to take on extra workers if EPL would involve them in significant costs should they misjudge the state of the economy. On this reasoning, employment might be smoothed over the business cycle, but not necessarily be higher or lower on average.

However, there are more subtle analyses of what might occur. Firms might not alter their hiring and firing behaviour, but instead push down average wages (on the lines suggested in Chapter 4) to compensate for the risk of redundancy payouts and other costs. But this is easier to do in competitive labour markets. Where unions are strong and resist wage cuts, or where wages are close to minimum wage level and therefore cannot be pushed down further, the impact is likely to be more marked on employment. Firms may choose to substitute capital equipment for labour as the real costs of employing workers rises as a consequence of EPL. At an economy-wide level, investment in capital-intensive industries rather than labour-intensive industries might become more attractive. This may imply that those countries with long-standing and expensive EPL will tend to specialise in manufacturing rather than services, and in sectors which are less sensitive to demand fluctuations, which raise the costs of EPL.

Hiring standards might also alter. As we have already seen, even in a recession firms are always taking on some employees. As there will be more individuals applying for a smaller number of available jobs, firms may take the opportunity to raise their entry standards, asking for more qualifications or more prior experience. Younger workers and those with fewer skills will be at the back of the queue. When hiring picks up, these new standards may be maintained and this will make it more difficult for individuals to be re-engaged, particularly if their skills have depreciated through lack of practice and not being able to keep up with changes in the work environment.

Another possibility is that employers will try to avoid the costs associated with EPL by making temporary or fixed-term appointments, or by contracting work out to other firms. Faced with higher unemployment, governments may facilitate this by allowing the proliferation of temporary contracts,[14] which may be the only realistic chance of employment for some groups of workers. This can lead to labour market dualism, where 'insiders' with permanent well-paid jobs have a much better deal than 'outsiders' with insecure and poorly paid employment.

Evidence

Systematic attempts to test hypotheses about the effects of EPL began with Lazear's (1990) cross-country study of the impact of severance pay on employment. Using aggregate data for 20 countries from 1956 to 1984, Lazear claimed to find that dismissal pay was negatively related to the employment–population ratio, labour force participation and hours worked, and positively associated with the unemployment rate. This appeared to be a pretty damning indictment of one type of EPL. However, later work tended to cast doubt on some of the simpler conclusions about job protection.

Over the last 25 years hundreds of articles have examined the evidence on these issues.[15] Some broad conclusions on the economic impact of EPL are as follows.

Firstly, the effects on overall employment and unemployment and average wages are ambiguous, as theory suggests. Many studies find lower employment and higher unemployment[16] as

---

14 France and Spain, with high scores on the OECD employment protection indicators for 2013, had 16.2 per cent and 23.1 per cent respectively of their employees on fixed-term contracts, as against 6.2 per cent in the UK.

15 Skedinger (2010) and OECD (2013) provide partial reviews of this literature.

16 The effects of EPL on unemployment are clearly influenced by other variables, such as the level of unemployment benefits and the conditions attached to them. The composition of the unemployed may also change, together with the average length of unemployed spells.

a result of strong employment protection legislation, but other equally rigorous approaches find no effect: very few studies, however, suggest that employment is boosted by EPL.

Secondly, both hirings and firings seem to be reduced by EPL; those countries with higher employment protection indicator scores have lower employee turnover, which is associated with reduced structural change.

Thirdly, there is wide agreement that temporary employment contracts proliferate where employment protection is stronger.

Fourthly, there is some evidence that productivity is reduced by employment protection. It is sometimes argued on theoretical grounds that, as firms facing high levels of EPL display lower labour turnover may have higher recruitment standards and invest more in training (Deakin 2012), they should display higher productivity. But the evidence suggests otherwise: for instance, Autor et al. (2007) use data from US states (which have different degrees of job protection as a result of gradual erosion of the 'contract at will' by judicial decisions at state level) and find that employment flows and firms' entry rates decline with employment protection, while capital is substituted for labour and total factor productivity falls.

Finally, most studies show that there are very different effects for different members of the workforce. Employment prospects worsen for young workers and other disadvantaged groups, while middle-aged males benefit most in terms of protected jobs and wages.

Apart from these economic effects, it is interesting to see that a number of studies suggest that employment protection legislation has little effect on subjective feelings of job security. Clark and Postel-Vinay (2009) even find that workers paradoxically feel less secure in countries where jobs are more protected. It is possible that this may be because outsiders do not feel protected, as they are locked into a succession of temporary contracts, while insiders fear that, if they were to lose jobs, they would find it very difficult to get a new one of a comparable quality.

Probably a majority of economists now take the view that the negative effects of employment protection legislation have been a significant element in the high levels of unemployment, poor job creation record and segmented labour markets experienced in many countries. This has led to the policy recommendation that restrictions on dismissals should be reduced, and the distinction between temporary and permanent employment should be eroded. Some progress has been made in this direction; the OECD (2013: 67) reports that:

A clear tendency towards reducing the strictness of employment protection is observable over the past decade, mostly focused on regulations governing individual and collective dismissals. Between 2008 and 2013, in particular, more than one third of OECD countries undertook some relaxation of these regulations, with reforms concentrated in countries with the most stringent provisions at the beginning of the period.

Alternatives to standard employment

This verdict may be rather optimistic, though. In many cases the changes have been superficial and have had little impact.[17] Moreover, we have seen increasing restrictions on the use of alternatives to standard employment models. These restrictions are intended to give employees more job security by limiting employer discretion.

---

17 For instance, in France successive administrations have tried with scant success to reduce employment protection. In 2016 President Hollande's attempt to make it slightly easier to dismiss workers saw proposals watered down but nevertheless facing extensive and violent protests as well as such strong parliamentary opposition that they had to be forced through by Presidential decree.

Agency workers

One example is the Agency Workers Regulations, implemented by the Conservative–Liberal Democrat coalition in 2011 in response to an EU directive. Employment agencies have long provided a range of services for UK employees and employers, including the provision of genuine temporary employment (for example, providing people to fill in for permanent staff who are ill or on leave, or extra assistance at times when demand for an organisation's services is abnormally high). Workers are screened by agencies and thus save employers time in the short run, and in the slightly longer term avoid employers having to take workers on permanently when they might be unsatisfactory or when the demand for services is so variable that permanent posts cannot be justified. The agency worker gets the benefit of employment more quickly than he or she could find it otherwise, and the temporary nature of the work avoids long-term commitment which he or she would otherwise perhaps find difficult to offer because of personal circumstances. Agencies have for many years had an important role in areas of the UK labour market such as hotels and catering, nursing, acting and modelling, reception and secretarial work and security services.

In many other European countries, however, agencies have been looked on with suspicion as a means by which employers could evade employment protection legislation and exploit workers. In some countries, notably Italy and Greece, they were banned outright until relatively recently. The Agency Workers Directive was a response to this suspicion. The ensuing regulations give agency workers the same basic employment conditions after twelve weeks working for an organisation in the 'same role' as those that would have been applied if they were recruited directly by the hirer. These are such conditions as access to training, holiday pay, automatic pension enrolment and notice periods. Even from day one of a temporary agency assignment the worker is now entitled to the same access to job vacancies as permanent members of the hiring organisation's staff, and to collective facilities such as staff canteens, childcare and transport services.

Despite the considerable concern expressed by employers about the regulations, they seem not to have made a great deal of difference. Undoubtedly, some users of agency workers have experienced an increase in their costs, but overall the impact has been muted. After an initial dip in employment of agency workers, probably associated with the recession, their employment has risen again.

The TUC, smelling a rat, has accused the UK government of failing to implement the EU's Agency Workers Directive properly and called for a ban on the controversial 'Swedish derogation' clause. This clause exempts an agency from having to pay workers the same rate of pay as those employed by the hiring organisation so long as the agency directly employs the workers and guarantees to pay them for at least four weeks during the times when work is unavailable.[18] Agency workers are then considered to be employed by the agency and can be hired out to other employers without triggering the 12-week rule.

In Sweden, where the clause originates, workers still receive equal pay once in post and 90 per cent of normal pay between assignments. But the TUC claims[19] that in some UK workplaces agency staff are being paid much less than permanent staff, despite doing the same job. It also found that 'Swedish derogation' contracts are used regularly in UK call centres, food production and logistics firms. The Labour Party has also expressed concern about this alleged loophole in the regulations.

---

18 Once again it is likely that the cost of this apparent improvement in the conditions of agency workers is ultimately paid in the form of reduced wages, as the analysis of Chapter 4 suggests. While this seems to lend support to the TUC argument, it points to the weakness of all employment mandates considered as redistributory mechanisms.

19 http://www.cipd.co.uk/pm/peoplemanagement/b/weblog/archive/2013/09/02/ban-swedish-derogation-to-end-pay-abuses-says-tuc.aspx (accessed 20 July 2016).

Zero-hours contracts

Another controversial area has been the use of 'zero-hours' contracts (ZHC). These are a type of contract where employees have no guaranteed hours of work but agree to be potentially available. Estimates of the scale of such contracts differ. An Office of National Statistics estimate for November 2015, based on an employer survey, gave a figure of 1.7 million active contracts (with a further 2 million where no work was provided in the fortnight covered by the survey). However, the Labour Force Survey for the fourth quarter of 2015, based on responses by individuals, suggested that only just over 800,000 people were on such contracts.[20] The LFS figure has risen in recent years, in part because people are now much more aware of the nature of these contracts,[21] but may still underestimate the numbers. However, many workers will have more than one ZHC, while some workers with full-time jobs may do additional work on zero-hours contracts, so the number of contracts overestimates the numbers of workers solely dependent on ZHC. A best guess would be that around 3 per cent of employees were on this type of contract in 2015.

ZHC have been around for many years in the retail and hospitality industries, where demand fluctuates from month to month and even day to day. Their use has spread more recently, as Table 7 demonstrates, to other sectors including healthcare, education and public services. Nor are these contracts used simply by profit-making employers trying to squeeze their wage bill. A

---

20 https://www.ons.gov.uk/employmentandlabourmarket/peopleinwork/ earningsandworkinghours/articles/contractsthatdonotguaranteeaminimum numberofhours/march2016 (accessed 9 March 2016).

21 Until recently, many people would not have been aware of the term 'zero-hours contract' and would have recorded themselves as part-time workers or some other category. On a personal note, my son was unaware that he had been on a ZHC for over a year until I explained what the term meant.

Table 7   Level and rate of people on zero-hours contracts,
by industry October to December 2015

	In employment on a zero-hours contract (thousands)	UK, not seasonally adjusted Per cent of people in employment on a zero-hours contract
Production including agriculture	50	1.3
Construction	31	1.4
Wholesale and retail	66	1.6
Accommodation and food	189	11.6
Information, finance, professional	40	0.8
Admin and support services	52	3.3
Public admin	15	0.8
Education	60	1.8
Health and social work	179	4.4
Transport, arts, other services	117	3.5

Source: Labour Force Survey.

survey of employers by the Chartered Institute of Personnel and Development (CIPD 2013) found that a third of voluntary sector organisations used zero-hours contracts, along with a quarter of public sector employers and 17 per cent of private sector firms. Not all such jobs are low paid, as many seem to assume. In a TV question session before the 2015 election, Jeremy Paxman put David Cameron on the back foot by demanding 'could you live on a zero-hours contract?' Cameron was poorly briefed and waffled: he should have replied, 'It all depends. If I were a hospital consultant, a lawyer or a university lecturer working on such a contract, as many do, I certainly could'.

It is easy to see ZHC as exploitative. Unions have probably been too quick to generalise from hard cases where individuals are unhappy with their arrangements,[22] but even some better-off ZHC employees point to difficulties in securing mortgages or consumer loans without a regular fixed income (a problem they share with many self-employed people). Despite this, research suggests that the large majority of people working on zero-hours contracts are happy to do so; indeed, they are on average happier with their jobs than people on more conventional contracts (CIPD 2013).

For this type of contract has the advantage of offering opportunities to many people who would find it difficult to take regular work at fixed times.[23] These include full-time students (with class timetables which change from term to term, limiting their ability to take fixed-hours jobs), who constitute about a quarter of all ZHC employees, and people with children and other care responsibilities. They are free to take shifts, or refuse them, on a day-to-day basis as their availability alters. Other people on zero-hour contracts include people available for occasional extra work in addition to their main job (for instance, hospital consultants and university lecturers), and semi-retired individuals who want to work occasionally but not on a fixed weekly basis. The availability of ZHC may be partly responsible for the recent increase in the numbers working past state pension age, something which is not as marked elsewhere in Europe. In some ways these contracts thus resemble other forms of work such as freelancing and self-employment.

Zero hours arrangements are not ideal for all workers, though, and politicians have duly threatened action. The Coalition banned 'exclusive' ZHC arrangements, where employers who

---

22 For example, Unite 'believes that in general zero-hours contracts are unfair, creating insecurity and exploitation for many ordinary people struggling to get by'. http://web.archive.org/web/20130811185613/http:/www.unitetheunion.org/news/governmentmustacttohaltriseinzerohours/ (accessed 9 March 2016).

23 Only just over a third of ZHC employees want to work more hours than they currently do.

cannot guarantee work nevertheless impose restrictions on employees working for other firms. The Labour Party suggested in the run-up to the 2015 election that people who work regularly on a ZHC for more than eight hours a week should be able to request a permanent contract, and that workers should be paid for cancelled shifts. Others would go further: in his 2015 campaign for the Labour Party leadership, Jeremy Corbyn pledged to ban zero-hours contracts outright.[24]

This would be a serious mistake. Zero-hours contracts helped to keep levels of joblessness down during the recession, at a time when many other European countries with less flexible labour markets saw staggering levels of unemployment. Banning ZHC would be detrimental to both employers and employees. There are always going to be short-term fluctuations in demand[25] which affect staffing requirements. With a ban on ZHC, some work (for example, opening restaurants on quiet evenings) would become uneconomic, or would be done cash-in-hand in the shadow economy. Zero-hours contracts would have to be consolidated into a smaller number of part-time permanent contracts for people who could commit to fixed hours. Opportunities would then disappear for some groups who are unable to work regular hours, including single parents and students.

Self-employment

Another deviation from the standard employment model is self-employment. As Figure 10 suggests, self-employment jobs have grown faster than employee jobs since the recession. This has led some commentators to argue that many of the self-employed are not in 'real' jobs, but are forced to scrabble around

---

24 See http://www.theguardian.com/uk-news/2015/aug/20/zero-hours-contracts -offered-to-a-quarter-of-all-unemployed (9 March 2016).

25 LFS data show that there is a strong seasonal pattern in the use of zero-hours contracts, something which critics appear not to have noticed.

Figure 10 Share of self-employed workers in total employment and self-employed hours in total hours

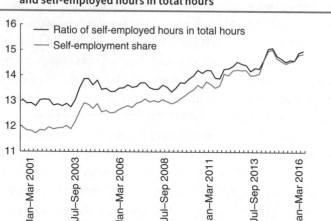

Source: https://www.ons.gov.uk/employmentandlabourmarket/peopleinwork/
employmentandemployeetypes/articles/trendsinselfemploymentintheuk/
2001to2015 (accessed 20 July 2016).

for freelance work. On this view, the apparent post-2010 jobs 'miracle' is phoney. Employers are cynically outsourcing work which should be done by those in regular employment. They get the work done more cheaply because they can avoid many of the costs of employing people directly, ranging from office space to auto-enrolment in pension schemes, but workers suffer in terms of lower wages and benefits and growing insecurity.

There are now over four and a half million self-employed in the UK, about 15 per cent of the workforce. There will always be some working for themselves who are not in a good place, but a look at the detail of the figures suggests a much more optimistic picture.

For one thing, what seems to be the basic premise of the critics – that the numbers entering self-employment were rising faster than overall employment – is mistaken. The bulk of the increase in numbers was rather because there was a sharp fall in those *leaving* self-employment. This means that more were persisting in self-employed status (a result partly attributable to more of the older self-employed working on after state pension age), and less were exiting to employment, unemployment or inactivity.

For another, there is little evidence of correlation at the industry level between employee jobs lost and increasing numbers of self-employed. This suggests that the belief that outsourcing is driving self-employment needs qualification.

The government's position, give or take some traditional concerns about tax-dodging by construction workers, is that self-employment is a 'good thing'. People striking out in business for themselves show enterprise, may boost growth and reduce the benefit bill. On average the self-employed report themselves as happier than the employed. The vast majority are not seeking employee status, and those self-employed who are working part-time are less likely to want to work more hours than the part-timers with employee status.

There is reason to believe that the numbers of self-employed will continue to increase in the longer term. There is a rising trend in higher-skilled workers such as managers and professionals becoming self-employed, often as consultants. The numbers of self-employed women – historically under-represented among the self-employed – are growing faster than those of men, and in a wider range of occupations than in the past when hairdressing, cleaning and childcare accounted for most women with this status. And as the greying of the population gathers pace, the tendency of older workers to have higher levels of self-employment will continue to boost numbers. Although younger workers are far less likely than older workers to be self-employed, their numbers are growing too – and are already much higher than in most continental European countries.

Changes in technology have facilitated changes in work patterns. The internet has made it far easier to work at home (over half the self-employed regularly work from home, as opposed to about 6 per cent of full-time employees) and to obtain business online. It is much easier to contact suppliers and customers, and business registration is easier.

Freely chosen self-employment – which seems to be the case for most – may be good for the economy, but does it require any help from the state? There have been dozens of schemes to boost self-employment over the years: they have not had much impact. Offering grants, cheap premises or finance to target groups usually has a significant 'deadweight' effect as these schemes encourage those who would have succeeded anyway. Training schemes, though no doubt worthy, similarly have little long-term impact.

It is probably better to concentrate on dismantling barriers to self-employment such as excessive occupational regulation, over-complex tax requirements and the difficulties faced when the self-employed begin to take on employees, rather than short-lived and ineffective subsidies.

The 'gig' economy

One contributor to the future growth of self-employment is likely to be the emergence of the 'gig' economy. There have always been business projects that have brought people together for a specific event ('gig') or series of events, but which could not constitute a permanent employment relationship. Historically, one-off construction projects were an example. Others include exhibitions, arts events and entertainment performances, and pop-up shops.

Recently, there has been much attention paid to the emergence of computer applications (apps) which widen the scope of the gig economy. Apps such as Uber, which enables individuals to act as on-demand taxi-drivers either in their spare time or as a full-time job, or TaskRabbit, which enables households to outsource various chores, are challenging traditional forms of employment based on the firm (Rogers 2015).

The existence of firms, as Ronald Coase (1937) pointed out many years ago, is predicated on the need to reduce transactions costs, such as those involved in sourcing, negotiating and monitoring work arrangements. The new apps set out standard contractual arrangements such as price, and can ensure the quality of work through prior checking of workers and consumer rating systems. For a modest fee, rather than the overheads necessarily associated with a regular business firm, the app owners enable workers to operate flexibly and consumers to get rapid and inexpensive access to many services without extensive search.

Some commentators have seen the gig economy as the future of work, with traditional employment collapsing – in service sectors in particular. This is possible, but other observers are more downbeat. It has been pointed out[26] that many app-provided services do not display significant economies of scale, which may limit their scope. In many fields where traditional firms are tempted to outsource further via apps, there may be issues about how necessary training and updating could be managed.

There is also little evidence that, so far at least, large numbers of workers have chosen to work full-time in the gig economy.[27] Rather, apps enable those with constraints on their time (such as students or parents of small children) to work more effectively on a part-time basis.

Another factor which may inhibit the spread of the gig economy is the increasing interest which regulators are taking in this type of employment. This may be intended to protect the consumer – although easy reporting and rating mechanisms via apps make company response to consumer complaints far faster

---

26 See, for example, http://www.economist.com/news/briefing/21637355-freelance
-workers-available-moments-notice-will-reshape-nature-companies-and
(accessed 26 March 2016).

27 http://www.resolutionfoundation.org/media/blog/the-gig-economy-revolutionis
ing-the-world-of-work-or-the-latest-storm-in-a-teacup/ (accessed 26 March 2016).

than in the past.[28] It may be driven by fear that taxes will be lost, particularly where apps operate across national frontiers. It is very likely to be pushed by pressure from interested parties (such as those operating London black cabs, who are bitterly opposed to Uber). It may be driven by concern that existing labour standards – in areas such as minimum wages, working time, paid holidays and parental leave – will be undermined.

In the US, these concerns have been taken very seriously.[29] Judges have been considering cases where some Uber drivers are suing to have themselves declared employees, in order to access various employment rights. A lasting decision in their favour could compromise the whole app business model and probably bankrupt Uber if it had to recompense all drivers. This danger has led two US economists, Seth Harris and Alan Krueger (2015), to propose a new legal category of 'independent worker' for those occupying the grey area between traditional employee status and that of fully independent contractor. However, something similar to this status ('worker' rather than employee or self-employed) already exists in the UK and has not reduced the demands in some quarters for regulation: a 'class action' employment tribunal case is currently being pursued against Uber. Similar cases have been started in France and Germany.

It is not clear as yet how this will conclude. If the claims are upheld, and companies such as Uber are forced to become employers in the conventional sense, job opportunities will probably be lost. It will also inevitably be the case that the extra costs of conventional employment will be passed on to the consumer in higher prices and to the new 'employees' in terms of a larger slice of pay being taken by the 'employer' to compensate.

---

28 Uber drivers who perform badly can be instantly fined and taken out of the system for a period. Customers who report problems can be reimbursed more or less simultaneously.

29 See *The Economist*, 'Part-time palaver', http://www.economist.com/node/21665025 (accessed 26 March 2016).

Conclusions

This chapter has shown that employment protection legislation has complicated effects on labour markets. It benefits those who keep their jobs in economic downturns (although workers may pay for this benefit in terms of lower pay in the long run), but reduces hiring in periods of economic recovery. It benefits 'insiders' at the expense of 'outsiders' such as young labour market entrants, the unskilled and other disadvantaged groups. It may hinder productivity and economic growth in the longer term.

Attempts by employers to circumvent strict EPL may lead, where regulations permit, to a proliferation of temporary contracts, contracted-out work, agency employment and other forms of alternative employment. While such alternatives have attractions even in an environment where EPL is weak, employment patterns may be distorted if businesses choose them simply because permanent contracts have been artificially made too expensive.

It is right to recognise that employees value job security, but such a preference should not necessarily mean that employers are forced to continue indefinitely with an employment contract which has become too expensive to maintain. And attempts to ban alternative, more flexible, forms of contract restrict individual choice and may not benefit those who are offered greater 'protection'.

In the American context, Arnow-Richman has made the point that the increasing emphasis on having 'just cause' for dismissal, rather than the contract-at-will, is mistaken. She prefers to give workers some protection by giving 'just notice' (Arnow-Richman 2012: 325):

> Rather than constrain employer discretion to terminate, a better approach ... would assist workers in the inevitable situation of job loss ... employers would remain free to terminate at

will, but would be obligated to pay for that right by providing advance notice or severance pay.

This would, she argues, bring employment law into line with contract law, which has always required contracting parties to provide reasonable notice of terminating an agreement. Arnow-Richman's position is similar to that of venture capitalist Adrian Beecroft, who created a stir in the UK by recommending to Prime Minister David Cameron that the concept of unfair dismissal be scrapped. His proposal (Department for Business, Innovation and Skills 2012) was that businesses should be able to dismiss an employee without giving a reason. Under his plan for 'compulsory no-fault dismissal', sacked employees would have the right to a hearing and financial compensation, but dismissal would be much simpler and its costs limited and predictable. The coalition shied away from this proposal as a result of pressure from the Liberal Democrats, but it is an idea with some appeal and well worth revisiting.

PART 4

CONCLUSIONS

12 WHAT NOW?

There is a misleading belief around, pushed most assiduously by the trade union left but all too often acquiesced in by people who should know better, that UK businesses operate in a Wild West-style unregulated labour market where they are free to exploit workers to an extent unmatched in most developed countries.

This book has shown that, on the contrary, considerable employment regulation has existed in this country for many years, and has grown particularly rapidly in recent decades – to an extent that it damages economic performance and prospects.

Such regulation can often be quite consciously promoted to protect the particular privileges of groups of workers, or to boost the election chances of politicians, or to serve corporate interests. It frequently does little to benefit the workforce as a whole, and though it may boost the incomes and working conditions of some groups of workers, this is frequently at the expense of other, perhaps more vulnerable, people. It inhibits structural change, and causes productivity to grow more slowly. It does little to boost economic growth.

Perhaps more fundamentally, by preventing people taking up jobs which they might otherwise have enjoyed, or by preventing employers from offering work they might otherwise have offered, inappropriate or excessive regulation erodes personal freedom and choice in subtle ways. It contributes to a culture of dependency where individuals seek support and redress from the state rather than their own efforts, and employers need permissions and exemptions before they can undertake new enterprises which could benefit the community. It stigmatises non-standard forms of employment and contractual practices and demonises particular groups of employers and employees. But regulation is not always driven simply by self-interest, political cynicism or populist spite. A repeated theme in this book has been that policymakers and the public, with the best will in the world, often misunderstand situations where regulation is attempted. Many apparently undesirable labour market phenomena – redundancies, zero-hours contracts, unpaid internships – may partly be the consequence of government interventions elsewhere rather than intrinsic to free labour markets.

Most importantly, I have stressed throughout that in the long run the costs of regulation tend to fall largely on consumers and workers rather than the businesses and shareholders who are popularly seen as either villains or, more benignly, inexhaustible resources to fund social objectives. Moreover, employment laws often have unforeseen and unintended consequences, which then give rise to further potentially damaging interventions.

Proposals to deregulate employment are portrayed as benefiting business interests and boosting profits. Superficially, this may sometimes seem to be the case. But in a competitive environment excess profits do not last long. Of more importance are the wider long-term benefits which flow from liberalisation of labour markets: greater economic opportunities, more innovation, higher employment, productivity gains and ultimately sustainable increases in real wages.

Some who accept the argument for liberal labour markets in principle – like many in the current government – fall prey to complacency. The UK's labour market, despite the restrictions documented in this book, has performed pretty well in recent years by comparison with many other developed countries, particularly those in continental Europe which have more extensive regulation. Our unemployment rate has fallen to pre-crisis levels, while hundreds of thousands of extra jobs have been created,[1] so why do we need to deregulate?

Further, it may be argued that some countries – perhaps Germany, Austria and one or two of the Scandinavian economies – continue to do as well as the UK, if not at times better, in terms of employment, GDP growth and living standards, despite being more heavily regulated. So maybe we needn't worry too much about raising minimum wages, restricting zero-hours contracts, putting workers on company boards or whatever new wheeze our hyperactive politicians and policy wonks come up with.

Such thinking is dangerous. Leaving aside the looming issue of Brexit, the UK labour market is not free of problems. Despite relatively low unemployment (albeit higher than fifty years ago), there is a real problem with young people. Youth unemployment remains far too high. There are also big differences in employment and unemployment rates between regions and between ethnic groups. Productivity performance has been poor. International comparisons suggest that the educational and skill levels of the UK workforce are weak, one possible reason why immigrants took, for example, nearly 40 per cent of the increase in jobs between end-2013 and end-2014. Real wages have grown only slowly since the recession ended. And while more-heavily-regulated countries may sometimes have performed well, they have often had other advantages[2] to offset apparently more restrictive employment legislation.

---

1 As jobs in a dynamic economy are created and destroyed all the time, the net increase in employment is only a partial measure of the job-creating performance of the labour market.

2 Economic dynamism and consequent job creation are also affected by such factors as natural resource endowments, a skilled workforce, good schools, high rates of investment, a simple and equitable tax system, a benefit system which incentivises job search, product market competition, a more efficient public sector, efficient land use and so forth. We need action on many of these areas.

Barriers to deregulation

Despite the temptations of complacency, some politicians have tried to push for deregulation – but so far without much success. Regulation tends to suffer from a 'ratchet' effect.[3] Once implemented, it is very difficult to reverse even if the intervention seems unsuccessful. A more likely response is to increase the scale and scope of the intervention to see if that works any better.

With legislation resulting from EU initiatives, the concept of the *acquis* has institutionalised this one-way progression. New members have to accept all existing EU rules, and unpicking them would involve wholesale renegotiation which countries are unwilling to take on. Brexit may offer the UK a chance to break free, but as I argued in Chapter 5, the pressures for regulation are in large part domestic in origin.

More generally, regulation creates vested interests which fight to maintain their privileges, while critics lack cohesion and usually have only a limited economic interest in the issue at hand. But this is not a simple dichotomy. 'Outsiders' who lose out through regulation may not even know that they have an interest at all. For instance, an occupation protected by licensing (such as the private investigators, dental hygienists and driving school instructors mentioned in Chapter 6) may not be even considered as a career choice by people without the unnecessarily restrictive qualifications demanded. If licensing were dropped, they might well want to move into the field, but they are not sufficiently aware of or concerned about this possibility to organise to seek removal of the relevant regulation.

Businesspeople who are critical of regulation in general may be reluctant to push the argument when it comes to particular issues affecting them directly. This may be because, once a

---

3   An expression first used by the libertarian economist Robert Higgs.

regulation's effects have been absorbed, it is a type of 'sunk cost', built into the business model. Take, for instance, the requirement to offer workers a minimum number of days' leave. If this regulation were to be removed, new firms might come in offering slightly higher rates of pay in return for shorter holidays. This might give cost advantages to the new entrants. Existing firms would find it difficult to match the higher pay, as reducing holiday entitlements would create problems with their established workforce: they would therefore resist this deregulation. Maintaining the stock of existing regulation thus acts as a barrier to entry by new businesses.

As for employees, the concept of the 'endowment effect' is of relevance. Behavioural economists (Kahneman 2011) observe that in experimental situations people ascribe greater value to things they possess than they would be willing to pay for them if they had to buy them. For example, participants given a mug and offered the chance to sell it require more money to compensate for the mug's loss than they were prepared to pay to buy such a mug. Something of the same kind may hold in relation to a mandated benefit. People may be prepared to sacrifice £X a week in pay to get shorter working hours, but would require more than £X to go back to working the original hours, a situation which makes deregulation more difficult for policy-makers as they may need to overcompensate to attract political support from voters.

Regulators themselves are an inhibiting factor. Once a government department or regulatory body is charged with overseeing a set of regulations, its employees understandably tend to the view that their work is essential, and indeed probably needs to be expanded in new directions.

A recent example is the Gangmasters' Licensing Authority. Set up after a tragedy involving Chinese shellfish collectors, it does not seem to have had a great deal to do, despite substantial staffing (89 in 2011), and was supposedly considered for scrapping under the last government's 'Red Tape Challenge'.[4] However, it persuaded the government that its work was of vital importance and has now been rebranded as the 'Gangmasters and Labour Abuse Authority' with a brief to focus on 'modern slavery',[5] although investigating such crime is surely the responsibility of the police and UK Visas and Immigration.

Modest measures of deregulation

If deregulation of the labour market is desirable, how can these barriers be overcome?

Under the Coalition there was a half-hearted attempt at slowing regulation with the 'one in–one out' principle that any further regulation should be offset by repeal of some existing laws. This did not work very well; what the process appeared to involve was the government wanting to pass a new law and then searching for some obscure or outdated rule to be scrapped, with little attempt to ensure that the costs and benefits were in any sort of balance.

It is untrue to say that there was *no* deregulation of employment under the Coalition: the minimum period before protection against unfair dismissal was increased from one year to two years, employees were given the right to waive some employment rights in exchange for shares in new businesses, and the consultation period before large-scale redundancies was reduced. However, the 'one in–one out' policy was not a conspicuous success, with the Coalition effectively adding more laws than it repealed. And since the 2015 general election, the Conservatives have upped the pace of regulation with a range of new laws, most notably

---

4   http://www.mirror.co.uk/news/uk-news/gangmasters-licensing-authority
-could-be-scrapped-85502 (accessed 15 August 2016).

5   Modern slavery encompasses slavery, human trafficking, forced labour and
domestic servitude. https://www.gov.uk/government/publications/modern
-slavery-uk-action-to-tackle-the-crime (accessed 15 August 2016).

those relating to the new National Living Wage, the Apprenticeship Levy and auto-enrolment in pension schemes. A listing of additions to employment law – from various sources – is given in Table 8.

Perhaps the government could adopt a simple moratorium on any further employment regulation over the next five years, maybe by yet another 'double lock' or declaratory legislation. This might stop knee-jerk, ill-considered legislation whenever some new media scandal about employment conditions blows up (though it would not prevent expanding interpretation of existing laws by the courts).

A moratorium would be popular among employers, whose concern is often as much with the *flow* of new regulation as with the *stock* of existing employment law, and it would not trouble the general public too much. However, this would do nothing to reverse the damaging effects of past legislation or to open up new opportunities for businesses and workers.

And a moratorium would not necessarily prevent further political meddling with employment matters. Legal compulsion is not the only way: 'persuasion'[6] is also a weapon in the meddler's armoury. For a long time ACAS codes of practice have been 'recommended': although not compulsory, failure to comply counts against employers at tribunals. Under the Coalition we had 'targets' for proportions of women in top company boardrooms rather than legally backed quotas. Similarly, there may in future be more exhortation for firms to implement the Living Wage for their employees, to reduce the gender pay gap by x per cent a year, to introduce new targets for employment of those with disabilities, and to have stronger minority ethnic representation on boards.

The problem is that, even absent coercion, these are not good policies, for the reasons outlined earlier. And the fact that firms

---

6   Usually in the Mafia-style format: 'do this or else something nasty will happen'.

Table 8   Increased employment regulation since 2010

Requirement	Comment
Abolition of default retirement age	
Adoption leave extended and pay increased	
Agency Workers Directive implemented	Agency workers given employee rights after 12 weeks
Annual reports on whistleblowing required	
Anti-slavery statements required annually	Medium-size and large firms
Apprenticeship levy	0.5 per cent on wage bills over £3 million. Apprenticeship title legally controlled.
Auto-enrolment in pension schemes	Rising employer contributions over time to 3 per cent of payroll
Director of Labour Market Enforcement appointed	
Fines for employers in tribunal cases	In addition to costs and payments to employees
Flexible working request rights extended to all employees	
Gangmasters and Labour Abuse Authority given extended remit and new powers	
Gender pay gaps required to be published by larger organisations	'League tables' to be published
Holiday pay extended to cover sales commission	
Jail sentences for employers of illegal immigrants	In addition to heavier fines
Levy on employing non-EU nationals	£1,000 per year
Minimum wage non-compliance: stricter penalties	
National Living Wage introduced	Rising over time to 60 per cent of median earnings
Obesity now classified as a disability and thus a 'protected status'	
Occupational regulation extended	For example, childcare workers, private investigators
Parental leave sharing and extension to grandparents	
Part-time education or training compulsory for school-leavers up to age 18	

Table 8   Continued

Requirement	Comment
Recruitment advertising restricted outside UK	
Wider definition of employee	Tribunal cases have found some gig workers are employees
Working Time Directive regulations extended	
Zero-hours contracts exclusivity outlawed	Status of all ZH contracts now under investigation by working party

This is a partial listing of new regulatory requirements, great and small, placed on business by government since the 2010 general election. Some result from UK legislation and regulations, others from the European Commission, the European Court of Justice or decisions by employment tribunals or other UK courts.

are not under a legal obligation[7] to carry out a mandate may be of little practical significance: if firms feel obliged to acquiesce because they otherwise face moral opprobrium (with reputational damage possibly affecting their sales) rather than the threat of a fine or criminal sanctions, they still bear a cost as a result of the policy. This cost, like other costs, will tend to be passed on to consumers and employees and may mean lost jobs, distortions to pay structures and higher prices. A relatively easy policy switch for a government which wanted to reduce the role of the state in employment matters would be to abandon non-statutory targets such as the proportion of women on company boards and scrap the plan for gender pay league tables.

Another tempting partial reform is to exempt small firms from some elements of employment regulation, which often has a disproportionate effect on these businesses. In this way smaller businesses are encouraged, while the bulk of employees in larger businesses, and in the public sector get the presumed benefits of regulation. This again often appears to be a harmless soft option to policymakers.

---

7   And therefore not subject to detailed parliamentary scrutiny.

However, there are unintended consequences of such exemptions. For (Garicano et al. 2013: 3)

> when managers are confronted with legislation that introduces a cost of acquiring a size that is beyond a certain threshold, they may choose to stay below the threshold and remain at an inefficiently small size.

In France, for example, there is a highly significant cut-off point at 50 employees. Once this figure is reached, French firms must set up a works council with a budget, a health and safety committee and a profit-sharing plan. They face other new obligations such as fuller and more frequent reporting to the tax authorities, greater financial liability for worker accidents and higher firing costs for redundant workers.

These obligations surely explain why France has over twice as many businesses with 49 employees as those with 50 employees.[8] Thus the average size of workplace in France is considerably smaller than that in the US, where there are no significant step increases in regulation.

Garicano et al. argue that the different size distributions which this produces are an important element in explaining productivity differentials between France and the US. Too many French firms remain inefficiently small in size, and produce too large a share of output because of their cost advantage in relation to firms which are just over the 50-employee exemption limit. They also point out that there are distributional consequences: the profits of small firms rise while wages tend to fall as a consequence of lower productivity. If, however, wages are prevented from falling because of minimum wages and union power – both significant issues in France – employment and output will be

---

8   See Figure 11. Similar 'cliffs' occur in Italy, where increased regulatory requirements kick in at 10 employees and at 15 employees (Melchiorre and Rocca 2013). Italy has an exceptionally large number of 'micro-businesses' with very few employees.

Figure 11 Number of firms by employment size in France

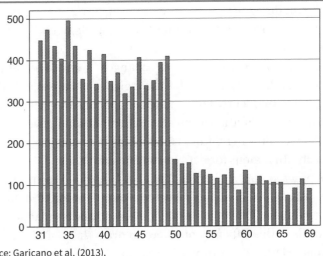

Source: Garicano et al. (2013).

lower. In a simulation, Garicano and his colleagues suggest that the overall effect of employment regulation in France is to reduce output by between 1 and 5 per cent of GDP, depending on the degree of wage flexibility assumed.

So providing partial exemptions from employment regulation, while popular with the small business lobby, may lead to unanticipated negative consequences.[9] If there are to be exemptions, they should perhaps only be for micro-businesses, perhaps just for those employing one or two people.[10] But the adverse

9   They may also be understandably unpopular with employees. In April 2015 a European Court of Justice decision confirmed that 3,200 ex-employees of Woolworths, and 1,200 former staff at the Ethel Austin clothing chain were not entitled to compensation after their firms closed, as they had worked in stores employing less than 20 people, the cut-off point for redundancy consultation. Those working in larger stores, however, received significant compensation of up to 60 days' pay. See http://www.theguardian.com/business/2015/apr/30/former-woolworths -workers-lose-battle-for-compensation (accessed 28 May 2015).

10 Including households employing nannies or cleaners.

consequences of regulation are not confined to small businesses; nor should deregulation be limited in this way. In any case, as I have argued throughout this book, the costs do not fall solely on businesses.

Another way in which modest changes in employment regulation might be implemented is through decentralisation. While the call has frequently been made to repatriate key elements of employment regulation from the EU to national governments, and thus to allow regulatory competition, a case is less often put to devolve to regions (or nations) within countries.

As pointed out in Chapter 7, regionalisation of the minimum wage was considered but rejected when Gordon Brown was prime minister. One of the problems which always plagues such proposals is the difficulty of where to draw the boundaries in a crowded island: travel-to-work areas have grown with the development of long-distance commuting, making it more difficult to define local labour markets. You don't want situations where The Moon Under Water on one side of a street pays its minimum wage bar staff at one rate, while those in The Eagle and Child across the road are paid another.

Different policies for the East and West Midlands, for example, might not make a great deal of sense. However, it is interesting to see that the Scottish National Party has expressed interest in devolved power to set a separate (higher) minimum wage for Scotland.[11] We should devolve this power, together with the ability to vary other forms of regulation such as the apprenticeship levy to Northern Ireland and Wales (both distinct territories) as well as Scotland, as part of a new federal structure in the UK such as

---

11 See http://www.snp.org/media-centre/news/2014/nov/sturgeon-calls-devolution
    -minimum-wage (accessed 28 May 2015). The SNP wants to help employers adjust to
    a higher minimum by reducing their national insurance contribution. This wouldn't
    help with the majority of minimum-wage employees who are under 21 (for whom
    employers don't pay contributions) or who work part time (employers do not have to
    make contributions for those working less than 23 hours a week at the NMW rate).

that advocated by Booth (2015). American states and Canadian provinces set their own minimum wages and have their own industrial relations legislation: something similar in the UK would stimulate regulatory competition, something conspicuously lacking in unitary states such as ours.

A more radical approach

If a more fundamental assault on regulation were to be undertaken, and large swathes of employment regulation were to be considered for abolition rather than devolution or partial exemptions, Brexit offers the opportunity for wholesale review not only of legislation coming from the EU but also of domestically inspired regulation.

One strategy could be to introduce a 'sunset' clause to a large body of existing employment legislation – perhaps all that developed since the 1960s. A date would be set when, if not renewed by Parliament, the legislation would lapse. A major review of employment law could then be undertaken, with a strong case having to be made to retain laws which involved significant costs for little obvious benefit: the default position being to drop laws which couldn't show clear benefits.

This proposal is essentially that put forward by Iain Mansfield (2014) in his prizewinning essay on Brexit, where he proposes a Great Repeal Bill[12] which would bring about, within three years of leaving the EU, a comprehensive review of all EU-based legislation – leading, where appropriate, to repeal. My suggestion is focused on employment regulation, rather than EU-based regulation in

---

12 Modelled on the 2011 Public Bodies Act, which gave broad powers to scrap unnecessary regulatory bodies and quangos. Mrs May, as part of the Brexit preparations, has borrowed the name for a bill which will be very different from Mansfield's suggestion, as it would simply embed into UK law all existing EU-derived legislation. See https://www.theguardian.com/politics/2016/oct/02/theresa-may-great-repeal-bill-eu-british-law (accessed 5 November 2016).

general, and it would cover solely UK-generated rules, such as those relating to minimum wages and unfair dismissal, as well.

Though there would be strong resistance, such a scenario would offer an opportunity to make a strong and coherent case for greater liberalisation of labour markets, and an opportunity to spell out exactly how regulation impacts on wages, employment and living standards in practice.

No doubt liberal economists would be under pressure to reveal their hands and to state exactly what regulation they thought should remain. Some might go with the clarity of Richard Epstein's vision of the unfettered 'contract at will'. Others might take a more pragmatic view.

At the moment there are approaching 100 different areas in which employment law constrains businesses and employees. This has costs to businesses, but also to consumers, employees, those who unsuccessfully seek work, and taxpayers who pick up the tab when people are squeezed out of the workforce by excessive regulation. Growth is slower than it need be, and earnings lower than they could be.

There may be a small core of regulation which classical liberals are prepared to accept. For example, I would suggest the following to cut the areas of regulation down to just five, which are probably compatible with the views of most advocates of free markets.

First, it seems reasonable to place some restrictions on the hours worked and types of jobs undertaken by children and young people, although there should be a reconsideration of exactly how much protection is provided and to what age.

Second, safety considerations probably require some limitations on hours worked in areas such as transport and health care. To allow employers and employees complete freedom to set hours may impose risks on the general public – a particular concern while public transport operators and hospitals remain effective monopolists and consumers and patients have little choice.

Third, employment contracts need to be enforceable cheaply and effectively. Where employees face substantial costs in, say, recovering unpaid wages, there needs to be an affordable and timely mechanism to resolve disputes.

Fourth, recognising that dismissal without any notice at all can be very destructive to employees, we may need a form of no-fault dismissal with some minimum level of compensation, perhaps on the lines suggested in Adrian Beecroft's report.[13]

Finally, it is rather difficult to imagine that in today's world that there should not be some form of anti-discrimination legislation, despite its often perverse effects. However, legislation should be much more tightly drawn to minimise the subjectivity of discrimination offences, and there should be limits on the compensation which can be claimed.

There may be other elements that could be added to this list, but it is clear that any such list would be a great deal shorter than that covering today's UK employment legislation.

It needs patiently to be explained that, as noted above, much employment regulation does very little to benefit employees as a whole. Though it may protect and boost the incomes of some groups of workers, this is often at the expense of other, perhaps more vulnerable, people. It certainly does nothing to boost economic growth.

More fundamentally, it erodes personal freedom and choice in subtle ways and contributes to a culture of dependency, with an ever-growing concentration of power in the hands of politicians and government functionaries. Even if we do not go all the way with Richard Epstein's conception of the contract at will, we should be a lot closer to that vision than we currently are.

---

13 In principle, as argued earlier, employers and employees could negotiate optimum levels of compensation when determining contracts. However, the existence of welfare benefits for those who lose their jobs distorts the choices facing employees and would probably lead to suboptimal levels of privately negotiated compensation.

Over the last half century there has been an accelerating shift towards the view that politicians are better judges of how employment ought to be structured and rewarded than employers and employees engaged in free markets. This shift should now be comprehensively reversed.

REFERENCES

Aaronson, D., French, E. and Sorkin, I. (2016) Fast food, slow results. *EA* Spring: 34–37.

ACAS (2015) Employment relations comment, March.

Acemoglu, D. and Angrist, J. D. (2001) Consequences of employment protection? The case of the Americans with Disabilities Act. *Journal of Political Economy* 109: 915–57.

Adams, R. B. and Ferreira, D. (2009) Women in the boardroom and their impact on governance and performance. *Journal of Financial Economics* 94: 291–309.

Adams, S. and Neumark, D. (2005) The effects of living wage laws: evidence from failed and derailed living wage campaigns. *Journal of Urban Economics* 58: 177–202.

Addison, P. (1993) *Churchill on the Home Front 1900–1955*. London: Pimlico.

Ahern, K. R. and Dittmar, A. K. (2012) The changing of the boards: the impact on firm valuation of mandated female board representation. *Quarterly Journal of Economics* 127(1): 137–97.

Akyol, M., Neugart, M. and Pichler, S. (2015) A tradable employment quota. *Labor Economics* 36: 48–63.

Arabsheibani, G. R., Marin, A. and Wadsworth, J. (2005) Gay pay in the UK. *Economica* 72(186): 333–47.

Arnow-Richman, R. (2012) From just cause to just notice in reforming employment termination law. In *Research Handbook on the Economics of Labor and Employment Law* (ed. C. L. Estland and M. L. Wachter). Northampton, MA: Edward Elgar.

Arrow, K. J. (1973) The theory of discrimination. In *Discrimination in Labor Markets* (ed. O. Ashfelter and A. Rees). Princeton University Press.

Autor, D. H. (2003) Outsourcing at will: the contribution of unjust dismissal doctrine to the growth of employment outsourcing. *Journal of Labor Economics* 21(1): 1–42.

Autor, D., Kerr, W. R. and Kugler, A. D. (2007) Does employment protection reduce productivity? Evidence from US states. *Economic Journal* 117: F189–F217.

Ayres, I., Vars, F. E. and Zakariya, N. (2005) To insure prejudice: racial disparities in taxicab tipping. *Yale Law Journal* 144: 1613–74.

Azariadis, C. (1975) Implicit contracts and underemployment equilibria. *Journal of Political Economy* 83: 1183–202.

Baily, M. (1974) Wages and employment under uncertain demand. *Review of Economic Studies* 41: 37–50.

Balcock, L. and Laschever, S. (2003) *Women Don't Ask: Negotiation and the Gender Divide*. Princeton University Press.

Bambra, C. and Pope, D. (2006) What are the effects of anti-discrimination legislation on socioeconomic inequalities in the employment consequences of ill-health and disability? *Journal of Epidemiology and Community Health* 61: 421–26.

Bartley, M. (1994) Unemployment and ill-health: understanding the relationship. *Journal of Epidemiology and Community Health* 48: 333–37.

Bator, F. M. (1958) The anatomy of market failure. *Quarterly Journal of Economics* 72(3): 351–79.

Becker, G. S. (1957) *The Economics of Discrimination*. Chicago University Press.

Becker, G. S. (1993) [1964] *Human Capital: A Theoretical and Empirical Analysis with Special Reference to Education*, 3rd edn. Chicago University Press.

Becker, G. S. (2011) *The Challenge of Immigration: A Radical Solution*. London: Institute of Economic Affairs.

Bell, B. and Van Reenen, J. (2012) Firm performance and wages: evidence from across the corporate hierarchy. Centre for Economic Performance Discussion Paper 1088. http://cep.lse.ac.uk/pubs/down load/dp1088.pdf (accessed 17 March 2015).

Ben-Galim, D. and Thompson, S. (2013) *Who's Breadwinning? Working Mothers and the New Face of Family Support*. London: Institute for Public Policy Research.

Bennett, J. M. (2010) Compulsory service in Late Mediaeval England. *Past and Present* 209: 7–51.

Berle, A. A. and Means, G. C. (1932) *The Modern Corporation and Private Property*. New York: Macmillan.

Bettio, F. and Verashchagina, A. (2013) Current tax-benefit systems in Europe: are they fair to working women? In *Gender and the European Labour Market* (ed. F. Bettio, J. Plantegna and M. Smith). Abingdon: Routledge.

BIS (2015) *National Minimum Wage: Government Evidence for the Low Pay Commission on the Additional Assessment*. Department for Business, Innovation and Skills.

Black, D. A. (1995) Discrimination in an equilibrium search model. *Journal of Labor Economics* 13(2): 309–334.

Blaug, M. (1958) The classical economists and the Factory Acts – a re-examination. *Quarterly Journal of Economics* 72(2): 211–26.

Booth, P. (2014) In the dock: market failure. *EA* Autumn: 4–6.

Booth, P. (2015) *Federal Britain: The Case for Decentralisation*. London: Institute of Economic Affairs.

Booth, S., Persson, M. and Scarpetta, V. (2011) *Repatriating EU Social Policy: The Best Choice for Jobs and Growth?* London: Open Europe. http://www.openeurope.org.uk/Content/Documents/Pdfs/2011EUsocialpolicy.pdf (accessed 10 July 2014).

Borjas, G. J. (2013) *Labor Economics*, 6th edn. New York: McGraw-Hill.

Bourne, R. and Snowdon, C. (2016) *Never Mind the Gap: Why We Shouldn't Worry about Inequality*. Institute of Economic Affairs Discussion Paper 70.

Brochu, P. and Green, D. A. (2013) The impact of minimum wages on labour market transitions. *Economic Journal* 123(573): 1203–35.

Brodie, D. (2003) *A History of British Labour Law 1867–1945*. Oxford: Hart.

Bryan, M., Salvatori, A. and Taylor, M. (2012) *The Impact of the National Minimum Wage on Earnings, Employment and Hours through the Recession.* Low Pay Commission.

Bryson, A. (2007) The effect of unions on wages. http://www.newunion ism.net/library/organizing/Bryson%20-%20The%20Effect%20of% 20Trade%20Unions%20on%20Wages%20%202007.pdf (accessed 7 May 2015).

Bryson, A. (2014) Union wage effects. http://wol.iza.org/articles/union -wage-effects-1.pdf (accessed 7 May 2014).

Bryson, A. and Forth, J. (2011) Trade unions. In *The Labour Market in Winter: The State of Working Britain* (ed. P. Gregg and J. Wadsworth), pp. 255–71. Oxford University Press.

Bryson, A. and Kleiner, M. K. (2010) The regulation of occupations. *British Journal of Industrial Relations* 48: 670–75.

Bryson, A., Charlwood, A. and Forth, J. (2006) Worker voice, managerial response and labour productivity: an empirical investigation. *Industrial Relations Journal* 37: 438–55.

Buchanan, J. M. and Thirlby, G. F. (eds) (1981) *LSE Essays on Cost.* London School of Economics.

Campbell, D. (2008) Breach of contract and the efficiency of markets. In *The Legal Foundation of Free Markets* (ed. S. F. Copp). London: Institute of Economic Affairs.

Card, D. and Krueger, A. B. (1994) Minimum wages and employment: a case study of the fast-food industry in New Jersey and Pennsylvania. *American Economic Review* 84: 772–93.

Carpenter, D., Krepper, L., Erickson, A. C. and Ross, J. K. (2015) Regulating work: measuring the scope and burden of occupational licensure among low – and moderate-income occupations in the United States. *Economic Affairs* 35(1): 3–20.

Chang, H.-J. (2013) Decent wages or a breadline economy: it's a no-brainer. *The Guardian,* 8 November.

CIPD (2013) Zero-hours contracts: myth and reality. http://www .cipd.co.uk/binaries/zero-hours-contracts_2013-myth-reality.pdf (accessed 8 March 2016).

Clark, A. and Postel-Vinay, F. (2009) Job security and job protection. *Oxford Economic Papers* 61: 207–39.

Clemens, J. and Wither, M. (2014) the minimum wage and the great recession: evidence of effects on the employment and income trajectories of low-skilled workers. National Bureau of Economic Research Working Paper 20724.

Coase, R. (1937) The nature of the firm. *Economica* 4: 386–405.

Conlon, G. and Patrignani, P. (2011) The returns to higher education qualifications. BIS Research Paper 45. London: Department for Business, Innovation and Skills.

Conlon, G., Patrignani, P. and Mantovani, I. (2015) The death of the saturday job: the decline of earning and learning among young people in the UK. UK Commission for Employment and Skills. https://www.gov.uk/government/publications/the-death-of-the-saturday-job-the-decline-in-earning-and-learning-amongst-young-people-in-the-uk (accessed 3 November 2016).

Connolly, S. and Gregory, M. (2008) Moving down: women's part-time work and occupational change in Britain 1991–2001. *Economic Journal* 118(526): F52–F76.

Conyon, M. J. (2006) Executive compensation and incentives. *Academy of Management Perspectives* 20: 25–44.

Dar, A., Canagarajah, S. and Murphy, P. (2003) Training levies: rationale and evidence from evaluations. http://siteresources.worldbank.org/INTLM/Resources/TrainingLevies.pdf (accessed 18 November 2015).

D'Arcy, C., Plunkett, J. and Wilson, T. (2014) *Minimum Wage Act II*. London: Resolution Foundation.

Darwall, R. (2006) *A Better Way to Help the Low Paid*. London: Centre for Policy Studies.

Deakin, S. (2003) The contract of employment: a study in legal evolution. ESRC Centre for Business Research, University of Cambridge, Working Paper 203.

Deakin, S. (2012) The law and economics of employment protection legislation. In *Research Handbook on the Economics of Labor and*

Employment Law (ed. C. L. Estland and M. L. Wachter). Northampton, MA: Edward Elgar.

Department for Business, Innovation and Skills (2012) Employment Law Review Report (Beecroft).

Department for Business, Innovation and Skills (2014) The impact of the Working Time Regulations on the UK labour market: a review of evidence. BIS Analysis Paper 5.

Department for Business, Innovation and Skills (2015) Apprenticeships Levy: employer owned apprenticeships training. https://www.gov.uk/government/uploads/system/uploads/attachment_data/file/455101/bis-15-477-apprenticeships-levy-consultation.pdf (accessed 10 March 2016).

De Simone, J. and Schumacher, E. J. (2004) Compensating differentials and AIDS risk. National Bureau of Economic Research Working Paper 10861.

Dickens, R., Riley, R. and Wilkinson, D. (2012) Re-examining the impact of the National Minimum Wage on earnings, employment and hours: the importance of recession and firm size. Report to the Low Pay Commission. London: NIESR.

Doleac, J. L. and Stein, L. C. D. (2013) The visible hand: race and online market outcomes. *Economic Journal* 123: F469–F492.

Dolton, P. and Bondibene, C. R. (2012) The international experience of minimum wages in an economic downturn. *Economic Policy* 69: 99–142.

Donohue, J. J. (2005) The law and economics of antidiscrimination law. John M. Olin Center for Studies in Law, Economics, and Public Policy Working Papers 290. http://digitalcommons.law.yale.edu/lepp_papers/290 (accessed 1 Jan 2016).

Donohue, J. J. (2007) Antidiscrimination law. In *Handbook of Law and Economics,* Volume 2 (ed. A. M. Polinsky and S. Shavell). Amsterdam: Elsevier.

Drydakis, N. (2014) Sexual orientation and labor market outcomes. *IZA World of Labor.* Available at: http://wol.iza.org/articles/sexual-orientation-and-labor-market-outcomes.pdf (accessed 24 February 2015).

Dullroy, J. (2015) Freelancers unite to get sickness and other employment benefits. *The Guardian*, 14 January. http://www.theguard ian.com/money/2015/jan/14/freelance-payment-sickness-leave (accessed 2 March 2015).

Engerman, S. L. (2003) The history and political economy of international labor standards. In *International Labor Standards: History, Theory and Policy Options* (ed. K. Basu, H. Horn, L. Roman and J. Shapiro). Oxford: Blackwell.

Epstein, R. (1984) In defense of the contract at will. *University of Chicago Law Review* 51(4): 947–82.

Epstein, R. (1992) *Forbidden Grounds: The Case Against Employment Discrimination Laws*. Cambridge, MA: Harvard University Press.

Epstein, R. (2004) *Free Markets Under Siege*. London: Institute of Economic Affairs.

Estavao, M. and Sa, F. (2006) Are the French happy with the 35-hour workweek? IMF Working Paper WP/06/251. https://www.imf.org/external/pubs/ft/wp/2006/wp06251.pdf (accessed 3 March 2005).

European Commission (2006) Green Paper: Modernising labour law to meet the challenges of the 21st century. http://www.euro parl.europa.eu/meetdocs/2004_2009/documents/com/com _com(2006)0708_/com_com(2006)0708_en.pdf (accessed 1 March 2016).

Faggio, G., Gregg, P. and Wadsworth, J. (2011) Job tenure and job turnover. In *The Labour Market in Winter* (ed. P. Gregg and J. Wadsworth). Oxford: Oxford University Press.

Fetter, F. W. (1980) *The Economist in Parliament: 1780–1868*. Durham, NC: Duke University Press.

Financial Reporting Council (2014) The UK Corporate Governance Code https://www.frc.org.uk/Our-Work/Publications/Corporate-Go vernance/UK-Corporate-Governance-Code-2014.pdf (accessed 23 March 2015).

Financial Services Authority (2009) The Turner Review: A regulatory response to the global banking crisis. http://www.fsa.gov.uk/pubs/other/turner_review.pdf (accessed 23 March 2015).

Flight, H. (2014) Why wage subsidies are not the best way to help the poorest paid in Britain. *City AM*, February 2014.

Frank, R. H. and Cook, P. J. (1995) *The Winner-Takes-All Society.* New York: The Free Press.

Freeman, R. B. and Medoff, J. L. (1984) *What Do Unions Do?* New York: Basic Books.

Fresh Start Project (2012) Options for change. Green Paper: Renegotiating the UK's relationship with the EU. http://www.eufreshstart.org/downloads/fullgreenpaper.pdf (accessed 9 July 2014).

Fresh Start Project (2013) Manifesto for change: a new vision for the UK in Europe. http://www.eufreshstart.org/downloads/manifesto forchange.pdf (accessed 9 July 2014).

Friedman, M. (1963) *Capitalism and Freedom.* Chicago: Phoenix.

Gabaix, X. and Landier, A. (2008) Why has CEO pay increased so much? *Quarterly Journal of Economics* 123(1): 49–100.

Galindo-Rueda, F. and Periera, S. (2004) The impact of the National Minimum Wage on British firms. Report to the Low Pay Commission.

Garicano, L., Lelarge, C. and Van Reenan, J. (2013) Firm size distortion and the productivity distribution: evidence from France. IZA Discussion Paper 7241.

Gertler, P. J., Shah, M. and Bertozzi, S. M. (2005) Risky business: the market for unprotected commercial sex. *Journal of Political Economy* 113: 518–50.

Goldin, C. and Rouse, C. (2000) Orchestrating impartiality: the impact of 'blind' auditions on female musicians. *American Economic Review* 90: 715–41.

Gomez, R., Bryson, A., Kretschmer, T. and Willman, P. (2009) Employee voice and private sector workplace outcomes in Britain 1980–2004. Centre for Economic Performance, Discussion Paper 924. http://cep.lse.ac.uk/pubs/download/dp0924.pdf (accessed 7 May 2015).

Gordon, D. F. (1974) A neoclassical theory of Keynesian unemployment. *Economic Inquiry* 12: 431–49.

Gorton, G. and Schmid, F. (2000) Class struggle inside the firm: a study of German codetermination. National Bureau for Economic Research Working Paper 7945.

Grampp, W. D. (1979) The economists and the combination laws. *Quarterly Journal of Economics* 93: 501–22.

Grazier, S. (2007) Compensating wage differentials for risk of death in Great Britain: an examination of the Trade Union and Health and Safety Committee Impact. University of Swansea Working Paper.

Greenwood, J., Guner, N., Kocharkov, G. and Santos, C. (2014) Marry your like: assortative mating and income inequality. *American Economic Review* (Papers and Proceedings) 104(5): 348–53.

Gregg, P. and Gardner, L. (2015) *A Steady Job? The UK's Record on Labour Market Security and Stability since the Millennium.* London: Resolution Foundation.

Groshen, E. (2011) Temporary layoffs in the Great Recession. Liberty Street Economics. http://libertystreeteconomics.newyorkfed .org/2011/04/temporary-layoffs-during-the-great-recession.html (accessed 1 November 2016).

Gruber, J. (1994) The incidence of mandated maternity benefits. *American Economic Review* 84: 622–41.

Harper, B. (2000) Beauty, stature and the labour market: a British cohort study. *Oxford Bulletin of Economics and Statistics* 62: 771–800.

Harris, J. (1998) *William Beveridge: A Biography*, 2nd edn. Oxford University Press.

Harris, S. D. and Krueger, A. B. (2015) A proposal for modernizing labor laws for 21st century work: the 'independent worker'. http://www.brookings. edu/research/papers/2015/12/09-modernizing-labor-laws-for-the-in dependent-worker-krueger-harris (accessed 26 March 2016).

Hasseldine, J., Woodward, T. and Hansford, A. (2006) The burden of complying with employment and environmental regulation. CIMA Research Executive Summaries Series 2(7).

Hayek, F. A. (1976) The atavism of social justice. In *New Studies in Philosophy, Politics, Economics and the History of Ideas.* London: Routledge and Kegan Paul.

Health and Safety Executive (2004) Attitudes towards health and safety: a quantitative survey of stakeholder opinion. http://www.hse.gov.uk/research/misc/attitudes.pdf (accessed 12 February 2015).

Heywood, J. S., Siebert, W. S. and Xiangdong, W. (2005) The implicit costs and benefits of family friendly work practices. IZA Discussion Paper 1581.

Hicks, J. R. (1932) *The Theory of Wages*. London: Macmillan.

HM Government (2014) Review of the balance of competences between the United Kingdom and the European Union: social and employment policy. https://www.gov.uk/government/uploads/system/up loads/attachment_data/file/332524/review-of-the-balance-of-com petences-between-the-united-kingdom-and-the-european-un ion-social-and-employment-policy.pdf (accessed 1 March 2016).

HMRC and ONS (2013a) *Child and Working Tax Credits Statistics, December 2013*. London: Her Majesty's Revenue and Customs and Office for National Statistics.

HMRC and ONS (2013b) *Child and Working Tax Credits Statistics. Finalised Annual Awards*. London: Her Majesty's Revenue and Customs and Office for National Statistics.

Home Office (2007) The economic and fiscal impact of immigration: a cross-departmental submission to the House of Lords Select Committee. https://www.gov.uk/government/uploads/system/uploads/atta chment_data/file/228936/7237.pdf (accessed 8 May 2015).

HomRoy, S. (2014) Was Adam Smith right? Evidence of compensating differential in CEO pay. *The Manchester School* (published online). http://onlinelibrary.wiley.com/doi/10.1111/manc.12086/full (accessed 22 April 2015).

Hood, A., Joyce, R. and Phillips, D. (2014) Policies to help the low-paid. In *IFS Green Budget 2014* (ed. C. Emmerson, P. Johnson and H. Miller). London: Institute for Fiscal Studies.

House of Commons Library (2010) How much legislation comes from Europe? Research paper 10/62. http://www.parliament.uk/business/ publications/research/briefing-papers/RP10–62/how-much-legisla tion-comes-from-europe (accessed 9 July 2014).

Howe, M. (2016) Transforming the UK's relationship with the EU: the legal framework. In *Breaking up Is Hard To Do: Britain and Europe's Dysfunctional Relationship* (ed. J. R. Shackleton and P. Minford). London: Institute of Economic Affairs.

Humphris, A., Kleiner, M. and Koumenta, M. (2011) Analysing policies regulating occupations in Britain and the US. In *Employment in the Lean Years: Policy and Prospects for the Next Decade* (ed. D. Marsden). Oxford University Press.

Hunt, C. J. (2012) Sex versus class in two British trade unions in the early twentieth century. *Journal of Women's History* 24(1): 86–110.

Hutton, W. (2011) Hutton review of fair pay in the public sector. http://webarchive.nationalarchives.gov.uk/20130129110402/http:/www.hm-treasury.gov.uk/d/hutton_fairpay_review.pdf (accessed 5 July 2016).

Hyde, A. (2012) Intellectual property justifications for restricting employee mobility: a critical appraisal in light of the economic evidence. In *Research Handbook on the Economics of Labor and Employment Law* (ed. C. L. Estland and M. L. Wachter). Northampton, MA: Edward Elgar.

Institute for Fiscal Studies (2014) *The Green Budget 2014*. London: IFS.

Iosua, E. E., Gray, A., McGee, R., Landhuis, C. E., Keane, R., Healand, M. and Hancox, R. J. (2014) Employment among schoolchildren and its associations with adult substance abuse, psychological well-being and academic achievement. *Journal of Adolescent Health* 55: 542–48.

Jensen, M. C. and Meckling, W. H. (1976) Theory of the firm: managerial behaviour, agency costs and ownership structure. *Journal of Financial Economics* 3(4): 305–60.

Jensen, M. C. and Murphy, K. J. (1990) Performance pay and top management incentives. *Journal of Political Economy* 98: 225–64.

Johnson, O. (1969) The 'last hour' of Senior and Marx. *History of Political Economy* 1(2): 359–69.

Jolls, C. (2012) Bias and the law of the workplace. In *Research Handbook on the Economics of Labor and Employment Law* (ed. C. L. Estland and M. L. Wachter). Northampton, MA: Edward Elgar.

Jones, O. (2014) How Ed Miliband can harness the right's tactics to bring in a wave of left-wing populism in 2014. *The Independent*, January 2014.

Kahneman, D. (2011) *Thinking, Fast and Slow*. London: Allen Lane.

Keane, M. P. (2011) Labor supply and taxes: a survey. *Journal of Economic Literature* 49: 961–1075.

Kirk, E., McDermont, M. and Busby, N. (2015) Employment tribunal claims: debunking the myths. University of Bristol Policy Report 1/2015. http://www.bris.ac.uk/media-library/sites/policybristol/doc uments/employment_tribunal_claims.pdf (accessed 29 February 2015).

Kis-Katos, K. and Schulze, G. G. (2005) Regulation of child labour. *Economic Affairs* 25(3): 24–30.

Kleiner, M. M. (2015) *Guild-Ridden Labor Markets*. Kalamazoo, MI: W. E. Upjohn Institute for Employment Research.

Kleiner, M. M. and Krueger, A. B. (2010) The prevalence and effects of occupational licensing. *British Journal of Industrial Relations* 48: 676–87.

Knowles, D. (2013) Romanians are already here, being paid £30 a day. *The Times*, November 2013.

Koumenta, M., Humphris, A., Kleiner, M. and Pagliero, M. (2014) Occupational regulation in the EU and UK: prevalence and labour market impacts. https://www.gov.uk/government/uploads/system/up loads/attachment_data/file/343554/bis-14-999-occupational-regu lation-in-the-EU-and-UK.pdf (accessed 1 July 2016).

Kuhn, P. (2004) Is monopsony the right way to model labor markets? A review of Alan Manning's *Monopsony in Motion*. *International Journal of the Economics of Business* 11(3): 369–78.

Kuhn, P. and Villeval, M. C. (2015) Are women more attracted to co-operation than men? *Economic Journal* 125(582): 115–40.

Lakey, J. (2008) State age protection laws and the Age Discrimination in Employment Act. *Journal of Law and Economics* 51: 433–60.

Lancaster, R., Ward, R., Talbot, P. and Brazier, A. (2003) Costs of compliance with health and safety regulations in SMEs. Health and Safety Executive Research Report 174.

Lawton, K. and Pennycock, M. (2012) *Beyond the Bottom Line: The Challenges and Opportunities of Paying a Living Wage*. London: Resolution Foundation.

Lazear, E. P. (1990) Job security provisions and employment. *Quarterly Journal of Economics* 105: 699–726.

Leaker, D. (2008) The gender pay gap in the UK. *Economic and Labour Market Review* 2: 19–24.

Legrain, P. (2016) Freedom of movement. In *Breaking Up Is Hard to Do: Britain and Europe's Dysfunctional Relationship* (ed. P. Minford and J. R. Shackleton). London: Institute of Economic Affairs.

Leibenstein, H. (1966) Allocative efficiency vs. x-efficiency. *American Economic Review* 56(3): 392–415.

Leonard, T. C. (2005) Eugenics and economics in the progressive era. *Journal of Economic Perspectives* 19(4): 207–22.

Le Roux, S., Lucchino, P. and Wilkinson, D. (2013) An investigation into the extent of non-compliance with the National Minimum Wage. Report to the Low Pay Commission.

Liddle, R. J. and McCarthy, W. E. J. (1972) The impact of the prices and incomes board on the reform of collective bargaining: a preliminary survey of specific pay references. *British Journal of Industrial Relations* 10(3): 412–39.

Lofstedt, R. E. (2011) *Reclaiming Health and Safety for All: An Independent Review of Health and Safety Legislation*. Department for Work and Pensions Cm 8219.

London Assembly Economic Committee (2014) Fair pay: making the London Living Wage the norm.

Longhi, S. and Platt, L. (2008) Pay gaps across equality areas. Equality and Human Rights Commission Research Report 9.

Low Pay Commission (2012) National Minimum Wage – Low Pay Commission report 2012.

Machin, S., Manning, A. and Rahman, L. (2003) Where the minimum wage bites hard: introduction of minimum wages to a low wage sector. *Journal of the European Economic Association* 1(1): 154–80.

Mankiw, G. (2014) Help the working poor, but share the burden. *New York Times*, 4 January 2014.

Manning, A. (2003) *Monopsony in Motion: Imperfect Competition in Labor Markets*. Princeton University Press.

Mansfield, I. (2014) *A Blueprint for Britain: Openness Not Isolation*. London: Institute of Economic Affairs.

Marin, A. and Psacharapoulos, G. (1982) The reward for risk in the labor market: evidence from the United Kingdom and a reconcilation with other studies. *Journal of Political Economy* 90: 827–53.

Mazzucato, M. (2013) *The Entrepreneurial State: Debunking Public vs. Private Sector Myths*. London: Anthem Press.

McCrary, J. (2007) The effect of court-ordered hiring quotas on the composition and quality of police. *American Economic Review* 97(1): 318–53.

McKean, R. N. (1965) The unseen hand in government. *American Economic Review* 55: 496–506.

McKechnie, J., Hobbs, S., Simpson, A., Howieson, C. and Semple, S. (2011) *The Regulation of Child Employment and Options for Reform*. London: Department for Education

McKinsey and Company (2007) Women matter: gender diversity, a corporate performance driver.

Meer, J. and West, J. (2013) Effects of the minimum wage on employment dynamics. National Bureau of Economic Research Working Paper 19262.

Melchiorre, M. and Rocca, E. (2013) The unintended consequences of Italy's labour laws: how extensive labour regulation distorts the Italian economy. *Economic* Affairs 33(2): 156–73.

Metcalf, H. (2009) Pay gaps across the equality strands: a review. Equality and Human Rights Commission Research Report 14.

Mill, J. S. (2006, first published 1859) *On Liberty*, published together with *The Subjection of Women*. London: Penguin.

Minogue, K. (2012) *The Servile Mind: How Democracy Erodes the Moral Life*. New York: Encounter.

Mirza-Davies, J. (2015a) Apprenticeships Statistics: England. House of Commons Library Briefing Paper 06113, 25 June.

Mirza-Davies, J. (2015b) Apprenticeships Policy, England. House of Commons Library Briefing Paper 03052, 2 September.

Morgan, S. and Carrier, H. (2014) The transition from education to work. In *Gender Inequality in the Labour Market in the UK* (ed. G. Razzu). Oxford University Press.

Neumark, D. and Stock, W. (2006) The labor market effects of sex and race discrimination laws. *Economic Inquiry* 44(3): 385–419.

Neumark, D. and Wascher, W. (1995) The effect of New Jersey's minimum wage increase on fast-food employment; a re-evaluation using payroll records. National Bureau of Economic Research Working Paper 5224.

Neumark, D. and Wascher, W. (2004) Minimum wages, labour market institutions and youth employment: a cross-national analysis. *Industrial and Labour Relations Review* 57(2): 223–48.

Neumark, D. and Wascher, W. (2007) Minimum wages and employment. *Foundations and Trends in Microeconomics* 3(1–2): 1–182.

Neumark, D., Thompson, M. and Koyle, L. (2012) The effects of living wage laws on low-wage workers and low-income families: what do we know? *IZA Journal of Labor Policy* 1: 11.

Niederle, M. and Vesterland, L. (2007) Do women shy away from competition? Do men compete too much? *Quarterly Journal of Economics* 122(3): 1067–101.

Niemietz, K. (2012) *Redefining the Poverty Debate. Why a War on Markets Is No Substitute for a War on Poverty.* London: Institute of Economic Affairs.

Office for Budget Responsibility (2015) Office for Budget Responsibility Economic and Fiscal Outlook, July 2015. http://budgetresponsibility.org.uk/docs/dlm_uploads/July-2015-EFO-234224.pdf (accessed 5 July 2016).

O'Connor, S. (2015) Fall in real wages prompts 40% rise in workers with second jobs. *Financial Times*, 26 January 2015.

OECD (2008) The price of prejudice: labour market discrimination on the grounds of gender and ethnicity. *OECD Employment Outlook*, Chapter 3. Paris: OECD.

OECD (2013) Protecting jobs, enhancing flexibility: a new look at employment protection legislation. *OECD Employment Outlook 2013*, Chapter 2. Paris: OECD.

Oi, W. (1962) Labor as a quasi-fixed factor. *Journal of Political Economy* 70: 538–55.

Orton, M. and Rowlingson, K. (2007) *Public Attitudes to Economic Inequality.* York: Joseph Rowntree Foundation.

Owen, G. (1999) *From Empire to Europe: The Decline and Revival of British Industry Since the Second World War.* London: Harper Collins.

Parker, H. M. D. (1957) *Manpower: A Study of Wartime Policy and Administration.* London: HMSO.

Pennycock, M., Cory, G. and Alakeson, V. (2013) *A Matter of Time: The Rise of Zero-hours Contracts.* London: The Resolution Foundation.

Phelan, J. (1994) The paradox of the contented female worker: an assessment of alternative explanations. *Social Psychology Quarterly* 57(2): 95–107.

Phelps, E. S. (1972) The statistical theory of racism and sexism. *American Economic Review* 62: 659–61.

Pickering, J. F. (1971) The prices and incomes board and private sector prices: a survey. *Economic Journal* 81(322): 225–41.

Pigou, A. C. (1920) *The Economics of Welfare.* London: Macmillan.

Plunkett, J. and Hurrell, A. (2013) *Fifteen Years Later: A Discussion Paper on the Future of the UK National Minimum Wage and Low Pay Commission.* London: The Resolution Foundation.

Pyper, D. and Dar, A. (2015) Zero-hours contracts. House of Commons Briefing Paper 06553. http://researchbriefings.files.parliament.uk/documents/SN06553/SN06553.pdf (accessed 9 March 2016).

Quigley, T. J., Crossland, C. and Campbell, R. J. (forthcoming) Shareholder perceptions of the changing impact of CEOs: market reactions to unexpected CEO deaths. *Strategic Management Journal.*

Reed, H. (2013) *The Economic Implications of Extending the Living Wage to All Employees in the UK.* Colchester: Landman Economics.

Richardson, R. (1991) Trade unions and industrial relations. In *The British Economy since 1945* (ed. N. F. R. Crafts and N. Woodward). Oxford: Clarendon Press.

Riley, R. (2013) Modelling demand for low skilled/low paid labour: exploring the employment trade-offs of a living wage. National Institute of Economic and Social Research Discussion Paper 404.

Robertson, D. J. (1961) *A Market for Labour*. London: Institute of Economic Affairs.

Rogers, B. (2015) The social costs of Uber. *University of Chicago Law Review Dialogue* 82(3): 85–103. https://lawreview.uchicago.edu/page/social-costs-uber (accessed 28 March 2016).

Rosen, S. (1981) The economics of superstars. *American Economic Review* 71: 845–58.

Rowthorn, R. (2014) *Large-scale Immigration: Its Economic and Demographic Consequences for the UK*. London: Civitas.

Sabia, J. J. and Nielsen, R. B. (2012) *Can Raising the Minimum Wage Reduce Poverty and Hardship? New Evidence from the Survey of Income and Program Participation*. Washington: Employment Policies Institute.

Sack, P. (2013) The Midas touch: gold-plating of EU employment directives in UK law. London: Institute of Directors. http://www.iod.com/influencing/policy-papers/regulation-and-employment/the-midas-touch-goldplating-of-eu-employment-directives-in-uk-law (accessed 9 July 2014).

Sanandaji, N. (2015) *Scandinavian Unexceptionalism: Culture, Markets and the Failure of Third-Way Socialism*. London: Institute of Economic Affairs.

Schick, A. and Steckel, R. H. (2010) Height as a proxy for cognitive and non-cognitive ability. National Bureau of Economic Research Working Paper 16570.

Schneider, F. and Williams, C. C. (2013) *The Shadow Economy*. London: Institute of Economic Affairs.

Schönberg, U. and Ludsteck, J. (2014) Maternity leave legislation, female labour supply, and the family wage gap. *Journal of Labor Economics* 32(3): 469–505.

Schuettinger, R. L. and Butler, E. F. (1979) *Forty Centuries of Wage and Price Controls: How Not to Fight Inflation*. Washington, DC: The Heritage Foundation.

Schulten, T. (2010) A European minimum wage policy for a more sustainable wage-led growth model. http://www.social-europe.eu/2010/06/a-european-minimum-wage-policy-for-a-more-sustainable-wage-led-growth-model/ (accessed 10 July 2014).

Shackleton, J. R. (1992) *Training Too Much?* London: Institute of Economic Affairs.

Shackleton, J. R. (1998) Industrial relations reform in Britain since 1979. *Journal of Labor Research* 19: 581–609.

Shackleton, J. R. (2002) *Employment Tribunals: Their Growth and the Case for Radical Reform*. London: Institute of Economic Affairs.

Shackleton, J. R. (2007) Britain's labor market under the Blair governments. *Journal of Labor Research* 28: 454–76.

Shackleton, J. R. (2008) *Should We Mind the Gap? Gender Pay Differentials and Public Policy*. London: Institute of Economic Affairs.

Shackleton, J. R. (2012) Wellbeing at work: any lessons? In *... and the Pursuit of Happiness* (ed. P. Booth). London: Institute of Economic Affairs.

Siebert, W. S. (2006) Labour market regulation in the EU-15: causes and consequences – a survey. IZA Discussion Paper 2430, Bonn.

Siebert, W. S. (2015) The simple economics of wage floors. In *Flaws and Ceilings: Price Controls and the Damage They Cause* (ed. C. Coyne and R. Coyne). London: Institute of Economic Affairs.

Skedinger, P. (2010) *Employment Protection Legislation: Evolution, Effects, Winners and Losers*. Cheltenham: Edward Elgar.

Snowdon, C. (2010) *The Spirit Level Delusion: Fact-Checking the Left's New Theory of Everything*. Democracy Institute/Little Dice.

Snowdon, C. (2012) *Sock Puppets: How the Government Lobbies Itself and Why*. IEA Discussion Paper 39. London: Institute of Economic Affairs.

Snowdon, C. (2013) *Euro Puppets: the European Commission's Remaking of Civil Society.* IEA Discussion Paper 45. London: Institute of Economic Affairs.

Snowdon, C. (2015) *Selfishness, Greed and Capitalism: Debunking Myths about the Free Market.* London: Institute of Economic Affairs.

Sowell, T. (2013) Why racists love the minimum wage laws. *New York Post*, 17 September.

Stewart, M. B. and Swaffield, J. K. (2008) The other margin: do minimum wages cause working hours adjustments for low-wage workers? *Economica* 75(297): 148–67.

Summers, L. (1989) Some simple economics of mandated benefits. *American Economic Association Papers and Proceedings* 79(2): 177–83.

Taylor, C. (2010) *Health and Safety: Reducing the Burden.* London: Policy Exchange.

Tebbit, A. (2009) Does the government 'gold-plate' EU employment directives? London: Institute of Directors.

Thévenon, O. and Solaz, A. (2013) Labour market effects of parental leave policies in OECD countries. OECD Social, Employment and Migration Working Papers 141. Paris: OECD Publishing.

Timmons, E. J. and Thornton, R. J. (2010) The licensing of barbers in the USA. *British Journal of Industrial Relations* 48: 740–57.

Toynbee, P. (2014) If you want to curb immigration, pay workers a living wage. *The Guardian*, 2 January.

Tullock, G. (2006) *The Vote Motive.* London: Institute of Economic Affairs.

Urwin, P. (2011) *Self-employment, Small Firms and Enterprise.* London: Institute of Economic Affairs.

Veljanovski, C. (ed.) (2015) *Forever Contemporary – The Economics of Ronald Coase.* London: Institute of Economic Affairs.

Wachter, M. L. (2012) Neoclassical labor economics: its implications for labor and employment law. In *Research Handbook on the Economics of Labor and Employment Law* (ed. C. L. Estland and M. L. Wachter). Northampton, MA: Edward Elgar.

Wadsworth, J. (2009) Did the National Minimum Wage affect UK prices? Centre for Economic Performance, LSE, Discussion Paper 0947.

Wallis, P. (2007) Apprenticeship and training in premodern England. Working papers on the nature of evidence: how well do 'facts' travel? 22/07. http://www.lse.ac.uk/economicHistory/pdf/FACTSPDF/2207 Wallis.pdf (accessed 18 November 2015).

Weichselbaumer, D. and Winter-Ebmer, R. (2007) The effect of competition and equal treatment laws on gender wage differentials. *Economic Policy* 22: 235–87.

Weingast, B. (1995) The economic role of political institutions: market-preserving federalism and economic development. *Journal of Law, Economics, & Organization* 20(1): 1–31.

Williams, N. and Mills, J. A. (2001) The minimum wage and teenage employment: evidence from time series. *Applied Economics* 33: 285–300.

Wilkinson, R. and Pickett, K. (2009) *The Spirit Level: Why Equality Is Better for Everyone*. London: Penguin.

Wolf, A. (2009) *An Adult Approach to Further Education*. London: Institute of Economic Affairs.

Wolf, A. (2015) Fixing a broken training system: the case for an apprenticeship levy. London: Social Market Foundation. http://www.smf .co.uk/wp-content/uploads/2015/07/Social-Market-Foundation -Publication-Alison-Wolf-Fixing-A-Broken-Training-System-The -Case-For-An-Apprenticeship-Levy.pdf (accessed 18 November 2015).

Woods, T. E. Jr (2007) The unanswered questions of the just wage. In *Catholic Social Teaching and the Market Economy* (ed. P. Booth). London: Institute of Economic Affairs.

ABOUT THE IEA

The Institute is a research and educational charity (No. CC 235 351), limited by guarantee. Its mission is to improve understanding of the fundamental institutions of a free society by analysing and expounding the role of markets in solving economic and social problems.

The IEA achieves its mission by:

- a high-quality publishing programme
- conferences, seminars, lectures and other events
- outreach to school and college students
- brokering media introductions and appearances

The IEA, which was established in 1955 by the late Sir Antony Fisher, is an educational charity, not a political organisation. It is independent of any political party or group and does not carry on activities intended to affect support for any political party or candidate in any election or referendum, or at any other time. It is financed by sales of publications, conference fees and voluntary donations.

In addition to its main series of publications, the IEA also publishes (jointly with the University of Buckingham) a refereed academic journal, *Economic Affairs*.

The IEA is aided in its work by a distinguished international Academic Advisory Council and an eminent panel of Honorary Fellows. Together with other academics, they review prospective IEA publications, their comments being passed on anonymously to authors. All IEA papers are therefore subject to the same rigorous independent refereeing process as used by leading academic journals.

IEA publications enjoy widespread classroom use and course adoptions in schools and universities. They are also sold throughout the world and often translated/reprinted.

Since 1974 the IEA has helped to create a worldwide network of 100 similar institutions in over 70 countries. They are all independent but share the IEA's mission.

Views expressed in the IEA's publications are those of the authors, not those of the Institute (which has no corporate view), its Managing Trustees, Academic Advisory Council members or senior staff.

Members of the Institute's Academic Advisory Council, Honorary Fellows, Trustees and Staff are listed on the following page.

The Institute gratefully acknowledges financial support for its publications programme and other work from a generous benefaction by the late Professor Ronald Coase.

The Institute of Economic Affairs
2 Lord North Street, Westminster, London SW1P 3LB
Tel: 020 7799 8900
Fax: 020 7799 2137
Email: iea@iea.org.uk
Internet: iea.org.uk

Institute of
Economic Affairs

Director General & Ralph Harris Fellow	Mark Littlewood
Director of Research	Dr Jamie Whyte

Managing Trustees

Chairman: Neil Record

Kevin Bell
Robert Boyd
Robin Edwards
Sir Michael Hintze
Professor Patrick Minford

Professor Mark Pennington
Bruno Prior
Professor Martin Ricketts
Linda Whetstone

Academic Advisory Council

Chairman: Professor Martin Ricketts

Graham Bannock
Dr Roger Bate
Professor Alberto Benegas-Lynch, Jr
Professor Christian Bjornskov
Professor Donald J Boudreaux
Professor John Burton
Professor Forrest Capie
Professor Steven N S Cheung
Professor Tim Congdon
Professor Christopher Coyne
Professor N F R Crafts
Professor David de Meza
Professor Kevin Dowd
Professor David Greenaway
Dr Ingrid A Gregg
Dr Samuel Gregg
Walter E Grinder
Professor Steve H Hanke
Professor Keith Hartley
Professor David Henderson
Professor Peter M Jackson
Dr Jerry Jordan
Dr Lynne Kiesling
Professor Daniel B Klein
Dr Mark Koyama
Professor Chandran Kukathas
Dr Tim Leunig
Dr Andrew Lilico

Professor Stephen C Littlechild
Professor Theodore Roosevelt Malloch
Dr Eileen Marshall
Professor Antonio Martino
Dr John Meadowcroft
Dr Anja Merz
Professor Julian Morris
Professor Alan Morrison
Professor D R Myddelton
Paul Ormerod
Professor David Parker
Professor Victoria Curzon Price
Professor Colin Robinson
Professor Pascal Salin
Dr Razeen Sally
Professor Pedro Schwartz
Professor J R Shackleton
Jane S Shaw
Professor W Stanley Siebert
Dr Elaine Sternberg
Professor James Tooley
Professor Nicola Tynan
Professor Roland Vaubel
Dr Cento Veljanovski
Professor Lawrence H White
Professor Walter E Williams
Professor Geoffrey E Wood

Honorary Fellows

Professor Michael Beenstock
Sir Samuel Brittan
Professor Richard A Epstein
Professor David Laidler

Professor Deirdre McCloskey
Professor Chiaki Nishiyama
Professor Vernon L Smith
Professor Basil S Yamey

Other books recently published by the IEA include:

Quack Policy – Abusing Science in the Cause of Paternalism
Jamie Whyte
Hobart Paper 173; ISBN 978–0–255–36673–1; £10.00

Foundations of a Free Society
Eamonn Butler
Occasional Paper 149; ISBN 978–0–255–36687–8; £12.50

The Government Debt Iceberg
Jagadeesh Gokhale
Research Monograph 68; ISBN 978–0–255–36666–3; £10.00

A U-Turn on the Road to Serfdom
Grover Norquist
Occasional Paper 150; ISBN 978–0–255–36686–1; £10.00

New Private Monies – A Bit-Part Player?
Kevin Dowd
Hobart Paper 174; ISBN 978–0–255–36694–6; £10.00

From Crisis to Confidence – Macroeconomics after the Crash
Roger Koppl
Hobart Paper 175; ISBN 978–0–255–36693–9; £12.50

Advertising in a Free Society
Ralph Harris and Arthur Seldon
With an introduction by Christopher Snowdon
Hobart Paper 176; ISBN 978–0–255–36696–0; £12.50

Selfishness, Greed and Capitalism: Debunking Myths about the Free Market
Christopher Snowdon
Hobart Paper 177; ISBN 978–0–255–36677–9; £12.50

Waging the War of Ideas
John Blundell
Occasional Paper 131; ISBN 978–0–255–36684–7; £12.50

Brexit: Directions for Britain Outside the EU
Ralph Buckle, Tim Hewish, John C. Hulsman, Iain Mansfield and Robert Oulds
Hobart Paperback 178; ISBN 978–0–255–36681–6; £12.50

Flaws and Ceilings – Price Controls and the Damage They Cause
Edited by Christopher Coyne and Rachel Coyne
Hobart Paperback 179; ISBN 978–0–255–36701–1; £12.50

Scandinavian Unexceptionalism: Culture, Markets and the Failure of Third-Way Socialism
Nima Sanandaji
Readings in Political Economy 1; ISBN 978–0–255–36704–2; £10.00

Classical Liberalism – A Primer
Eamonn Butler
Readings in Political Economy 2; ISBN 978-0-255-36707-3; £10.00

Federal Britain: The Case for Decentralisation
Philip Booth
Readings in Political Economy 3; ISBN 978-0-255-36713-4; £10.00

Forever Contemporary: The Economics of Ronald Coase
Edited by Cento Veljanovski
Readings in Political Economy 4; ISBN 978-0-255-36710-3; £15.00

Power Cut? How the EU Is Pulling the Plug on Electricity Markets
Carlo Stagnaro
Hobart Paperback 180; ISBN 978-0-255-36716-5; £10.00

Policy Stability and Economic Growth – Lessons from the Great Recession
John B. Taylor
Readings in Political Economy 5; ISBN 978-0-255-36719-6; £7.50

Breaking Up Is Hard To Do: Britain and Europe's Dysfunctional Relationship
Edited by Patrick Minford and J. R. Shackleton
Hobart Paperback 181; ISBN 978-0-255-36722-6; £15.00

In Focus: The Case for Privatising the BBC
Edited by Philip Booth
Hobart Paperback 182; ISBN 978-0-255-36725-7; £12.50

Islamic Foundations of a Free Society
Edited by Nouh El Harmouzi and Linda Whetstone
Hobart Paperback 183; ISBN 978-0-255-36728-8; £12.50

The Economics of International Development: Foreign Aid versus Freedom for the World's Poor
William Easterly
Readings in Political Economy 6; ISBN 978-0-255-36731-8; £7.50

Taxation, Government Spending and Economic Growth
Edited by Philip Booth
Hobart Paperback 184; ISBN 978-0-255-36734-9; £15.00

Universal Healthcare without the NHS: Towards a Patient-Centred Health System
Kristian Niemietz
Hobart Paperback 185; ISBN 978-0-255-36737-0; £10.00

Sea Change: How Markets and Property Rights Could Transform the Fishing Industry
Edited by Richard Wellings
Readings in Political Economy 7; ISBN 978-0-255-36740-0; £10.00

Other IEA publications

Comprehensive information on other publications and the wider work of the IEA can be found at www.iea.org.uk. To order any publication please see below.

Personal customers

Orders from personal customers should be directed to the IEA:

Clare Rusbridge
IEA
2 Lord North Street
FREEPOST LON10168
London SW1P 3YZ
Tel: 020 7799 8907. Fax: 020 7799 2137
Email: sales@iea.org.uk

Trade customers

All orders from the book trade should be directed to the IEA's distributor:

NBN International (IEA Orders)
Orders Dept.
NBN International
10 Thornbury Road
Plymouth PL6 7PP
Tel: 01752 202301, Fax: 01752 202333
Email: orders@nbninternational.com

IEA subscriptions

The IEA also offers a subscription service to its publications. For a single annual payment (currently £42.00 in the UK), subscribers receive every monograph the IEA publishes. For more information please contact:

Clare Rusbridge
Subscriptions
IEA
2 Lord North Street
FREEPOST LON10168
London SW1P 3YZ
Tel: 020 7799 8907, Fax: 020 7799 2137
Email: crusbridge@iea.org.uk